SITTING IN DARKNESS

AMERICA AND THE LONG 19th CENTURY
General Editors: David Kazanjian, Elizabeth McHenry, and Priscilla Wald

Black Frankenstein: The Making of an American Metaphor
Elizabeth Young

Neither Fugitive nor Free: Atlantic Slavery, Freedom Suits, and the Legal Culture of Travel
Edlie L. Wong

Shadowing the White Man's Burden: U.S. Imperialism and the Problem of the Color Line
Gretchen Murphy

Bodies of Reform: The Rhetoric of Character in Gilded-Age America
James B. Salazar

Empire's Proxy: American Literature and U.S. Imperialism in the Philippines
Meg Wesling

Sites Unseen: Architecture, Race, and American Literature
William A. Gleason

Racial Innocence: Performing American Childhood from Slavery to Civil Rights
Robin Bernstein

American Arabesque: Arabs and Islam in the Nineteenth Century Imaginary
Jacob Rama Berman

Racial Indigestion: Eating Bodies in the Nineteenth Century
Kyla Wazana Tompkins

Idle Threats: Men and the Limits of Productivity in Nineteenth-Century America
Andrew Lyndon Knighton

The Traumatic Colonel: The Founding Fathers, Slavery, and the Phantasmatic Aaron Burr
Michael J. Drexler and Ed White

Unsettled States: Nineteenth-Century American Literary Studies
Edited by Dana Luciano and Ivy G. Wilson

Sitting in Darkness: Mark Twain's Asia and Comparative Racialization
Hsuan L. Hsu

SITTING IN DARKNESS

MARK TWAIN'S ASIA AND
COMPARATIVE RACIALIZATION

Hsuan L. Hsu

NEW YORK UNIVERSITY PRESS
New York and London

NEW YORK UNIVERSITY PRESS
New York and London
www.nyupress.org

© 2015 by New York University
All rights reserved

References to Internet websites (URLs) were accurate at the time of writing.
Neither the author nor New York University Press is responsible for URLs that
may have expired or changed since the manuscript was prepared.

LIBRARY OF CONGRESS CATALOGING-IN-PUBLICATION DATA

Hsu, Hsuan L., 1976-
Sitting in darkness : Mark Twain's Asia and comparative racialization / Hsuan L. Hsu.
pages cm
Includes bibliographical references and index.
ISBN 978-1-4798-8041-6 (hardback) — ISBN 978-1-4798-1510-4 (pb)
1. Twain, Mark, 1835-1910—Criticism and interpretation. 2. Twain, Mark, 1835-1910—
Knowledge—Asia. 3. Asian Americans in literature. 4. Chinese in literature. I. Title.
PS1342.A7H78 2015
818'.409—dc23
2014040534

New York University Press books are printed on acid-free paper,
and their binding materials are chosen for strength and durability.
We strive to use environmentally responsible suppliers and materials
to the greatest extent possible in publishing our books.

Manufactured in the United States of America

10 9 8 7 6 5 4 3 2 1

Also available as an ebook

The Person Sitting in Darkness is almost sure to say: "There is something curious about this—curious and unaccountable. There must be two Americas: one that sets the captive free, and one that takes a once-captive's new freedom away from him, and picks a quarrel with him with nothing to found it on; then kills him to get his land."
Mark Twain, "To the Person Sitting in Darkness"

Mark Twain's reprimand of the imperialist aggressive powers and sympathy for the anti-colonialist Asian and African people are especially significant to us. This is the part of his literary heritage we should value most.
Lao She, "Mark Twain: Exposer of the 'Dollar Empire'" (a speech delivered in Beijing, 1960)

Contents

List of Illustrations	ix
Acknowledgments	xi
Introduction: "Coolies" and Comparative Racialization in the Global West	1
1. "A Witness More Powerful than Himself": Race, Testimony, and Twain's Courtroom Farces	27
2. Vagrancy and Comparative Racialization in *Huckleberry Finn* and "Three Vagabonds of Trinidad"	53
3. "Coolies" and Corporate Personhood in *Those Extraordinary Twins*	83
4. A Connecticut Yankee in the Court of Wu Chih Tien: Imperial Romance and Chinese Modernization	109
5. Body Counts and Comparative Anti-imperialism	139
Conclusion: Post-racial Twain?	167
Notes	171
Works Cited	209
Index	229
About the Author	244

Illustrations

Figure I.1.	True Williams, "John Chinaman in New York"	20
Figure 1.1.	Harry Williams, "Ah Sin"	46
Figure 2.1.	George Root, "Tramp! Tramp! Tramp! or the Prisoner's Hope"	63
Figure 2.2.	Colophon image from Frank Bellew, *The Tramp: His Tricks, Tallies, and Tell-Tales, With All His Signs, Countersigns, Grips, Pass-Words, and Villainies Exposed*	67
Figure 3.1.	"The Mill Among the Mill-Hands"	99
Figure 3.2.	G. Frederick Keller, "'What Shall We Do With Our Boys?'"	101
Figure 4.1.	The "Orientals"	121
Figure 4.2.	"The Explosion"	126
Figure 4.3.	Daniel Beard, "Another Miracle"	128
Figure 4.4.	Daniel Beard, "After the Explosion"	129
Figure 5.1.	"Indians and Chinamen"	145
Figure 5.2.	"A Memorial for the Perpetuation of My Name"	161
Figure 5.3.	Twain's calculations for the monument to King Leopold	164

Acknowledgments

While all its shortcomings are my own, writing this book has been a collaborative process enriched by conversations with colleagues, friends, and students over the last six years. The arguments presented here benefited from exchanges with undergraduates in my courses on U.S. literature and Mark Twain at Yale and the University of California, Davis, as well as provocative questions from audiences at the American Studies Association, the American Literature Association, the Modern Language Association, the Society of Nineteenth-Century Americanists, the University of Illinois Urbana-Champaign, the University of Tokyo, Northwestern University, Claremont Graduate University, Loyola University in Chicago, the University of Michigan, Oxford University, and the University of Notre Dame.

Lawrence Buell, Colin Dayan, Wai Chee Dimock, Gordon Hutner, Colleen Lye, Samuel Otter, Priscilla Wald, and Edlie Wong offered encouragement, criticism, and support at crucial stages of the project. I'm also grateful for the generous guidance provided by established Mark Twain scholars such as Shelley Fisher Fishkin, Susan Harris, Bruce Michelson, Linda Morris, and R. Kent Rasmussen, as well as Neda Salem's guidance at the Mark Twain Papers, Bancroft Library, University of California, Berkeley.

My research was supported by generous grants and prizes from the American Council of Learned Societies, the Center for Advanced Study in the Behavioral Sciences, the UC Davis Humanities Institute, the National Endowment for the Humanities, the Western Literature Association, and *American Literature*. Previous versions and excerpts from the Introduction, Chapter 2, and Chapter 4 were published as "Sitting in Darkness: Mark Twain and America's Asia," *American Literary History*, vol. 25, no. 1 (Spring 2013); "Vagrancy and Comparative Racialization in *Huckleberry Finn* and 'Three Vagabonds of Trinidad,'" *American Literature*, vol. 81, no. 4 (December 2009); and "A Connecticut Yankee in the Court of Wu Chih Tien: Mark Twain and Wong Chin Foo," *Common*

Place, vol. 11, no. 1 (October 2010). I am grateful to the publishers of these journals for permission to reprint portions of those articles here. Gordon Hutner's invitation to participate in *American Literary History*'s "Second Book Project" symposium and special issue was especially helpful, as it first prompted me to imagine this project as a book.

At NYU Press, Eric Zinner provided encouragement and advice throughout the process; the press's referees offered rigorous and incisive feedback that I have found indispensable in revising this book. I'm also grateful to Mac Layne and Cara Shipe for proofreading the manuscript in its final stages and to Grace Kowles for producing the index.

The English department at UC Davis and the Center for Advanced Study in the Behavioral Sciences have been ideal work environments, not least because of the fellowship and intellectual engagement of my colleagues Beth Freeman, Danielle Heard, Mark Jerng, Kathleen Frederickson, Jonathan Levy, Martha Lincoln, Michael Makovski, Desiree Martín, John Marx, Timothy Schroeder, Matthew Stratton, Julie Sze, and Mike Ziser. Beyond the academy, I'm grateful for the love and support of friends and family—particularly Kang, Hsiang-Lin, Kang Jr., Lin, Cristina, Jason, Kile, Kalissa, Myron, and Beenash. Like Twain's novels, much of this book was written in feline company, thanks to a stray cat named Jasper.

Introduction

"Coolies" and Comparative Racialization in the Global West

As the unexpected bestselling status of his autobiography and the controversy over the NewSouth edition of *Tom Sawyer* and *Huckleberry Finn* (in which pejorative terms for blacks and Native Americans have been replaced with "slave" and "Indian" throughout) attest, Mark Twain's incisive literary treatments of U.S. history's darker episodes continue to fascinate and provoke twenty-first century readers.[1] For a broad international[2] audience, Twain exemplifies how literary form and style can be mobilized against racist institutions; at the same time, his writings have provided key test cases for critical conversations about the possibilities and limitations of canonical engagements with blackness and empire.[3] But whereas Toni Morrison's reading of the "Africanist" presence at the center of *Huck Finn* has given rise to illuminating scholarship on blackness and its multiracial analogues in canonical American literature,[4] historical dynamics of comparative racialization raise questions about how "Africanist" representations intersected with representations of Chinese immigrants in a period when the figure of the indentured "coolie" laborer blurred boundaries between traditional notions of freedom and servitude. *Sitting in Darkness* draws on recent scholarship on Asian immigration, U.S. imperialism, race theory, and legal history to situate Twain's race fiction in a comparative perspective: in the intersectional contexts of Chinese Exclusion and Jim Crow, even historical novels about antebellum slavery registered fluctuating connections between immigration policy, imperialist ventures, and anti-black racism.

Although this book focuses on the explicit and implicit comparisons that Twain drew between different racial groups over the course of his career, his writings also provide occasions to think through broader methodological issues, such as how literature can articulate tensions between different racial groups, how to critique processes of comparative racialization without reproducing their logic of analogy, and how readings that attend to shifting institutions of structural racism can complement accounts that focus on racial prejudice. The book's title, which I take from Twain's trenchant essay, "To the Person Sitting in Darkness" (1901), refers not only to the underrepresented status of the Chinese and their supposed lack of enlightenment but also to how Western imperialism marginalized and exploited numerous racialized and colonized populations. Twain's ironic figure for a colonized subject bereft of Christianity and modernity recapitulates a range of captives from his earlier writings: Chinese immigrants sentenced to imprisonment by San Francisco's police courts, Injun Joe locked away in a cave, the prolonged captivity of Jim in the last chapters of *Huck Finn*. If it invokes the possibility of analogizing colonized Chinese and Filipino subjects with figures of "darkness" frequently linked to African Americans, "To the Person Sitting in Darkness" also attends to the different ways in which Boers, Chinese Boxers, and Filipino revolutionaries were subjugated. In addition to arguing that treatments of race in Twain's era should be read comparatively and demonstrating the importance of Chinese immigration and U.S. transpacific relations in his writings, *Sitting in Darkness* experiments with modes of reading that analyze how the shifting legal, material, and discursive grounds of racialization manifest in literary form. Rather than engaging in a traditional single-author study, this book uses Twain's career as an occasion to rethink the intersections between topics often kept distinct in studies of the literature of the Gilded Age: imperialism, Chinese Exclusion, Jim Crow, the rise of corporations, and the development of the U.S. West.

This introductory chapter will set the stage for my study by describing and framing the archive of Twain's career-long engagements with questions of migration, war, and colonialism raised by U.S. relations with China and the Philippines. These writings underscore the role of comparative racialization in the post-Reconstruction United States and throughout Twain's writings by showing how Twain critiqued not just antiblack stereotypes but also laws, geographies, and economic relations that comparatively and differentially racialized African Americans, Asian Americans, Native Americans, Filipino nationalists, and other groups. Understanding Twain's fictional engagements with racism and colonialism requires an assessment of the discursive, legal, and extralegal means whereby racialized groups were compared, differentiated, and repressed in a period marked by massive demographic shifts and diverse forms of racial and imperial violence.

I. Mark Twain and Comparative Racialization

When Mark Twain headed west in 1861 after serving for two weeks in the Missouri state militia, he distanced himself from the battlefields of the Civil War but not from the political and cultural dynamics of slavery. "Lighting out" for Virginia City and San Francisco—where Twain's professional writing career took off[5]—was only a viable option because the Compromise of 1850 had organized territories acquired from Mexico in the Treaty of Guadalupe Hidalgo around a series of agreements concerning the future expansion of slavery. Although California was admitted as a free state in 1850, proslavery Democrats had considerable influence in the state's government, and early legislatures "denied blacks voting rights, prohibited African American court testimony, and banned black homesteading, jury service, and intermarriage with whites";[6] the state assembly even passed a bill that—had it not been blocked by state senator David Broderick—would have banned the immigration of free blacks into California. Setting the stage for virtually unprosecutable acts of racist violence by whites, the first session of the state legislature stipulated in 1850 that "no black or mulatto person, or Indian, shall be allowed to give evidence in favor of, or against a white man";[7] the California Supreme Court's decision in *People v. Hall* (1854) extended this exclusion to Chinese witnesses.[8] If the U.S. West taught Twain an appreciation of vernacular narrative, brash humor, and the social and economic dynamics of boom towns, it also exposed him to volatile scenarios of comparative racialization in which antiblack laws and customs were adapted and imposed upon a range of racial groups. Spending his formative years in the South and West, Twain witnessed a broad post–Civil War redefinition of white citizenship that encompassed western Indian wars and immigration restrictions as well as the effects of Emancipation. As historian Joshua Paddison explains, "Widening our conception of Reconstruction to include the West highlights interconnections between African American, Native American, Asian American, and Mexican American history and demonstrates that the multiracial, multireligious encounters that made the West a zone of tumultuous cultural contact also indelibly shaped national politics."[9]

Whereas he is best known for a handful of novels about southern slavery and feudal England, Twain produced, throughout the arc of his career, a shadow archive of writings about China, Chinese immigrants, and transpacific imperialism. Twain's interest in the Chinese extends from his early writings about Chinese criminals and settlements in the U.S. West to his late polemics against the brutal indemnities imposed by the United States and its European allies in the wake of the Boxer uprising. Biographer Forrest Robinson attributes Twain's departure from San Francisco (and a crucial turning point in his career) to his published criticisms of racist policing: "His now seasoned nose for trouble led him into conflict with the San Francisco police, who took umbrage when he criticized them in print for corruption and mistreatment of the Chinese. Clemens beat a temporary retreat to the Sierra foothills, where, in the cabin of Jim Gillis on Jackass Hill in Tuolumne County, he first heard the story of the frog that would make him famous."[10] Shelley Fisher Fishkin also traces Twain's shift toward fiction as a mode of social critique to his writings about the Chinese in San Francisco: when the *San Francisco Daily Morning Call* refused to run an outraged article Twain had written about the persecution of a Chinese man, "Twain quickly learned that exposés of racism in San Francisco would not be printed in newspapers there. So he started writing a different kind of story, one with the same subject but an alternate strategy, and published it in a paper in the next state and in a national magazine."[11] Like Fishkin, Martin Zehr suggests that Twain's concern with the Chinese provoked an important transition in his writing style: "Twain's writing is influenced in a stylistic sense in conjunction with his experience of the Chinese. Almost from the beginning, Twain's writing about the Chinese is permeated with an intentional editorial flavor, not unlike [sic] any of his early western journalism, i.e., never strictly journalistic."[12] In California, Nevada, and Hawai'i, Twain witnessed and wrote about a new post–Civil War system of racial inequality based on the policing of movement, the segregation of public space, settler colonialism, overseas economic interests, and the production of uneven vulnerabilities to premature death[13] years before he began publishing novels set in the antebellum South. Twain's writings about the Chinese thus provide a basis for reading his entire corpus in the contexts of comparative racialization and comparative colonialism.

Twain's most well known novels thematize the relationship between the industrial, post-Reconstruction era and race relations in the antebellum South. Even *A Connecticut Yankee*, which ostensibly takes place in medieval Europe, is structured around the contrast between its Yankee protagonist and an honor-based, feudal, and serf-holding society that would have resonated with contemporaneous representations of the South. Thus, Twain's fiction insistently returned to the social, demographic, and cultural transformations wrought by Emancipation, industrial capitalism, and immigration on an unprecedented scale. Although his commentaries on Chinese populations in San Francisco and western mining towns may appear far removed from the settings and black-white motifs of novels like *The Adventures of Huckleberry Finn* and *Pudd'nhead Wilson*, they initiated a career-long engagement with Chinese immigrants and U.S. transpacific relations that influenced Twain's depictions of African Americans and other racialized subjects.

While scholars have long noted Twain's numerous writings about Chinese immigrants, Asian laborers in Hawai'i, the Boxer Rebellion, and the U.S.-Philippine War, this archive has been marginalized within his body of work. *Sitting in Darkness* is the first extensive study of Twain's representations of Asians. Although the Chinese writer Lao She noted the significance of "Mark Twain's reprimand of the imperialist aggressive powers and sympathy for the anticolonialist Asian and African people" in his 1960 speech "Mark Twain: Exposer of the 'Dollar Empire,'" U.S. critics have only recently begun to integrate Twain's insights concerning Asiatic racialization with his writings about slavery and Reconstruction.[14] Margaret Duckett presents an overview of Twain's treatments of Chinese immigrants in *Mark Twain and Bret Harte* (1964) but attributes Twain's increasingly sympathetic attitudes toward the Chinese primarily to his wish to achieve something like "the current popularity of Bret Harte" by emulating Harte's relatively complex representations of Chinese characters.[15] In "Mark Twain, 'The Treaty with China,' and the Chinese Connection," Martin Zehr draws an implicit analogy between Twain's Chinese and African American characters. "In both instances," he argues, "Twain's transformation is a product of a developing empathy that is, in turn, a product of his often-demonstrated ability to successfully adopt the perspective of the other in his writings."[16] Shelley Fisher Fishkin draws this analogy more explicitly in her lucid discussion of Twain's satirical sketches about anti-Chinese laws and customs, "What Have the Police Been Doing?" (1866) and "Disgraceful Persecution of a Boy" (1870): "When Twain took up the subject of racism in *Adventures of Huckleberry Finn*, the time, the place, and the race would be different. But the central question would be the same: How can a society that debases human lives on a mass scale consider itself civilized?"[17] While these arguments help us understand Twain's stance toward public opinion and his sympathetic engagement with the humanity of Chinese immigrants, their reliance on empathy and analogy downplays the historical specificity of the "Chinese Question." Why were Chinese characters and stereotypes so popular in the decades following the Civil War? What historical conditions support analogies between African American and Chinese subjects—and what conditions are obscured by such analogies?

In a critical assessment of "the Afro-Asian analogy," Colleen Lye details "the limitations placed on Asian American politics when Asian racialization is attributed to a white supremacy that is by temporal and conceptual priority antiblack."[18] If framing Twain's Chinese plots as analogues of his narratives about slavery highlights his critiques of racial prejudice and his capacity to empathize with racial "others," it also risks falling into an ahistorical framework of formal equivalence in which "the Chinese [in the western states] were placed in the 'mental compartment which in the East had been reserved for blacks.'"[19] Twain's texts about the Chinese were not just practice runs for his later antislavery novels or early exercises in interracial empathy: instead, they rehearsed and often satirized a range of discourses about the Chinese. Some of these discourses did take the form of analogy: for example, the California Supreme Court prohibited Chinese testimony in *People v. Hall* by reasoning that the state's ban on "black" testimony was intended to refer to anyone who was not "white."[20] However, even analogically imposed laws could have divergent effects: the ban on testimony had a particularly devastating effect for the Chinese in California because they were already subject to a "foreign miners' tax" that would make them vulnerable to being robbed and displaced by white men against whom they could not testify. The most influential racial analogy of the time was the notion that Chinese migrant laborers were "coolies" serving under terms of indenture analogous to antebellum slavery.[21] By using the term "coolie" to analogize Chinese workers with slaves, anti-Chinese agitators differentiated Chinese laborers *from* free black and white workers. Racial analogies could produce either convergent or divergent effects when they colluded with preexisting conditions. Twain's narratives dramatize the historical conditions that ground specific instances of interracial comparison, as well as their convergent or divergent consequences. Rather than focus on the "nonwhite, African-like (or Africanist) presence"[22] that Morrison taught us to interrogate, *Sitting in Darkness* focuses on Twain's interventions in a system of differential racialization that functions at regional, national, and transnational scales. Drawing on the considerable scholarship exploring how U.S. literary whiteness is haunted by blackness, I consider how black and Asiatic figures inflect and haunt *one another* throughout Twain's corpus.

By focusing on popular and legal responses to Asian immigrant laborers, *Sitting in Darkness* attempts to produce historically nuanced accounts showing how Twain's writings function not only as anachronistic satires of antebellum slaveholding society but also as critical anatomies of his own era's racial politics. For, as Lisa Lowe and Moon-Ho Jung have shown, Chinese immigrants represented an emergent form of racialized labor that unsettled existing notions of freedom and slavery. In a stunning reading of the 1807 British parliamentary debates concerning the introduction of coolies to the West Indies at the moment of emancipation, Lowe writes, "The Chinese coolie appears in colonial and parliamentary papers as a *figure* for this world division of labor, a new racial mode of managing and dividing laboring groups through the liberal promise of *freedom* that would commence with the end of slavery."[23] In his historical account of how the figure of the "coolie" intersected with discourses of slavery after Emancipation, Jung argues that "the construction of coolies formed a crucial ingredient in redefining blackness and whiteness—and Americanness—when equality under the law (Reconstruction) and wage labor (industrialization) seemed to erode their meanings."[24] Far from being direct analogues for antebellum

African slaves, representations of the Chinese had specifically *modern* associations: Lye observes that "the Asiatic figures of early-twentieth-century American literature (despot, coolie, mask) referred not to persons but to a host of modernity's dehumanizing effects (laboring conditions, group entities, corporations)."[25] Jung notes that the "coolie" was ambiguously "identified with the past (slavery) and increasingly with the future (industrial capitalism and free trade)."[26] Lowe associates the "coolie" with "a modern racial governmentality in which a political hierarchy ranging from 'free' to 'unfree' was deployed in the management of the diverse labors of colonized peoples."[27] California in the postbellum decades was a vast experiment in the "modern racial governmentality" described by Lowe: a young settler-colonial state with an extractive economy whose laws attempted to racialize and control—through a carefully calibrated array of racial analogies and differentiations—a population that included displaced Native Americans, Mexican *Californios* who were naturalized by the Treaty of Guadalupe Hidalgo, legal and "illegal" Chinese migrants, black and white immigrants from the Eastern Seaboard, and immigrants from all over the world.

Moving beyond the model of racial analogy, recent monographs by Helen Jun and Julia Lee have examined the long history of intersections between African American and Asian American cultural production, mapping "the fertile but uneven terrain from which African American and Asian American interracial representations emerged."[28] Their analyses unearth striking patterns of interracial tension: for example, Jun argues that the nineteenth-century African American press deployed a discourse of "black Orientalism" that highlighted Chinese differences in order to argue for the relative assimilability of African Americans.[29] While scholars have analyzed the significance of "AfroAsian encounters"[30] amid the interracial tensions and varied race legislation of the late nineteenth century, we need a better understanding of how this dynamic field of cross-racial analogies and tensions played out in literary form. Perhaps because there were relatively few publishing outlets for Asian American, Mexican American, and Native American authors, literary scholars working on comparative racialization have tended to focus on treatments of interracial encounter by ethnic authors writing after 1900.[31] But since much of the legal and discursive groundwork of comparative racialization was established during struggles over

Reconstruction, Chinese Exclusion, and overseas imperialism, literary treatments of race during the decades between the Civil War and the U.S.-Philippine War—even texts that appear to feature only one racialized group or character—were all forged in the context of comparative racial thinking.

If the ongoing yet shifting dynamics of comparative racialization provide a historical context for this book, they also inform its methodology. While literary scholars including Jun and Lee have produced insightful and groundbreaking research by comparing texts produced by authors associated with different racial groups, this book focuses on the mechanisms of comparative racialization—the legal, spatial, and discursive techniques that were historically brought to bear—either analogically or differentially—on different racial groups. Twain's formal engagements with these mechanisms of racialization become more evident when we attend not only to explicit cross-racial connections but to the broader contexts of comparative racialization as well. Assuming that racialization was always implicitly (if not explicitly) comparative, I attend not only to the Africanist or Asiatic presence in literary narratives but also to the ghostly African American presence haunting Twain's accounts of Chinese immigrants and Filipino freedom fighters and to the Asian presences that haunt his treatments of African Americans.

Twain's race narratives bring literary techniques to bear on racial discourses that insistently compared and contrasted African American and Chinese immigrant populations. Whereas critics have shown how the formal complexities of Twain's works—such as dialect, irony, caricature, historical anachronism, courtroom farce, and incongruous endings—critique racist attitudes toward specific groups (chiefly African Americans), I argue that Twain's writings track the racial logic of his era by dramatizing comparisons and contrasts between racialized groups. The formal peculiarities of Twain's narratives—from the abrupt deus ex machina ending of *Ah Sin* to the "evasion" of *Huckleberry Finn* to the massacre of *Connecticut Yankee* to the self-conscious splitting of *Pudd'nhead Wilson* and *Those Extraordinary Twins*—reflect multiple, intersecting histories of migration, U.S. imperialism, and racial formation. Even when focusing on only one racialized character—Ah Sin, Injun Joe, or Jim—Twain's texts implicitly draw on and respond to the larger field of comparative racial discourse. To understand how Twain's treatments of racialized characters interrogate and sometimes move beyond the logic of racial analogy, *Sitting in Darkness* situates his writings in specific contexts and public debates—such as laws regulating testimony, vagrancy codes, discussions of corporate personhood, and debates concerning overseas empire—each of which had particular resonances with both transpacific migrations in the U.S. West and the racial politics of the South.

II. "Coolies for California": Race, Labor, and Empire

This study's emphasis on comparative racialization complicates understandings of Twain as either a western writer or a southern writer by focusing on connections between his novels about southern slavery and his earlier formative writings about the U.S. West and the Pacific—a transnational region that encompassed frontier mining settlements, San Francisco's police courts, Hawaiian sugar plantations, and eventually the sites of imperial battles and massacres in the Philippines. As Amy Kaplan and Stephen Sumida have pointed out, in many ways Twain's early career progressed eastward, gaining significant momentum from his dispatches from Hawai'i and his popular lectures on "Our Fellow Savages of The Sandwich Islands," as well as western pieces such as "Jim Smiley and His Jumping Frog" (1865) and *Roughing It* (1872).[32] Building on these accounts, I argue that Twain's experiences in the U.S. West and the Pacific—a transnational region that encompassed Nevada's mining settlements, San Francisco's police courts, Hawaiian sugar plantations, and eventually the sites of imperial battles and massacres in the Philippines—played a formative role in his writing.

In a September 26, 1866, travel dispatch published in the *Sacramento Daily Union*, Twain presents an uncharacteristically celebratory[33] assessment of the extraordinary productivity of Hawai'i's sugar plantations. Writing just a year after the Civil War, as business leaders throughout the nation were concerned with how to source cheap labor and commodities in the wake of Emancipation, Twain advocates Chinese "Coolies" as a promising and inexhaustible source of plantation labor. After identifying Kanaka plantation workers with the past ("day by day the Kanaka race is passing away"), Twain turns to Chinese contract laborers as the key not only to Hawai'i's productivity, but also to California's future prominence in the global economy. In a section entitled "Coolies for California," he predicts that

> You will have Coolie labor in California some day. It is already forcing its superior claims upon the attention of your great mining, manufacturing and public improvement corporations. You will not always go on paying $80 and $100 a month for labor which you can hire for $5. The sooner California adopts Coolie labor the better it will be for her. It cheapens no labor of men's hands save the hardest and most exhausting drudgery—drudgery which neither intelligence nor education are required to fit a man for—drudgery which all white men abhor and are glad to escape from.[34]

Although he frequently represents other racial groups as premodern and indolent, Twain introduces the "Coolie" as the "secret" to modernizing the state of California: "Give this labor to California for a few years and she would have fifty mines opened where she has one now—a dozen factories in operation where there is one now—a thousand tons of farm produce raised where there are a hundred now—leagues of railroad where she has miles to-day, and a population commensurate with her high and advancing prosperity."[35] After noting how several western corporations have already profited from Chinese laborers (the Pacific Railroad Company, for example, "pronounce it the cheapest, the best, and most quiet, peaceable and faithful labor they have tried"), Twain turns to the topic of transpacific commerce and its promise of U.S. economic supremacy:

> We have found the true Northwest Passage—we have found the true and only direct route to the bursting coffers of "Ormus and of Ind"—to the enchanted land whose mere drippings, in the ages that are gone, enriched and aggrandized ancient Venice, first, then Portugal, Holland, and in our own time, England—and each in succession they longed and sought for the fountain head of this vast Oriental wealth, and sought in vain. The path was hidden to them, but we have found it over the waves of the Pacific, and American enterprise will penetrate to the heart and center of its hoarded treasures, its imperial affluence. The gateway of

this path is the Golden Gate of San Francisco; its depot, its distributing house, is California—her customers are the nations of the earth; her transportation wagons will be the freight cars of the Pacific Railroad, and they will take up these Indian treasures at San Francisco and flash them across the continent and the vessels of the Pacific Mail Steamship Company will deliver them in Europe fifteen days sooner than Europe could convey them thither by any route of her own she could devise.[36]

Although the notion that the Chinese were "quiet" and "peaceable" laborers turned out to be misguided (in fact, Chinese workers protested inequitable laws and struck for better working conditions), Twain's dispatch from Hawai'i about California's Pacific future prophetically highlighted both the pivotal role of racialized labor in the state's economy and California's pivotal role in the nation's economic and imperial expansion.

For Twain, access to the Pacific Ocean and to Chinese immigrants promised to make California the center of the future global economy. California, he writes, "is about to be appointed to preside over almost the exclusive trade of 450,000,000 people—the almost exclusive trade of the most opulent land on earth."[37] Historians have described California's role in U.S. overseas expansion in similar terms: William Robbins writes, "From the beginning of the sea-otter trade along the northern Pacific coast at the close of the eighteenth century through the years of the California gold rush, the Pacific slope was tied to oceanic routes for travel, for trade, and to a significant degree—particularly in the case of San Francisco—for sources of investment capital. For more than two centuries, then, Pacific and Asian ties have been a geopolitical reality for the Far West. The transnational rail links that began to span North America during the last thirty years of the nineteenth century firmed and further integrated eastern ties to an area that could truly be seen as an increasingly international web of cultures, economies, and regions."[38] Gray Brechin notes that "the founding of California and its leading city were merely way stations on the course of empire in its eternal quest for metals and the energy necessary to acquire yet more of the same."[39] However, Twain's uncharacteristic use of hyperbolic, romantic language—"the bursting coffers of 'Ormus and Ind,'" "the land where the fabled Aladdin's lamp lies buried"[40]—also registers the fantastical nature of such projections, which presume both unhampered access to uneven commerce and the tractability of Chinese laborers.

Chinese immigrants played a crucial role in the development of California and the U.S. West. In addition to the more than twelve thousand Chinese workers who took part in constructing the Central Pacific Railroad, Chinese labor contributed to mining, farming, infrastructure, laundries, restaurants, and domestic service throughout the western states. Alexander Saxton notes that, "while Chinese were only one-twelfth of the total population" of California in the 1870s and 1880s, "they comprised a much larger fraction [between one-fifth and one quarter] of the labor force."[41] Particularly after the completion of the railroads, however, white workers perceived Chinese immigrants as unfair labor competition, and the state and federal government imposed a series of restrictions on Chinese immigrants culminating in the 1882 Exclusion Act, which prohibited the immigration of working-class Chinese men.

In the western United States, Chinese immigrants mixed and at times clashed with diverse ethnic groups as state and federal laws produced distinct racial categories. European immigrants consolidated their claims to "whiteness" in opposition not only to African Americans (who were socially and economically subordinated by Jim Crow laws) but also to Chinese migrants, Native Americans, and Mexican Americans. Even when they are not set in the West, Twain's writings frequently reflect his early exposure to laws that differentiated and disciplined California's multiracial labor force by imposing racial restrictions on landowning, employment, testimony, taxation, suffrage, mobility, and public space. Because Twain wrote about a range of racial and ethnic groups, including Irish and Italian immigrants, the Jewish diaspora, Mexican Americans, and Native Americans, this book considers how his writings about the Chinese intersect with his descriptions of Irish immigrants, his ambivalent depiction of Injun Joe, his farce about the Italian Cappello twins, and his critiques of the United States' treatment of Filipino colonial subjects.[42] However, I focus on Chinese immigrants and African Americans because they are the subjects of Twain's most complex writings on racism and comparative racialization and because his contemporaries persistently drew analogies and contrasts between the "Negro Problem" and the "Yellow Peril" during a period marked by the racial reshufflings of Reconstruction, post-Reconstruction, Chinese immigration, industrialization, and empire building.⁴³ As Jung notes, "Within the major social crises of the 1860s—battles over the legal, political, and social standing of slaves, masters, blacks, and whites in the United States—coolies represented a vexing anomaly whose contested status would reconstruct American identities after emancipation."⁴⁴

A formative location in Twain's development as a writer, California was the site of explosive struggles over racial inequality and immigration restrictions. On the one hand, southern Democrats imported discriminatory laws inspired by antebellum black codes into California, adapting them to apply to other racial groups.⁴⁵ On the other hand, white workers agitated for laws applying specifically to the Chinese, framing them as unassimilable "perpetual foreigners" in contradistinction from African Americans. California was both a settler colony and a pivotal node in overseas empire: "As the wealth of nature poured forth, it turned California into a financial center of global significance and the western pole of the national economy: The West was both colony and empire in the nineteenth century, with its own imperial center in San Francisco and peripheries from the Black Hills to the Aleutians, from Zacatecas to Hawai'i."⁴⁶ As a setting for comparative racialization and a key staging area for commercial and naval vessels setting out across the Pacific, California exposed Twain to social dynamics that would preoccupy him throughout the course of his career.

III. The Archive

While staying with his friend Steve Gillis's family in San Francisco, Twain wrote a parody of Edgar Allan Poe's "The Raven" titled "The Mysterious Chinaman" (1864–1865).⁴⁷ "Once upon a morning dreary," the poem's speaker hears a knock at his door and assumes it is "Maim" (probably Mary Elizabeth Gillis, to whom the poem was inscribed).⁴⁸ When he opens the door, however, the speaker discovers the domestic servant Ah Chung:

> Then this leathery wretch beguiling my sad fancy into smiling,
> By the grave and stern decorum of the countenance he bore—
> "Though thy crest be shorn and shaven, thou," I said, "art sure no Raven,

Ghastly, grim, and long-tailed scullion, wand'ring from the kitchen floor—
Tell me what thy lordly will is, ere you leave my chamber door"—
Quoth Ah Chung, "No shabby 'door.'" (hic!)⁴⁹

Probably because of its racist caricature of both the Chinese servant and his faulty command of the English language, Twain's critics and biographers have seldom commented on this poem. But if the poem disparages the Chinese worker by likening his pidgin speech to the nonsense of Poe's raven and by likening his queue to a tail, "The Mysterious Chinaman" also allegorizes the repeated entanglements between the United States and Asia that would characterize both his era and his career as a writer. The poem's compulsive return to Ah Chung and his refrain—modeled on the structure of "The Raven"—belies the speaker's dismissive claim that Chung's answer "little meaning, little relevancy bore." For beneath its humor and caricature, "The Mysterious Chinaman" is literally about an open door—a site of transracial encounter, foreign communication, and potential invasion. In this Gothic representation of a "Chinaman," repetition evokes the troubling intimacy of racialized labor: western states were already becoming dependent on Chinese migrant workers, and Chinese domestic laborers were already in American homes. Even in the opening stanzas of Twain's poem, when his speaker is innocently pondering "many a quaint and curious shirt that me and Steve has wore" and doing his "washing," he is performing a task frequently associated with Chinese workers.⁵⁰ Twain's poem highlights the unsettled boundaries of race, labor, gender, and nation that would characterize his later engagements with U.S.-Asia relations.

The Chinese played an important role in Twain's early newspaper writing. When his travel correspondence was serialized in the *Sacramento Daily Union* and the *Daily Alta California* in the 1860s, those newspapers were publishing numerous commentaries on the "Chinese Question." Twain's numerous articles about Chinese migrants in the *Virginia City Territorial Enterprise* and the *San Francisco Daily Morning Call* range from descriptions of Chinatown and Chinese buildings to descriptions of arrests and trials involving Chinese residents accused of various crimes. They include humorous representations that highlight the exotic language and appearance of Chinese residents, sensational accounts that dwell on their supposed immorality and uncivilized habits, and more sympathetic responses to the persecution of unoffending Chinese men. While these ambivalent representations of the Chinese resonate with popular depictions of African Americans as primitive, undisciplined, criminal, or passive, Twain more directly invoked longstanding debates concerning African Americans in the eastern states in other articles with titles such as "Miscegenation" and "Chinese Slaves." Twain's early writings sometimes voiced unsympathetic and patronizing attitudes that were common in journalists' accounts of Chinese immigrants, and these attitudes were reflected in his actions: he later reported that he and his friend Steve Gillis would amuse themselves by throwing beer bottles on the roofs of Chinese men's "wooden shanties covered with beatenout cans."[51] An 1869 poem attributed to Twain caricatures the queues of two "distinguished Chinamen" who were reportedly returning to California: "they'll waggle home, / And carry their tails behind them."[52]

Although Twain's early newspaper articles were only sometimes sympathetic to the Chinese, he developed a more critical perspective as he acquired firsthand experience of how the police, courts, and newspaper editors colluded to repress the Chinese. By 1864, Twain was using the Chinese as a foil for satirizing ideas about Western cultural superiority: for example, he attributed the criminal activities of Chinese immigrants—such as the smuggling of prostitutes and an attempt to sabotage a railroad—to Christianity and other "civiliz[ing]" influences.[53] Shortly after the Civil War, Twain's "Personal Habits of the Siamese Twins" (1869) even used the Chinese conjoined twins, Chang and Eng Bunker, to allegorize the difficulties of national reconciliation—effectively treating Chinese characters as emblems for the U.S. body politic.[54] Twain's outrage over the *San Francisco Call*'s racist editing practices led to a turning point in his career. As he recounts in his autobiography, a story about a "Chinaman" led to Twain's break from the "soulless drudgery" of journalism:

> Finally there was an event. One Sunday afternoon I saw some hoodlums chasing and stoning a Chinaman who was heavily laden with the weekly wash of his Christian customers, and I noticed that a policeman was observing this performance with an amused interest—nothing more. He

did not interfere. I wrote up the incident with considerable warmth and holy indignation. Usually I didn't want to read in the morning what I had written the night before; it had come from a torpid heart. But this item had come from a live one. There was fire in it and I believed it was literature—and so I sought for it in the paper next morning with eagerness. It wasn't there. . . . The foreman said Mr. Barnes had found it in a galley proof and ordered its extinction. [Barnes] said that the *Call* . . . gathered its livelihood from the poor and must respect their prejudices or perish.[55]

As I noted above, Fishkin has suggested that this incident helped precipitate Twain's shift from local journalism to satirical sketches and fiction with a wider circulation. Twain apparently held a grudge against the offending newspaper, which had suppressed the article because it "could not afford to alienate its Irish readers" for forty years (Twain either resigned or was fired as a result of the incident): "When news photos of the great San Francisco earthquake of 1906 arrived in the East, showing the *Call*'s building reduced to a skeletal frieze of ruins, Twain exulted, 'How wonderful are the ways of Providence!'"[56]

As Hsin-Yun Ou has shown, two men who became Twain's friends in the 1860s—Anson Burlingame and Reverend Joseph Hopkins Twichell—profoundly influenced his views about the Chinese. Burlingame, who invited Twain to visit him in Peking after the two met in Hawai'i in 1866,[57] worked to shore up China's autonomy and equality in its diplomatic negotiations with the United States. Twichell, whose close friendship with Twain began in 1868, worked tirelessly to support the rights of Chinese laborers and students in the United States. In the years following his acquaintance with Burlingame and Twichell, Twain wrote a number of critical sketches and stories focusing on U.S. relations with China. "The Treaty with China: Its Provisions Explained" (1868), published in the *New York Tribune*, praises the Burlingame Treaty for placing diplomatic relations on an equal footing by guaranteeing equality and reciprocity in international relations, diminishing foreign traders' extraterritorial privileges, relinquishing "practices of unnecessary dictation and intervention by one nation in the affairs or domestic administration of another,"[58] and granting rights (such as rights to testify in court, to access public schools, and to apply for naturalization) to Chinese immigrants. No longer constrained by the anti-Chinese sentiment of newspaper readers in California and Nevada, Twain expands upon a point he had made in passing in an 1866 article, "What Have the Police Been Doing?"[59]

> In San Francisco, a large part of the most interesting local news in the daily papers consists of gorgeous compliments to the "able and efficient" Officer This and That for arresting Ah Foo, or Ching Wang, or Song Hi for stealing a chicken; but when some white brute breaks an unoffending Chinaman's head with a brick, the paper does not compliment any officer for arresting the assaulter, for the simple reason that the officer does not make the arrest; the shedding of Chinese blood only makes him laugh. . . . I have seen dogs almost tear helpless Chinamen to pieces in broad daylight in San Francisco, and I have seen hod-carriers who help to make Presidents stand around and enjoy the sport. I have seen troops of boys assault a Chinaman with stones when he was walking quietly along about his business, and send him bruised and bleeding home.[60]

Twain leverages his regional experience as a former San Francisco resident to contextualize the treaty for his New York readers, emphasizing that political rights are essential to the safety and equal treatment of Chinese immigrants. Notably, "The Treaty with China" also departs from Twain's earlier endorsement of "coolie" labor by recommending measures that would break up "the infamous Coolie trade" by supporting the already considerable "'voluntary' emigration of Chinamen to California."[61]

Among the miscellaneous and frequently humorous "Memoranda" that Twain contributed to the *Galaxy Magazine* (in which Walt Whitman had recently published his cosmopolitan essay on democracy and aesthetics, *Democratic Vistas*) were five installments about Chinese immigrants: "Disgraceful Persecution of a Boy" (May 1870), "John Chinaman in New York" (September 1870), and three installments of the unfinished story, "Goldsmith's Friend Abroad Again" (October 1870, November 1870, and January 1871). In Chapter 1, I will consider how "Disgraceful Persecution" and "Goldsmith's Friend" deploy literary techniques such as irony and first-person narrative to expose the contradictions of racist laws and customs. "John Chinaman" stands out not only as (at least ostensibly) an account of "Chinamen" on the

Eastern Seaboard but also as an incisive treatment of both ethnic stereotypes and comparative racialization. In the piece, a correspondent recounts an encounter with "a Chinaman sitting before [a tea store] acting in the capacity of a sign" and proceeds to meticulously describe the man's clothing: "His quaint Chinese hat, with peaked roof and ball on top; and his long queue dangling down his back; his short silken blouse, curiously frogged and figured[;] his blue cotton, tight-legged pants tied close around the ankles, and his clumsy, blunt-toed shoes with thick cork soles."[62] However, when the liberally disposed narrator attempts to encourage the man and asks how he is being paid, the "Chinaman" responds in Irish brogue: "Divil a cint but four dollars a week and find meself; but it's aisy, barrin' the bloody furrin clothes that's so expinsive."[63] "John Chinaman" highlights the fictitious nature of ethnic stereotypes by exposing a "Chinaman" to be a "sign" produced by costume and by representing the Irish man through brogue ("brogue" is etymologically derived from a term for stout shoes, such as the man's "blunt-toed shoes with thick cork soles"). But it also places the two stereotypes of Chinese costume and Irish brogue in uncomfortable proximity: how do we know that this is an Irish man wearing clothing that looks Chinese, rather than a Chinese man speaking in accents that appear Irish? In the context of Irish Americans' animosity toward Chinese workers (whom they frequently perceived as unfair labor competition in this period), this short sketch emphasizes the socioeconomic vulnerabilities and cultural stereotypes that the two groups had in common.[64] True Williams's illustration of "John Chinaman in New York" (Figure I.1) for an early collection of Twain's sketches highlights the dual and reversible qualities of ethnic "signs" by presenting the title of the piece in reverse, as if seen through a window from inside the tea shop. The hybrid image of an Irish man in Chinese costume emphasizes that ethnic figures such as the "Chinaman" are inherently relational, indexing analogies and tensions between a range of racial and ethnic groups.

Although Twain had written about Virginia City's Chinatown in ethnographic terms in 1864, he later updated his description of the settlement's opium-smoking "vagabonds" and exotic foods in *Roughing It*, praising the Chinese as "quiet, peaceable, tractable, free from drunkenness, and . . . as industrious as the day is long."[65] While *Roughing It*'s assessment of the Chinese as a "tractable" and "industrious" race may

JOHN CHINAMAN IN NEW YORK.

AS I passed along by one of those monster American tea-stores in New York, I found a Chinaman sitting before it acting in the capacity of a sign. Everybody that passed by gave him a steady stare as long as their heads would twist over their shoulders without dislocating their necks, and a group had stopped to stare deliberately.

Is it not a shame that we, who prate so much about civilization and humanity, are content to degrade a fellow-being to such an office as this? Is it not time for reflection when we find ourselves willing to see in such a being, matter for frivolous curiosity instead of regret and grave reflection?

Figure I.1: True Williams, "John Chinaman in New York," in *Mark Twain's Sketches, New and Old* (Hartford, Conn.: American Publishing Co., 1875), 231. Courtesy of the Mark Twain Project, Bancroft Library, University of California, Berkeley.

appear less hostile than Twain's earlier accounts of their criminal activities, the equation of Chinese immigrants with industriousness also drew on popular stereotypes of the Chinese as a race of mindless laborers lacking in individuality: as Lye points out, "The coolie signifies . . . the prospect of [the body's] mechanical abstraction" under modern monopoly capitalism.[66] Twain's enthusiasm about coolie labor in his correspondence from Hawai'i and his later comments on Indian "coolie" laborers in Mauritius in *Following the Equator* (1897)[67] reinforce this view of the Asiatic migrant as mechanized laborer.

However, Twain's increased exposure to the Chinese in the U.S. West led to more nuanced treatments of Chinese racialization: with the exception of a passing reference in *Roughing It*,[68] he would never again employ the term "coolie" to refer to involuntary Chinese laborers in the United States. Moreover, Twain was involved with numerous projects that critiqued or presented alternatives to figurations of the "coolie": *Ah Sin* (1877)—which I discuss in Chapter 1—complicates the notion of Chinese docility by featuring a Chinese hero who strategically performs a tractable, inoffensive, and mindless persona in order to protect himself and his white friends. Twain's writings about conjoined twins—which I examine in Chapter 3—explore the contradictions between liberal individualism and new collective bodies such as corporations and impersonal laborers that were increasingly associated with Gilded Age capitalism and Chinese immigration. Chapter 4 considers Twain's relationships with two public figures—Yung Wing and Wong Chin Foo—who embodied a different form of Chinese modernity: not the "coolie" but the cosmopolitan intellectual working to strengthen China against foreign incursions. Twain's suggestion, in "Concerning the Jews" (1898), that the history of anti-Semitism has "the business aspect of a Chinese cheap-labor crusade" not only indicates parallels between the treatment of these ethnic groups but also avows that the racialization of Chinese and Jewish diasporas was rooted in anxieties about economic competition and falling wages.[69] "The Fable of the Yellow Terror" (1904–1905)[70]—a dystopian sketch about the threat of four hundred million Chinese subjects developing mastery of modern science and military technology—also invokes the industriousness of the Chinese, but only in the service of a broader critique of empire: in the fable, the Bees learned to use their stings and expand their sway from the Butterflies, when the latter sent missionaries, traders, and soldiers into the Bees' territory to force open their markets.

Twain's later writings about Asia turn from Chinese immigrants to the United States and Europe's imperialist interventions in China and the Philippines. After the United States decided to annex the Philippines and Guam in the wake of the War of 1898, Twain joined the New York Anti-Imperialist League and, according to Jim Zwick, became "the most prominent opponent of the Philippine-American War."[71] In "To the Person Sitting in Darkness" (1901), along with a number of shorter pieces collected by Zwick in *Mark Twain's Weapons of Satire: Anti-imperialist Writings on the Philippine-American War*, Twain focuses on the ethical implications of annexing the Philippines and opening China to trade and missionaries against the will of their inhabitants, as well as the war atrocities committed to ensure control over these populations. However, Twain insistently situated U.S. practices of racial domination in the broader context of comparative imperialism, comparing slavery to India's caste system, Jim Crow to Spanish colonial rule in the Philippines, the Boxer revolt to the Pawnee war. In "To My Missionary Critics" (1901)—a response to those who published shocked responses to his critique of Reverend William Scott Ament—Twain employs a series of anecdotes to draw analogies between the unfair and indiscriminate indemnities imposed on the Chinese for the Boxer uprising and the practices of Middle-Eastern despots and southern racists (530–531).[72] In "The United States of Lyncherdom" (1901), he makes the modest proposal that we import missionaries in China back into the United States to proselytize against the lynching of black men: "The light from the [lynching] fires flushes into vague outline against the night the spires of five thousand churches. O kind missionary, O compassionate missionary, leave China! come home and convert these Christians!"[73] Even in the sharp, satirical style of his later writings, Twain advocated for the international reciprocity and territorial sovereignty that had been at the heart of the Burlingame Treaty: "The Boxer is a patriot. He loves his country better than he does the countries of other people. I wish him success. The Boxer believes in driving us out of his country. I am a Boxer too, for I believe in driving him out of our country."[74] Beneath his caricature of nativist rhetoric, Twain uses chiasmus to emphasize an ethos of reciprocity between Americans and "Boxers," whom he describes as patriots struggling against foreign interventions and unequal treaties. Twain returns to the Boxer uprising in his unpublished piece, "The Chronicle of the Young Satan," where Satan cheerfully describes how the Chinese revolt precipitated by Christian missionaries "will be Europe's chance to rise and swallow China" and how, eventually, "the Turk and the Chinaman" will acquire Western guns "to kill missionaries and converts with."[75]

One of Twain's many passing references to the Chinese describes an unexpected scene of reading in the gold-mining town of Bendigo in Australia:

> I was taken to the hospital and allowed to see the convalescent Chinaman who had been attacked at midnight in his lonely hut eight weeks before by robbers, and stabbed forty-six times and scalped besides; . . . when I arrived this awful spectacle of piecings and patchings and bandagings was sitting up in his cot reading one of my books. (*FE*, 243)

Although this passage takes the form of a joke about an admirer who arranged for Twain to witness this unusual spectacle, it also gestures toward transpacific continuities between racial violence in Bendigo and the U.S. West—both settler colonies whose economies were grounded in resource extraction. It is unclear whether this passage's humorous hyperbole is poking fun at the suffering of the "Chinaman" or the racial violence of those who attacked him; what is clear is that Twain's host expects him to be pleased by a scenario that aligns his writings with the Chinese man's convalescence. Despite its improbability, this scene of cross-cultural and cross-racial reading suggests that the critiques of racism, imperialism, and structural violence found in Twain's books (and it is significant that he does not specify a title) concern the vulnerability of the Chinese diaspora as well as that of other groups. While Twain produced a rich and varied body of writings about the Chinese, I do not believe his engagements with Asia and Chinese immigrants are coextensive with these texts. Instead, the following chapters consider influences and resonances between Twain's commentaries on the Chinese and texts—such as *Tom Sawyer*, *Huckleberry Finn*, *A Connecticut Yankee*, and *Pudd'nhead Wilson*[76]—that do not mention China or the Chinese at all. Twain's comparisons between different racial groups and instances of colonialism—as well as the historical practices of comparative racialization that characterize his era—extend through all his writings.

In the half century that followed his earliest encounters with the Chinese in California and Hawai'i, Twain's perspectives on both race and writing shifted dramatically. After endorsing Chinese "coolies" as a source of cheap labor, Twain moved on to positive depictions of Chinese characters such as Ah Song Hi and Ah Sin, to critical treatments of issues—such as racialized vagrancy and "coolie" discourse—that affected Chinese migrant workers, to direct involvement with reformers' efforts to modernize China, and finally to strident criticisms of colonialism and cultural imperialism in and beyond Asia. Throughout these shifts in attitude and genre, however, Twain remained focused on material inequalities, which he frequently highlighted through cross-racial analogies and distinctions.

The first half of this book considers how the legal and social contexts of comparative racialization inflect Twain's narratives by juxtaposing his texts with landmark legal cases concerning testimony, vagrancy, and corporate personhood. Chapter 1, "'A Witness More Powerful than Himself': Race, Testimony, and Twain's Courtroom Farces," examines a range of responses to the *People v. Hall* case, which extended (through the logic of racial analogy) a ban on African American and Native American testimony against whites to the Chinese. After surveying critical responses to the decision by Chinese immigrants and their supporters, I conduct a comparative reading of the motif of testimony—including blocked or circuitous testimony—in Twain's writings about Chinese and African American court cases. Twain's courtroom farces in "Goldsmith's Friend," *Ah Sin*, and *Pudd'nhead Wilson* dramatize the consequences of laws that deny the ethical and political responsibilities of witnessing to racialized populations. Chapter 2, "Vagrancy and Comparative Racialization in *Huckleberry Finn* and 'Three Vagabonds of Trinidad,'" situates *Huck Finn* among a range of texts in which Twain and Bret Harte critiqued the laws, institutions, and historical inequities that produced uneven, racially differentiated access to mobility and public space throughout the U.S. West and South. The disproportionate use of vagrancy laws to criminalize Native American, Mexican, black, and Chinese subjects—many of whom had already been forcibly displaced by legal or extralegal means—grounds analogies between a range of texts and characters including the Chinese narrator of "Goldsmith's Friend," the "vagrant" Injun Joe, Pap Finn, Jim and Huck (who respectively experience their downriver voyage as paralyzing and liberatory), and the Chinese, Native American, and canine protagonists of Harte's little-known rewriting of *Huck Finn*, "Three Vagabonds of Trinidad."[77] Chapter 3, "'Coolies' and Corporate Personhood in *Those Extraordinary Twins*," situates *Those Extraordinary Twins* in two related contexts: the establishment of corporate personhood (along with Fourteenth Amendment protections for corporations) in *Santa Clara County v. Southern Pacific Railroad* (1886)[78] and popular representations of Chinese railroad workers as swarming, monstrous "coolie" masses functioning as collective—rather than individuated—agents. These contexts reframe both *Twins* (in which the conjoined twins are put on trial as a "corporation" for kicking Tom) and *Pudd'nhead Wilson* by connecting their antebellum settings with the industrial-era labor struggles in which U.S. notions of whiteness and racial difference were forged.

This book's later chapters develop comparative close readings across national boundaries in order to emphasize how Twain's writings connect the struggles of different nations, races, and colonized populations. Chapter 4, "A Connecticut Yankee in the Court of Wu Chih Tien: Imperial Romance and Chinese Modernization," reads *A Connecticut Yankee in King Arthur's Court* as both a satire of specific instances of Western imperialism (including in China) and a critical engagement with the emergent genre of historical romance. I juxtapose *A Connecticut Yankee* with two instances of Chinese modernization—Yung Wing's Chinese Educational Mission and Wong Chin Foo's novel *Wu Chih Tien*[79] (which Twain read and praised). Yung's attempt to educate Chinese boys in English and Western science is a suggestive precursor to Hank Morgan's project of educating medieval boys into modern Republican subjects. Wong's novel joins Twain in revising the conventions of historical romance, but Wong does so by presenting a democratic, modernizing, and masculine Chinese protagonist who allegorizes the anti-Manchu and anti-imperialist movement in China. Chapter 5, "Body Counts and Comparative Anti-imperialism," considers the development of Twain's anti-imperialist writings from his reflections on European colonialism in *Following the Equator* to his bitter criticisms of the

U.S.-Philippine War and the Western response to the Boxer uprising. Twain turns to abstract representational strategies—more appropriate to the genres of the nonfiction sketch, journalistic parody, fable, and collage than to novelistic fiction—that draw connections between different anti-imperial movements (Boer nationalists, Filipino revolutionaries, Chinese peasants, South Asian laborers, and blacks in the U.S. South) by highlighting how modern practices of state racism delineate, count, and manage racialized populations.

* * *

By reading Twain's writings in the context of legal battles over Chinese Exclusion, the displacement of Chinese settlers from the countryside to urban "Chinatowns," and the writings of early Chinese migrants, *Sitting in Darkness* shows how his picaresque plots, historical novels, courtroom farces, journalistic parodies, and anti-imperialist sketches critically engaged particular modes of comparative racialization at the level of literary form. A comparative approach has the benefit of shifting the focus of conversation from Twain's attitudes about racial stereotypes to how his works register and critique the structural inequalities that ground racial comparisons: who can testify in court, who can be employed by the state, who can vote or run for office, who can apply for citizenship, and who can move or stay still in public space. By examining how Twain deploys such issues of material inequality to ground and interrogate analogies between different racialized and colonized groups, I hope to extend our understanding of how his works mobilize literary form to expose and address not only racial prejudice but also structural modes of racism that function even in the absence of prejudicial intentions.

1

"A Witness More Powerful than Himself"

Race, Testimony, and Twain's Courtroom Farces

BOSTON: You've got to talk.
FERGUSON: Yes, or hang.
1ST MINER: Talk and hang both! (They all make a dive for ah sin who scrambles between their legs and upsetting one or two of them—jumps on table, seizes flat iron, shrieking and gibbering Chinese. Picture of consternation by miners. Quick curtain.)[1]

While the uncomfortable blend of farce, mob violence, and racist caricature presented in this scene from Twain and Bret Harte's collaborative play, *Ah Sin*, may not surprise readers familiar with similar mob scenes in *Huckleberry Finn*, *A Connecticut Yankee in King Arthur's Court*, and *Those Extraordinary Twins*, the double imperative—"Talk and hang both!"—invokes a predicament specific to nonwhite populations in California and other western states. When the California Supreme Court in *People v. Hall* (1854) extended the state's prohibition on "black" and "Indian" testimony to the Chinese, it both marked the Chinese population as a target for violent crimes and endangered those Chinese who attempted to bear witness to crimes. If the civic order required that subjects provide testimony in courts of law, the decision that Chinese were incompetent witnesses—grounded in both Chief Justice Hugh Murray's spurious racial science and in the popular suppositions about the vulgar and unbinding nature of Chinese oaths[2]—disabled their testimony. Thus, a Chinese witness who provided information about a crime might be in danger of retaliation if the culprit could not be convicted on the basis of Chinese evidence: as William Speer reports of one Chinese man who did not provide information about a robbery in Tuolomne County, "The reason why he did not go and give information to Mr. G. was that the facts could not be proven on account of their testimony being invalid, and he feared that, if left at large, his life would be taken by the robbers or their associates."[3] Whereas witnesses are generally empowered with the knowledge that their testimony can convict a criminal, this Chinese witness understood that talking about what he'd seen was much more likely to endanger him than to convict the robbers. Similarly, the Chinese laundryman in *Ah Sin* must negotiate the legislated vulnerability and impotence of Chinese testimony ("Talk and hang *both*.").

This chapter situates *Ah Sin*—a work that has been marginalized in the Twain canon by its formal idiosyncrasies and yellowface stereotypes—amid the public debates about the racialization of testimony precipitated by *People v. Hall*. The ban on testimony both responded to and reproduced the racialization of the Chinese as dishonest, "inscrutable," and withdrawn from civic life. If, in most western states and territories, "slyness was interpreted by courts as a character flaw that jeopardized Chinese participation in the criminal justice system,"[4] the lack of Chinese participation exacerbated both the criminalization of the Chinese and their apparently "sly" hesitance to present public testimony that could not hold up in court. Twain's responses to the prohibition on Chinese testimony highlight the political force inherent in the act of testifying, as well as the everyday forms of violence and injustice to which this legal disability subjected the Chinese. Reading *Ah Sin* as a response to California's prohibition on Chinese testimony also highlights how Twain's other courtroom farces—from his early journalism in the *San Francisco Daily Morning Call* to the troubling conclusion of *Pudd'nhead Wilson*—critique the political framing of what counts as "evidence" by interrogating the distinction between testimony and non-testimonial evidence. A closer look at historical responses to the *People v. Hall* decision elucidates the stakes of racialized and racializing evidence in the courtroom scenes of Twain's early sketches, *Ah Sin*, and *Pudd'nhead Wilson*.

I. People v. Hall and the Racialization of Testimony

"Of all the wrongs visited upon the Chinese in the period from 1850 to 1870," writes legal historian Charles McClain, "the ban on their testimony in the state's courts—not surprisingly, given its fateful implications—rankled most deeply, and the removal of this disability was consistently the chief item on the agenda of the community leadership."[5] The ban on Chinese testimony was established in *People v. Hall*, when the California Criminal Procedures' ban on black, mulatto, or Indian testimony against a white man was extended to the Chinese. Writing for the majority, California Supreme Court chief justice Hugh Murray argued that the term "Indian" applied to "the Mongolian, or Asiatic" because Christopher Columbus had mistaken the New World's inhabitants for Asian Indians; he also argued that the generic term "black" was intended to include all nonwhites.[6] The immediate consequences of the case anticipated its broader effects throughout California and other western territories influenced by California's laws: when *People v. Hall* reversed the conviction (on the testimony of three Chinese witnesses) and the death sentence of George W. Hall for the murder of Chinese miner Ling Sing in Nevada County,[7] it effectively announced that the Chinese could be killed with impunity provided that no white witnesses sympathetic to the Chinese were around. More broadly, the prohibition on testimony debarred Chinese immigrants from the capacity and civic duty to bear witness—a right that, as the communication theorist John Durham Peters explains, Western cultures associated with Enlightenment reason and manhood (in both ancient Greek and Latin, the same word denotes both "witness" and "testicle"; in German, *zeugen* means both "testify" and "procreate").[8]

If Murray's analogies between Chinese, "black," and "Indian" contributed to a "Negroization of Chinese immigrants" and an extension of racist laws that southern Democrats had brought west from slave states,[9] his opinion also set the Chinese apart as foreigners: "The anomalous spectacle of a distinct people, living in our community, recognizing no laws of this State except through necessity, bringing with them their prejudices and national feuds, in which they indulge in open violation of law; whose mendacity is proverbial . . . "[10] California's prohibition on Chinese testimony produced only a partial analogy between Chinese and African American subjects because the formal prohibition colluded with discursive and economic factors to intensify the racialization of Chinese immigrants. In addition to Murray's charges of "proverbial" "mendacity" and a refusal to recognize or abide by the state's laws, the Chinese were often viewed as unfair labor competition, linguistically inarticulate, inherently deceitful, and heathen. Ironically, their inability to testify reinforced these stereotypes, along with prevalent notions about Chinese stoicism: "In the nineteenth century suffering in silence becomes one of features [sic] of the Chinese most interesting and impressive to Western observers."[11]

These racial beliefs led California's legislature to adopt a new foreign miners' tax in 1852 (an 1850 version of the tax had been used to displace Mexican Americans from mining claims) targeting Chinese miners. Justified by the notion that the political and economic interests of Chinese immigrants were in China rather than the United States (the Chinese were wrongly accused of observing foreign laws and sending most of their earnings back to China rather than spending them in the United States)—as well as by sensationalist predictions that the United States would be overrun by millions of Chinese[12]—the new tax attempted to control the influx of Chinese immigrants in western mining camps in 1851–1852. This monthly tax became indispensable to California's economy, accounting for up to half of the state's revenue between 1852 and 1870.[13] Whereas taxation generally entails some measure of state protection and representation, the decision in *People v. Hall* undercut Chinese access to the protection of the courts. In fact, historian Sucheng Chan has suggested that the prohibition on Chinese testimony was in part intended to "handicap" Chinese miners who had been appealing "to the local courts when they were robbed of their gold dust either by other Chinese or by white miners or when they were evicted from claims they were working. Such action contradicts the stereotype of them as a people who insulated themselves from the larger society around them."[14] Chan's comments indicate the extent to which the ban on testimony produced the very conditions of social segregation and "foreignness" that were cited as reasons for taxing and legally disabling the Chinese.

The collusion of the Foreign Miners' Tax and the prohibition on testimony indicates how the racialization of the Chinese was both analogous to *and* divergent from that of other groups. Formally prohibited to testify in courts along with African Americans and Native Americans, the Chinese were rendered powerless against abusive collectors of a tax that expressly targeted them. As the Presbyterian minister William Speer wrote in "An Answer to the Common Objections to Chinese

Testimony; and an Earnest Appeal to the Legislature of California, for Their Protection by our Law" (1857),

> Scarce a man that reads this has not seen or heard of acts of barbarity and fraud on the part of "Foreign miners' tax collectors," that ought to have been severely punished; such as whipping, cutting, taking the blankets and tools of even those that have been sick, dating back their licenses one or two weeks in the month, snatching their dust when weighing out the amount due, charging $6 instead of $4 monthly, requiring one to pay for others, perhaps a stranger for a company of half-a-dozen, re-issuing old licenses, and the like.[15]

These widespread abuses by corrupt tax collectors—or by white men masquerading as tax collectors—could not be "severely punished" without the testimony of white witnesses. Speer suggests that, even when collected honestly, the exorbitant amount of the Foreign Miners' Tax (which, despite its name, was collected almost entirely from Chinese) "beggars [Chinese miners]. It drives them to the mountains and thickets like wild beasts. It fills them with hunger, sickness and despair. It turns them, what [sic] their honorable character with our trading population in the country shows is not necessary, into cheats and liars. It will in time fill our prisons."[16]

Foreign Miners' Tax collectors were not the only Californians who regularly attacked Chinese immigrants. Hostility toward the Chinese increased in the 1850s when surface mines were becoming scarcer and white placer miners struggled to compete with the rise of company mines (which used hydraulic and quartz mining and sometimes employed Chinese laborers).[17] Speer details some of the worst excesses enabled by the prohibition of Chinese testimony, including a band of masked desperados robbing and terrorizing Chinese settlements[18] and this brutal attack reported in the *Auburn Whig*:

> On the night of May 3d, about 12 o'clock, a party of eight or ten Chinamen, encamped on Shirt Twain Canon, about 150 yards above the Iowa Hill and Yankee Jim's trail, were attacked by a party of four Americans, when a scene of fiendish butchery was enacted, which makes the blood thrill with horror in the narration. Armed with the noiseless knife, these ruffians commenced their horrid work upon the helpless Asiatics.[19]

Speer argues that such crimes—which frequently included outright murder—would have repercussions well beyond the legally unprotected Chinese community, for "as long as crimes cannot be proven and punished before our Courts, upon Chinese testimony, so long must this great, wide-scattered, helpless class offer inducements for the commission of crime. They furnish a *school* for the increase, education and support of criminals."[20] In addition to inducing citizens to commit crimes under conditions of impunity, Speer notes that the ban on testimony barred Chinese immigrants from performing an important civic duty. Finally, the law was detrimental to the nation's international reputation: "In this question *our national character* is involved. The people of California are, to all the vast coasts of the Pacific Ocean, the representatives of Western Civilization—of the results of Christianity.... Men from every people under heaven are walking our streets, threading our mountain trails, sipping our streams, watching and, by the eternal axioms of right and wrong in every breast, judging of our principles by their fruits."[21]

Speer's arguments resonated with middle-class Chinese immigrants' criticisms of the prohibition on testimony. In an open letter responding to an anti-Chinese speech by California governor John Bigler, San Francisco merchant Lai Chun-chuen attacked *People v. Hall* by dissociating the Chinese from Native Americans: "[Your people] have come to the conclusion that we Chinese are the same as Indians and Negroes, and your courts will not allow us to bear witness. And yet these Indians know nothing about the relations of society; they know no mutual respect; they wear neither clothes nor shoes; they live in wild places and in caves."[22] In rejecting *People v. Hall*'s analogy, however, Lai reproduced stereotypes about Native Americans and conceded the notion that some racial groups should be disqualified from bearing witness. In a remonstrance to Congress written at the request of numerous Chinese businessmen in San Francisco sometime between 1856 and 1868, the merchant Pun Chi enumerated the "perpetual vexations of the Chinese" and devoted a section to "Fatal injuries unpunished" as a result of the prohibition on testimony: "Of how great wrongs is this the consummation! To the death of how many of us has it led!"[23] Pun Chi then named a number of murdered Chinese men whose killers were released without trial in the absence of a white witness. Although the law recognized no competent witness to these murders, Pun Chi's partial "catalogue of crimes" bore witness in print by naming the dead and detailing the incidents. In addition to criticizing specific laws such as the prohibition on testimony and the Foreign Miners' Tax, he presented a broad assessment of the shortcomings of California's legal "usages": "Murder is allowed to escape without the forfeit of life; robbery occurs without the apprehension of the offender. False rumors are made a pretext to arrest men; officers apprehend the innocent in order to oppress and fine them. They practice neither humanity nor justice. Their ambition and their schemes terminate simply in gold and silver. Justice demands that political institutions such as these should speedily be reformed, or you will meet with the scorn of the whole world."[24]

Whereas Lai Chun-chuen argued against *People v. Hall* by rejecting the idea that the Chinese are "the same as Indians and Negroes," Frederick Douglass's visionary speech on "Our Composite Nationality" (1869) aligned African American interests with those of Chinese immigrants and other exploited groups. Without relying on a simple logic of racial analogy, Douglass's concept of a "composite" nationality located the strength of the U.S. nation in the diversity of its population. In his impassioned defense of Chinese immigration, Douglass devoted several paragraphs to refuting key assumptions underlying the prohibition on Chinese testimony. Contesting the popular belief that "the Chinaman . . . is secretive and treacherous, and will not tell the truth when he thinks it for his interest to tell a lie," Douglass noted that Americans can "make it for [the Chinaman's] interest to tell the truth . . . by applying to him the same principle of justice that we apply to ourselves."[25] He further argued that, since civilizations are founded on trust, "the very existence of China for [five thousand years], and her progress in civilization, are proofs of her truthfulness."[26] Finally, Douglass refuted—and inverted—the notion that Chinese are unable to understand the sanctity of oaths by offering a cultural relativist assessment of the American custom of swearing on the Bible:

> The next objection to the Chinese is that he cannot be induced to swear by the Bible. This is to me one of his best recommendations. The American people will swear by anything in the heavens above or in the earth beneath. We are a nation of swearers. We swear by a book whose most authoritative command is to swear not at all. . . . If the Chinaman is so

true to his convictions that he cannot be tempted or even coerced into so popular a custom as swearing by the Bible, he gives good evidence of his integrity and his veracity.[27]

Insofar as the Bible itself prohibits swearing, Douglass suggested, it is Christians and not the Chinese who regularly violate the integrity of oaths. While he paused to note that southern gentlemen were turning to Chinese labor as a possible solution to the shortage of superexploited labor left in the wake of Emancipation, Douglass argued that granting legal and social equality to the Chinese would enable them to contribute to the nation's wealth and culture without devaluing the labor of other groups.

Even jurists who upheld *People v. Hall* had a difficult time legitimating racial prohibitions on testimony. When the California Supreme Court ruled that Hing Kee's testimony in the case of an alleged robbery by a white man was invalid in *People of the State of California v. Brady* (1870), for example, the court's opinion considered at length—only to subsequently dismiss—the possibility that the decision to render the Chinese incompetent witnesses before the law was made in bad faith:

> We can hardly conceive it possible that a legislative body in a Christian country would deliberately deprive its Courts and police of any proper means for the detection and prevention of crime; that it would willingly leave any class unprotected, so far as the commission of crimes against them are concerned; this would directly encourage crime, and lead inevitably to the demoralization of society, and consequently the insecurity of all. To withdraw from any class the protection of the police laws, through prejudice or from a desire to discourage their presence, would be inhuman and barbarous. *We cannot attribute* any such motives to a co-ordinate department of the Government, and *we must conclude* that the provisions of the law under consideration *were supposed* by the Legislature to provide every means for the detection and punishment of crime consistent with justice and the safety of the community.[28]

Despite its forced and heavily qualified conclusion—which professes trust in the good intentions of the legislature in spite of all appearances—this passage articulates a scathing critique of the law's actual effects. Simply because it "cannot attribute" prejudice to the

California Legislature, the Supreme Court upheld a decision that led to glaring structural inequalities resulting from Chinese immigrants' limited access to police protection.

As a young reporter writing regular accounts of arrests and court cases for the *San Francisco Daily Morning Call* in 1864, Twain had ample opportunity to witness the racist policing and trials that proliferated in the wake of *People v. Hall*. The following three reports attributed to Twain, written in the span of four days in September 1864, present a striking contrast between the treatment of Chinese and white suspects:

> in bad company.—A day or two since, while the employees of A. & E. Bartheimer, wholesale tobacco dealers on Battery street, were engaged in a portion of the building, leaving another portion exposed, three Chinamen were observed moving furtively about, with evident designs of pelf. Supposing the ground all clear, one of the Celestials carefully wrapped his handkerchief over a box of chewing tobacco, weighing twenty-one pounds, and valued at sixteen dollars and fifty cents, and decamped. Chase was given and two of the chaps were captured, together with the booty; the third made good his escape. The names thus added to the roll of infamy are Ah Chow and Ah Wen. Ah Chow declared that he was a belly good man, collector for one of the extensive Chinese Companies of the city, had nothing to do with the theft, wouldn't for anything have had anything to do with it. His reputation was at stake. His virtue rose indignant against the impeachment; could prove an immaculate character in Chinese, etc. But Ah Chow's declamation availed nothing. A certain magpie once got his neck wrung for being caught in bad company. *Etiam* Ah Chow. They were both ordered to appear this morning for sentence.
>
> discharged.—John Connor, one of the three men arrested for making hash of a Chinaman's head, was examined yesterday afternoon, before Judge Shepheard, and discharged. Silk and Benson, the other two, who are charged with assisting in the job, will be examined to-day.
>
> the battered chinaman case.—Andrew Benson and Wm. Silk, two of the triad who were charged with having pounded a Chinaman to pieces in a slaughter house, a few days since, were examined yesterday in the Police Court. Benson was discharged and Silk sent up to the County Court.[29]

In the first passage, the court convicted a Chinese man for being "caught in bad company" while dismissing his testimony (his "declamation availed nothing"); in the latter passages, by contrast, the police court discharged two of the three white men suspected of "making hash of a Chinaman's head." If many of Twain's news reports described Chinese suspects in denigrating or nonchalant ways that minimize their suffering (for example, he reported that a suspect named "Ah Sow "is an astonishing freak of nature, being unquestionably a male sow"[30] and referred to other Chinese suspects as "only fish of a very small fry [whose] proceedings were not worth their writing up"[31]), his apparent lack of interest in the plight of Chinese "criminals" and crime victims was in part due to his editors' preference for reports that affirmed racist policing practices. When Twain did write an outraged article on anti-Chinese violence and the arbitrary and incompetent practices of the city's police, his editors suppressed the article and he apparently received threats that led to his departure from San Francisco.[32]

Years later, in the satirical *Galaxy* essay "Disgraceful Persecution of a Boy" (1870), Twain wrote that "one of the principal recreations of the police, out toward the Gold Refinery, is to look on with tranquil enjoyment while the butchers of Brannan Street set their dogs on unoffending Chinamen, and make them flee for their lives"; he added in a footnote that "I have many such memories in my mind" and that one particularly violent incident "sticks in my memory with a more malevolent tenacity, perhaps, on account of the fact that I was in the employ of a San Francisco journal at the time, and was not allowed to publish it because it might offend some of the peculiar element that subscribed for the paper."[33] In addition to exposing how the "form" or template imposed by the editors on the "local items" of San Francisco's newspapers precluded any criticism of the police and courts, "Disgraceful Persecution" posed a question that Twain would return to in *Huckleberry Finn*: what kind of education do everyday reports that affirm racist violence convey to American children? The essay responded to the imprisonment of a boy for stoning Chinese men by enumerating the conditions—ranging from the Foreign Miners' Tax to how the San Francisco police, courts, and newspapers took advantage of vulnerable Chinese immigrants to enhance arrest statistics and produce glorified accounts of the "dare-devil intrepidity" of the police in arresting Chinese chicken thieves ("DP," 8)—that impressed upon the boy that a Chinaman had no rights that any man was bound to respect; that he had no sorrows that any man was bound to pity; that neither his life nor his liberty was worth the purchase of a penny when a white man needed a scapegoat; that nobody loved Chinamen, nobody befriended them, nobody spared them suffering when it was convenient to inflict it; everybody, individuals, communities, the majesty of the state itself, joined in hating, abusing, and persecuting these humble strangers. ("DP," 8–9)

By invoking Chief Justice Roger Taney's decision, in *Dred Scott v. Sandford* (1856), that black men could not become U.S. citizens because they were "so far inferior that they had no rights which the white man was bound to respect," Twain drew an implicit comparison between the noncitizen status of Chinese immigrants in his own era and that of blacks before the Civil War.[34] However, the Chinese man diverged from the status of the slave insofar as "neither his life nor his liberty was worth the purchase of a penny": his status as formally free laborers left the "Chinaman" vulnerable in distinctive ways, insofar as no master had a property interest in his well-being. Twain's revisions to "Disgraceful Persecution" introduce a term—at once aesthetic and social in its import—that links his interests in formal disjunctions and humorous juxtapositions[35] with the contradictions of law and racial thinking: whereas the *Galaxy* version of the sketch perceives a "sublimity of grotesqueness" in the law's punishment of a boy for an act that is perfectly consistent with anti-Chinese legislation, later versions of the essay call this a "sublimity of *incongruity*" ("DP," 9, emphasis added).

Twain turned to fiction as a strategy for engaging with these injustices in "Goldsmith's Friend Abroad Again," an unfinished work serialized in the *Galaxy* in 1870–1871 and, as I show in Chapter 2, an important antecedent to *Huckleberry Finn*.[36] "Goldsmith's Friend" features an incident probably based on the public stoning of a Chinese man that Twain had witnessed and attempted, in vain, to report in the *Call*:[37] after some Irish bystanders set a dog on him, the new immigrant Ah Song Hi is arrested for "disturbing the peace."[38] At his trial, the protagonist attempts to call four Chinese witnesses: "They saw it all. I remember their faces perfectly. They will prove that the white men set the dog on me when I was not harming them" ("GF," 468). But the police lawyer explains that this is impossible because "in this country white men can testify against Chinamen all they want to, but *Chinamen ain't allowed to testify against white men!*" Ah Song Hi, who believes in America's democratic ideals, responds with incredulity: "What a chill went through me! And then I felt the indignant blood rise to my cheek at this libel upon the Home of the Oppressed, where all men are free and equal—perfectly equal—perfectly free and perfectly equal. I despised this Chinese-speaking Spaniard for his mean slander of the land that was sheltering and feeding him" ("GF," 468). The final installment of "Goldsmith's Friend"—which describes the summary trials of Chinese prisoners—probably draws on Twain's own experiences writing up police court sentences for the *San Francisco Call*: "There were twelve or fifteen Chinamen in our crowd of prisoners, charged with all manner of little thefts and misdemeanors, and their cases were quickly disposed of, as a general thing. When the charge came from a policeman or other white man, he made his statement and that was the end of it, unless the Chinaman's lawyer could find some white person to testify in his client's behalf; for, neither the accused Chinaman nor his countrymen being allowed to say anything, the statement of the officers or other white person was amply sufficient to convict. So, as I said, the Chinamen's cases were quickly disposed of, and fines and imprisonment promptly distributed among them" ("GF," 469–470).

Twain described the larger social implications of *People v. Hall* in chapter 54 of *Roughing It*, which is dedicated to Chinese settlers in Virginia City, Nevada. "A Chinaman," he wrote,

> is a great convenience to everybody—even to the worst class of white men, for he bears the most of their sins, suffering fines for their petty thefts, imprisonment for their robberies, and death for their murders. Any white man can swear a Chinaman's life away in the courts, but no Chinaman can testify against a white man. Ours is the "land of the free"—nobody denies that—nobody challenges it. [Maybe it is because we won't let other people testify.] As I write, news comes that in broad daylight in San Francisco, some boys have stoned an inoffensive Chinaman to death, and that although a large crowd witnessed the shameful deed, no one interfered.[39]

This passage presents a condensed picture of many points detailed in Speer's more elaborate responses to anti-Chinese laws: the Chinese were easy prey to white criminals; they were liable to be wrongfully convicted of crimes committed by white men; theft, displacement, and discriminatory taxation also made Chinese immigrants more likely to be criminalized and imprisoned as vagrants, tax evaders, or thieves. The brutal scene of public stoning—one which Twain's early writings returned to repeatedly—subtly contests the prohibition on testimony by suggesting that the morally incompetent witnesses, in this case, are not the Chinese but the presumably white "crowd [that] *witnessed* the shameful deed" without interfering.

As Margaret Duckett has pointed out, Twain's writings and views about the Chinese were in part inspired by the national popularity of Bret Harte's treatments of Chinese characters.[40] In his autobiography, Twain observed that "Plain Language from Truthful James" had, within a week, brought Harte from obscurity to being "as notorious and as visible . . . as if it had been painted on the sky in letters of astronomical magnitude."[41] Although Harte's satirical poem was appropriated by anti-Chinese agitators, his short stories dramatized the social consequences of *People v. Hall*. "The Iliad of Sandy Bar" (*Overland Monthly* 1870)—in which, according to Axel Nissen, "Harte created his first Chinese character in fiction, maybe *the* first Chinese character in American fiction"[42]—begins with a violent altercation witnessed only by "a serious Chinaman, cutting wood before the cabin."[43] When the Chinese witness responds to Colonel Starbottle's questioning by remaining "stolid, indifferent, and reticent," the colonel "[runs] over the various popular epithets which a generous public sentiment might accept as reasonable provocation for an assault" and exclaims that "this yer's the cattle . . . that some thinks oughter be allowed to testify ag'in' a White Man!"[44] In "Wan Lee, the Pagan" (first published in *Scribner's Monthly* in September 1874), Harte narrated an incident similar to the one that prompted Twain's "Disgraceful Persecution of a Boy": the story's hospitable, cosmopolitan protagonist ends up "stoned to death in the streets of San Francisco, in the year of grace 1869, by a mob of half-grown boys and Christian school-children!"[45] Although their collaboration on *Ah Sin* produced a surprisingly unpopular play, Twain and Harte were well positioned to produce a dramatic assessment of anti-Chinese attitudes and laws.

II. Ah Sin and Nontestimonial Evidence

Twain and Harte's collaboratively authored play, *Ah Sin*, has been marginalized by critics as a failure among audiences and an embarrassing work indulging in repeated scenes of yellowface minstrelsy. The play was written specifically to feature the white actor Charles Parsloe, already well known for performing the role of a caricatured "Chinaman" in Harte's *Two Men of Sandy Bar* (1876).[46] While *Ah Sin* attempted to capitalize on the popularity of Chinese caricature, it is worth noting here that Twain worked on the play in the midst of composing *Huckleberry Finn*—a novel that channeled the conventions of blackface minstrelsy into a profound indictment of both slavery and post-Reconstruction race relations.[47] As Eric Lott notes in his groundbreaking study of antebellum blackface, minstrelsy is not a point of access to black cultural authenticity or an entirely hostile form of racist caricature but rather a complex process of "love and theft" in which white working-class performers and audiences both assimilated and disavowed black cultural practices.[48] Instead of merely lampooning its Chinese protagonist, *Ah Sin* offers a nuanced—if sometimes oblique—portrait of a Chinese immigrant's psychology and motives as influenced and circumscribed by racist legislation. Several early reviewers, and Twain himself, framed the play as a vehicle for the staging of an original Chinese character. Describing the play as a "course of public instruction" on the "Chinese question," Twain explained that "the whole purpose of the piece is to afford an opportunity for the illustration of this character. The Chinaman is going to become a frequent spectacle all over America by and by, and a difficult political problem, too. Therefore, it seems well enough to let the public study him a little on the stage beforehand."[49] Several reviewers praised the play's depiction of a "typical Chinaman," and one even claimed that the "singular" character of the "heathen Chinee" makes *Ah Sin* a "distinctively American play."[50] Others were less convinced by Parsloe's yellowface role, calling the play's title character nothing more than "a reflection of the American burlesque of the Chinaman"[51]—a burlesque that "fails to give any illustration of Chinese character whatever."[52] Noting that Parsloe was able to move on to another yellowface role as the character of Washee Washee in Joaquin Miller's *The Danites* (1877), Sean Metzger observes that "even if audiences had not accepted Harte and Twain's play, it seemed, they did validate Parsloe's performance as the kind of Chinaman they would pay to see. Concomitant with the increasing clamor to evacuate the land of Chinese people, Parsloe's performances offered a stand-in on which to project particular embodiments of Chineseness that audiences paid to sustain."[53]

If Parsloe's performance appealed to both spectators and many of the play's reviewers, why did *Ah Sin* fail to satisfy audiences? The critic Dave Williams attributes the play's failure to its critiques of anti-Chinese laws and stereotypes: "*Ah Sin,* a product of two of the era's leading writers, challenged audience expectations and paid the price for its daring."[54] But critics have also noted the play's formal incoherence—a quality they often attribute to Harte and Twain's collaborative process. The reviewer for the *New York Spirit of the Times*, for example, complains of the play's poor "literary execution" and its "ramshakly" construction;[55] more recently, Jerry Thomason claims that as a result of the collaborative process between Harte and Twain, "the play is often chaotic and the plot incoherent."[56] The play's political views are similarly incoherent: Harold Bush describes *Ah Sin* as an "embarrassingly stereotyped burlesque/drama (suggestive of Twain's halting response at times to issues of race),"[57] and both James Moy and Hsin-Yun Ou suggest that the play's formal messiness is a product of a tension between its authors' efforts to depict a dignified and sympathetic Chinese character and their desire to make money by catering to the public's preference for disparaging caricatures of the Chinese.[58] Brenda Murphy faults the play's allegedly anti-realist impulse "to represent as manipulated and convoluted a set of actions as is possible within the confines of conventional form, with the apparent object of removing the play as far from the commonplace action of real life as an active imagination can take it."[59] In revisiting *Ah Sin*, my aim is not to defend it against accusations of racism or to prove that Twain was sympathetic to the Chinese but, rather, to shift the interpretive focus from the play's racial stereotypes to its dramatization of structural racism.

Assembling a range of theatrical stereotypes and clichés, *Ah Sin* interweaves a murder plot, a marriage plot, a courtroom farce, and several instances of comic relief featuring songs, physical comedy, puns, and carelessly rendered pidgin English. When the affable old miner

Plunkett, who has a penchant for telling stretchers, plays a game of poker with the deceptive and calculating Broderick in the mining town of Deadwood, California, the laundryman Ah Sin decides to help Plunkett out by stealthily stacking the deck. Plunkett wins Broderick's mine, but when he discovers gold there in the evening, Broderick throws him over a cliff. Broderick pays Ah Sin, the only witness, to dispose of his bloodied jacket and subsequently attempts to frame the gentlemanly York (the male love interest in the play's courtship plot) for the murder. When a mob of white miners attempts to question Ah Sin about York's involvement at the end of Act 2, Ah Sin refuses to talk about the murder; only at the end of the play does Ah Sin finally produce his evidence before an improvised lynch court when Broderick asks him to simulate a bloodstain on York's jacket and bring it to the trial. Instead of York's stained jacket, Ah Sin produces Broderick's bloodied jacket, and the jury and spectators decide that Broderick is guilty of murdering Plunkett. At this point, Broderick offers Ah Sin half a stake in his rich mine and $10,000 to save him from being hanged, and Ah Sin produces Plunkett himself ("'Nother witness! Plunkee!" [*AS*, 95]), whom he has been nursing at his own home all along. In addition to Plunkett, Broderick, and York, Ah Sin's actions save the play's love plot: York's survival of the lynch trial will leave him free to marry the heiress Shirley Tempest, whom he has been courting throughout the play. While the plot empowers Ah Sin as the character who surreptitiously controls—even, in a sense, authors—all the action, the Chinese laundryman's actions and motives account for much of the play's apparent incoherence: as one reviewer notes, "*Ah Sin* does innumerable things without any conceivable motive. (Why, for instance, does he change the cards when *Broderick* and *Plunkett* are playing? Why does he hide *Plunkett* during these acts in his wash-house?) Is this a characteristic of the San Francisco Chinaman?"[60] These erratic actions appear quite reasonable when we read the play in light of the prohibition on Chinese testimony.

Ah Sin's status as a kind of deus ex machina who both creates (by stacking the poker deck) and resolves the play's potentially tragic predicaments anticipates two peculiar plot elements of *Huckleberry Finn*: Jim's quiet decision not to tell Huck that the corpse in the houseboat was his father's and Tom Sawyer's notorious decision to put off informing Jim of his freedom so that he and Huck could amuse themselves by pretending to free him from captivity. While these aspects of Twain's later novel have been historicized as responses to the realities of slavery and post-Reconstruction indebted servitude (Jim's silence about Pap's death ensures that Huck will continue on as a white travel companion, and critics have read the novel's supposedly flawed ending as an allegory for the immobilization of freedmen and the prolongation of black captivity in the post-Reconstruction era),[61] critics have not subjected the formal peculiarities of *Ah Sin* (often dismissed as a result of its collaborative authorship—as if Twain's other works, such as *Huckleberry Finn*, *Pudd'nhead Wilson*, and *Those Extraordinary Twins* did not involve difficult formal inconsistencies) to extended historical analysis. While my reading of the play draws on Randall Knoper's suggestion that Ah Sin's apparently erratic behavior represents a mode of subaltern "mimicry,"[62] I argue that the Chinese laundryman's motives and strategies—along with the formal incoherence of the text as a whole—represent historically informed responses to the debates precipitated by *People v. Hall*.

Ah Sin—whose farcical "court scene is ahead of anything of its kind before presented," according to the *Denver Daily Rocky Mountain News*[63]— explicitly thematizes the dynamics of witnessing, testimony, and evidence. The entire plot is structured by the Chinese witness's presence at the scene of Broderick's assault and the deferral of his (legally disabled) testimony. Beyond that, Ah Sin also acts as a witness to Broderick's dishonest poker playing, the lynch court's irregular procedures, and numerous scenes involving courtship and exchanged identities. On two occasions, Ah Sin proclaims his intention to "watchee" as events unfold; at York's trial for murder, he falls off a pile of boxes he has climbed, explaining that "me wantee *see* better" (*AS*, 90). Halfway through the play, a white mob attempts to force Ah Sin to tell them what he knows about Plunkett's disappearance; later, when York asks Ah Sin to vouch for him, the laundryman reminds him, "Chinaman evidence no goodee"; nevertheless, Broderick's trump card at the trial is York's apparently bloodstained jacket, which he has paid Ah Sin to fabricate and which he refers to as "the Chinaman's evidence." When he is admonished that "a Chinaman cannot testify in this court," Broderick replies that Ah Sin's physical evidence constitutes "a witness more powerful than himself" (*AS*, 83, 94). Insofar as the lynch court upholds *People v. Hall*'s ban on Chinese testimony, the play suggests a continuity between the extralegal racial injustices frequently carried out by white mobs and the letter of the law. The paradox underlying *Ah Sin*'s plot, however, is that Ah Sin is both an ideal, ubiquitous witness and legally disabled from testifying to anything he perceives. His strategic combination of deception, delay, and physical evidence empowers Ah Sin to bear witness to what he has seen: Broderick's murderous fight with Plunkett. By the end of the play—and in spite of his legal disability—Ah Sin is able to remove suspicion from York and bring Broderick to justice: as the latter puts it, "Devil take the Chinaman, he has put the rope around my neck" (*AS*, 95). Although the law designates him an "incompetent witness," Ah Sin proves to be the most perceptive witness in the play.

But why does Ah Sin wait until the end of the play to present Broderick's bloodied coat and reveal that Plunkett has been alive all along? Greed may have something to do with it: Ah Sin extracts half a mine and $11,000 from Broderick over the course of the play: $500 for helping dispose of the jacket, $500 for staining York's jacket and bringing it to the trial, and the rest for saving Broderick from lynching.[64] But the state's prohibition on Chinese testimony—which is observed even by the extralegal lynch court in Act 4—may also explain Ah Sin's reluctance to implicate Broderick when he is questioned by a group of angry white miners. Like other supposedly "inscrutable" Chinese who refused to provide information to the authorities during the era of *People v. Hall*, Ah Sin may realize that testifying would put him in danger of retaliation without providing the authorities with legally admissible evidence. (Tom Sawyer and Huck Finn face a similar dilemma in *Tom Sawyer*, when they decide not to testify against Injun Joe because they are terrified of retribution; Tom does eventually testify, in part because his testimony—unlike that of an Indian—is supported by law and custom in antebellum Missouri.) With Plunkett out of the picture, it would be Ah Sin's word against Broderick's, and no court in the state could hear a "Chinaman'"s testimony against a white man. Even when Ah Sin does produce the jacket, he is careful not to accuse Broderick himself: he allows the lynch court to discover for themselves that Broderick's name, not York's, is on the jacket's collar. Faced with the double imperative to "talk and hang *both*!"—to risk making a disempowered statement that would leave him vulnerable to retribution—Ah Sin instead performs the part of a fool (he "jabbers in Chinese" on numerous occasions) and cleverly deploys nontestimonial physical evidence to bear witness in his stead.

Harry Williams's "Ah Sin" (Figure 1.1)—a song written in 1877 expressly for Charles T. Parsloe and probably performed in some productions of *Ah Sin*—suggests that the Chinese laundryman had already learned about his legal disability firsthand. The song describes Ah Sin's marriage to an Irish girl and his subsequent discovery of his wife being kissed by an American ("Meli-can") man. In lines that are designated as *spoken* before the final verses, Ah Sin reports: "Me say, 'What for you kissee my little galee?' He get mad and kickee me down stairs. Policeman come along and say what's your name? Then I tellee him—."[65] The final lines of the song describe what happened in the wake of this assault: "P'lice man takee me to lockee up shop, puttse in a room and make me stay, Judge send me up for very long tim-ee me love Irish gal, she run 'way! Me catch sickee, feel likee die No can walkee, plenty much lame, if me catch-ee Meli-can man, Me break his nose-ee all the same!"[66] Williams's lyrics perform in miniature the tension that characterizes Twain and Harte's entire play: a tension between racial caricature and a critique of the racist criminal justice system. But if the song describes Ah Sin's inability to protect himself from punishment and wrongful criminalization in the past, he finds a way around the ban on testimony in the play. Ah Sin resorts to physical evidence as a surrogate for the testimony of Plunkett, who remains in hiding during the courtroom scene.

But why should Plunkett be out of the picture, when showing his face would prevent the possibility of a miscarriage of justice? As the *New York Sun* reviewer put it, "Why does [Ah Sin] hide *Plunkett* during these acts in his wash-house?" Even if Plunkett came forward and testified, his word might not hold water: from the beginning of the play, he is presented as a habitual liar who tells yarns about "champagne suppers," his "awful rich" mine, and his family (he tells Miss Tempest that York is his son and tells York she is his daughter; *AS*, 42). When Broderick accuses Plunkett of cheating at cards, he explains that no one will believe Plunkett's testimony: "Who will believe the champion liar of Calaveras . . . against a man of truth?" (*AS*, 54). Plunkett, it seems, would not be a credible witness; thus, while his appearance would

Figure 1.1: Harry Williams, "Ah Sin" (Detroit: Roe Stephens, 1877). Courtesy of the Lester S. Levy Collection of Sheet Music, Special Collections, Sheridan Libraries, Johns Hopkins University.

certainly absolve York and Broderick of murder, his testimony might be incapable of proving his claim to the mine he had won from Broderick in the poker game or of punishing Broderick for attempting to murder him. Ah Sin can only influence the white mob and lynch court by waiting for the ideal moment to intervene in their theatrical enactment of justice.

Ah Sin's motives for keeping the injured Plunkett at his house are less explicit, but several lines scattered throughout the play gesture toward an interracial friendship between them. Given that his testimony would not hold up even against a "champion liar" like Plunkett, it seems safe to assume that Ah Sin could not have held Plunkett against his wishes—so the incentive for their cohabitation is mutual. This is confirmed by an odd moment (one that several reviewers deemed absurd and incoherent)[67] that occurs just before the miners question Ah Sin in Act 2: as Plunkett's wife and daughter exit the stage, "plunkett *enters from house.*"

> Ah Sin. (*Pushing* plunkett *into house.*) Go inee, go inee. Go to bedee—I fetchee ginee—(*Hands in gin.*) You wife catchee, you catchee plenty hellee—(*Sits—fills cup and drinks.*) (AS, 68)

Ah Sin then becomes intoxicated in a comic sequence wherein he loses his cup, drinks from the bottle, declares he "No can keep eye up," staggers, and falls asleep on the table. But the brief glimpse of Plunkett serves to inform the audience that he is alive and contentedly drinking gin in Ah Sin's house while avoiding his wife. The play's concluding lines repeat this motif: when Plunkett appears in the court, his wife "*runs towards him—he tries to shrink out of sight*" (AS, 95). Plunkett, it seems, would rather get drunk with Ah Sin than "catchee plenty hellee" from his wife. Despite the use of comic, ethnic dialect here, Ah Sin's onstage drunkenness functions as both a surrogate and a complement to Plunkett's intoxication within the house: here, drinking gin is an interracial, homosocial activity. Like the canonical American novels that Leslie Fiedler discusses in his classic essay, "Come Back to the Raft Ag'in, Huck Honey!" *Ah Sin* "celebrate[s] . . . the mutual love of *a white man and a colored*" and thus indulges the white man's fantasy of "acceptance at the breast he has most utterly offended."[68] The suppressed and socially stigmatized intimacy (an interracial "stranger intimacy"[69] that the play itself only indicates in passing, incoherent lines) between the white miner and the Chinese laundryman "in the homosocial environment of frontier mining camps"[70] explains both Ah Sin's initial motive[71] for helping Plunkett win at cards ("Plunkee goodee me—no likee see Broderick swindly him" [*AS*, 51]) and his motive for waiting as long as possible to reveal that Plunkett has not been murdered. In addition to extorting money from Broderick, Ah Sin's delay allows him to enjoy the company of a friend.

Ah Sin's critique of the racialization of testimony takes several forms. Like Twain's account of the complicit witnesses of a public stoning, the play features several white characters who either perceive or interpret evidence incompetently; the intertwined plots put the audience in the position of desiring that Ah Sin's testimony be made public, since it is the key to punishing the villain and to enabling the consummation of the love plot, and the tension between Ah Sin's competence as a witness and his lack of access to protected speech conveys both the inequity and the social impracticality of invalidating the testimony of a considerable portion of the laboring population. Ah Sin's inability to testify does not endanger other Chinese characters (indeed, there are no other Chinese in the play's mining camp—a fact that suggests they may have recently been purged by exorbitant taxes and extralegal violence)[72] but honest and sympathetic white characters like Plunkett, York, and Miss Tempest.[73] Finally, *Ah Sin* challenges its audience to perceive and interpret evidence of socially and legally invalidated truths such as the humanity and competence of a Chinese man and the existence of intimacies between Chinese and white workers in a state where even children were taught to believe that "nobody loved Chinamen, nobody befriended them" ("DP," 9).[74] Ah Sin's presentation of Plunkett at the end of the play—so easily dismissed as either an absurd deus ex machina resolution or a comic attempt to defuse the threatening spectacle of a "Chinaman" having figuratively "put the rope around [the] neck" of a white man and literally pointed a gun at Broderick—obliquely attests to the fact that he and Plunkett have spent most of the play's four acts in each others' mutually chosen company.

Although *Ah Sin*'s critique of *People v. Hall* (like Twain's later satires of slaveholding society) would have been relatively uncontroversial in 1877 (the decision had already been reversed by the Civil Rights Act of

1870 and revisions to California's penal and civil codes in 1872),[75] beliefs about the deceitfulness and incompetence of "Chinamen" and struggles over evidence and testimony played important roles in the national debates that preceded the Chinese Exclusion Act of 1882 and the Geary Act of 1892 (whose requirement of "at least one credible white witness" echoes the earlier prohibition of Chinese testimony).[76] For example, *Chinese Immigration: The Social, Moral, and Political Effect of Chinese Immigration: Testimony Taken Before a Committee of the Senate of the State of California* (1876) painted a bleak picture of the character of Chinese immigrants and recommended renegotiating the Burlingame Treaty. Drawing exclusively on testimony from white observers, the California Senate Committee's report considered accusations that associated the Chinese with a range of social ills including "coolie" labor, prostitution, opium, disease, assassinations, a shadow government, and a lack of regard for the sanctity of oaths. The *Memorial of the Six Chinese Companies. An Address to the Senate and House of Representatives of the United States. Testimony of California's Leading Citizens* (1877) leveraged notions of evidence and testimony to refute the state senate's report. Noting that the senate's document omitted any consideration of the "Chinese side of the question" and even "suppressed the testimony of many of their witnesses who held contrary views," the *Memorial of the Six Chinese Companies*[77] counters the clearly biased evidence of the anti-Chinese report with the "Testimony of California's Leading Citizens." In reviewing the evidence, the Six Companies even suggest that California's senators lack credibility as witnesses; for example, after disproving the claim that not a single Chinese had been converted to Christianity, the *Memorial* comments: "We have been told that in American courts the rule of evidence is, that if a witness has been found incorrect in the statement of *some* facts, his whole testimony can be impeached. But in this case, your memorialists are charitable enough to assume that the State Senate Committee were debarred from obtaining this evidence from natural causes."[78] Whereas advocates of Chinese Exclusion often represented the Chinese as unfair labor competition and hostile to the white working class, *Ah Sin*'s oblique depiction of kindness and intimacy between its Chinese character and Plunkett indicates both the possibility of interracial working-class solidarity and the difficulty of perceiving or representing it under existing political conditions.

III. *"The Fingerprints That Will Hang You"*

By turning to object witnesses—Broderick's bloodied jacket and Plunkett's living body (much more important than Plunkett's testimony, given his penchant for lying)—as strategically orchestrated alternatives to Chinese testimony, *Ah Sin* at once critiques *People v. Hall* and reaffirms its outcome: the silencing of Chinese immigrants. Ah Sin, who engages in physical comedy routines throughout the play, is empowered as a witness in spite of his cultural incompetence and his occasional inability to speak: even in the final courtroom scene, he "*Jabbers a lot of Chinese*," speaks the indecipherable line "ti Kelly kee chow," and engages in unspecified "*Comic business*" (*AS*, 94). If Ah Sin is finally able to bear witness by producing Broderick's jacket—"a witness more powerful than himself"—*Pudd'nhead Wilson* explores the darker side of physical evidence, which could be used to extract information from uncooperative racialized "witnesses" and, on a larger scale, to police racialized populations.

The climactic trial of *Pudd'nhead Wilson* (which I analyze more closely in Chapter 3) echoes several elements of *Ah Sin*'s climactic courtroom farce: instead of providing verbal testimony, the racialized character Tom Driscoll presents conclusive physical evidence that identifies the culprit. In her commentary on "Tom Driscoll's demonstrative body," Emily Russell notes that the novel's trial scenes hinge upon a "principle of corporeal legibility" that extends well beyond Wilson's use of fingerprinting.[79] In addition to lecturing the jury at length on the supposedly infallible nature of corporeal fingerprint evidence, Wilson carefully observes Tom's nervous physical reactions to the proceedings. Tom becomes increasingly distressed, until "finally, in a page torn from a sentimental novel, the murderer swoons at the moment of his exposure: 'Tom turned his ashen face imploringly toward the speaker, made some impotent movement with his white lips, then slid limp and lifeless to the floor' (120). In this climactic moment, Tom's body becomes the only effective communicator and his speech is rendered impotent. Wilson finds Tom's collapse so demonstrative that he insists, 'He has confessed' (ibid.)."[80] Ironically, Wilson's discourse on fingerprinting extracts a physical confession from Tom, but not the fingerprints he was hoping for: Wilson's injunction to "make upon the window the finger-prints that will hang you!" causes Tom to faint.[81] Tom's failure to suppress his distress bears witness to not only his guilt but also an excess of emotion that racial science frequently attributed to nonwhites.

Whether by fainting or providing fingerprints, Tom Driscoll would provide physical evidence that trumps his speech: in the words of *Ah Sin*, "a witness more powerful than himself." In her comparison of the use of palmistry and fingerprints as modes of extracting physical evidence in *Pudd'nhead Wilson*, Sarah Chinn writes: "Where the palm-reading exercise was an attempt to construct a narrative and was executed among supposed equals, [the fingerprinting] display is designed to establish identities by separating out innocent from guilty and, as a consequence, white from black, legitimate citizens from chattel slaves."[82] Whereas *Ah Sin* was able to manipulate and exploit physical evidence, fingerprints and involuntary movements silence and disenfranchise Tom. Once shown to be a black man and a slave, his oral testimony becomes merely "some impotent movement with his white lips" (*PW*, 120). *Pudd'nhead* thus dramatizes a shift in the role of physical evidence as modern policing practices began to leverage physical evidence to identify criminals and to enforce laws that criminalized racialized subjects.

As historian Alfred McCoy has noted, a burst of inventions in the 1870s and 1880s fueled an "information revolution" in the United States: "New products and processes for the rapid compilation, codification, transmission, storage, and retrieval of information . . . invested the state with the potential for mass surveillance, allowing for the first time an advance beyond punishment of the few to control over the many."[83] Photographs, anthropometry, fingerprinting, and other forms of corporeal evidence contributed to the modernization of policing, but, given the racist laws and policing practices that Twain witnessed in San Francisco's courts and the South, more widespread policing would entail more effective enforcements of immigration restrictions, Jim Crow, and other forms of racial inequality. In 1883, for example, Harry Morse—a former sheriff employed by the Treasury Department to help investigate fraud at the San Francisco Custom House—proposed using thumbprints to identify Chinese immigrants;[84] although such proposals to use fingerprints were not implemented, customs officials used non-testimonial evidence including written descriptions, photographs, and anthropometric measurements to identify Chinese migrants.[85] Moreover, as McCoy demonstrates in *Policing America's Empire,* key developments in modern police surveillance were innovated by the U.S. colonial administration in the Philippines, working in a context of counterrevolution and indefinite civil liberties: within twenty years of adapting Alphonse Bertillon's photo identification system[86] and fingerprinting in 1901–1906, Manila's "Metropolitan Police would amass an extraordinary 'all embracing index' of alphabetized file cards for two hundred thousand Filipinos—the equivalent of 70 percent of Manila's entire population."[87] Finally, the widespread adaptation by police departments of Bertillonage, fingerprinting, and other techniques that allowed for the storage and transmission of physical evidence contributed to the racist practices of policing—including the uneven enforcement of vagrancy laws, which is the focus of the following chapter—that criminalized and disciplined African Americans, Mexican Americans, Native Americans, and Chinese immigrants in a range of local contexts.

2

Vagrancy and Comparative Racialization in *Huckleberry Finn* and "Three Vagabonds of Trinidad"

In his 1950 introduction to *Huckleberry Finn* (1884), T. S. Eliot provides a striking explanation for Twain's abrupt reversion to "the mood of *Tom Sawyer*" in the novel's final chapters. He explains that neither a tragic nor a happy ending would be appropriate, because

> Huck Finn must come from nowhere and be bound for nowhere. His is not the independence of the typical or symbolic American Pioneer, but the independence of the vagabond. His existence questions the values of America as much as the values of Europe; he is as much an affront to the "pioneer spirit" as he is to "business enterprise"; he is in a state of nature as detached as the state of the saint. In a busy world, he represents the loafer.[1]

For Eliot, Huck is a protomodernist protagonist, a nomadic "vagabond" shorn of personal history and local traits, belonging to no particular place and inhabiting a time that "has no beginning and no end."[2] Like the other tramps and loafers who populate Twain's writings, Huck embodies a negative freedom from a culture oriented toward business gain, "pioneer" settler colonialism, and territorially bound labor.

In the postbellum United States, however, unfettered mobility was criminalized as much as it was celebrated, and vagrancy was a flashpoint for profound cultural anxieties. As Indian Removal, Emancipation, roundups of Chinese immigrants, and the growth of large-scale agriculture displaced populations from the land they worked on and inhabited, not status, property ownership, or means of employment could be counted on to distinguish unemployed whites from other racial groups. Under such conditions, the romanticized figure of the independent white tramp could be sustained only through legal and representational processes of racialization that selectively precipitated, criminalized, and contained the displacement of nonwhites. Southern and western states thus instituted vagrancy laws that disproportionately criminalized populations displaced by various forms of racial exploitation and violence, removing or imprisoning racialized groups to more profitable locations, such as southern chain gangs, urban Chinatowns, and Indian reservations. Ironically, both Chinese men who were stereotyped as mechanical, deindividualized workers and black and Native American men—who were frequently described as undisciplined workers—were vulnerable to being first displaced by racially motivated violence and subsequently criminalized as vagrants. Like Twain's own move to Nevada and California during the Civil War, Huck's "lighting out for the territory" represents, not an escape from Southern racism, but a move from one arena of white supremacy to another.

Legal and discursive constructions of vagrancy perpetuate racial hierarchies through the ostensibly "race-blind" policing of public spaces, morals, and hygiene. Instead of racializing individuals through physical or sentimental stereotypes, the category of "vagrancy" targets spatial practices, or the ways in which bodies occupy and traverse space. While only some vagrancy laws explicitly targeted particular groups, they all enabled uneven policing and enforcement along racial lines. As Sau-Ling Cynthia Wong argues, "Race and ethnicity are [instrumental] in shaping perceptions of the American land, since they form the basis of a long tradition of legislative, not to mention informal, circumscription of spatial possibilities for certain groups."[3] Whereas Eliot highlights the cosmopolitan mobility with which Huck "questions the values of America as much as the values of Europe," I argue that Twain's novel and several of its key intertexts dramatize differences in access to *regional* mobility, or the ability to move about within and between regions that themselves depended upon the availability of differentiated groups of workers and unemployed labor reserves.[4] The historical fictions by Twain and Bret Harte examined in this chapter expose racial inequalities not only by interrogating stereotypes about bodies, dialects, and mental capabilities but also by dramatizing the racially uneven distribution of "spatial possibilities for certain groups."

This chapter reads *Huckleberry Finn*'s white vagabonds alongside legal, popular, and literary treatments of racialized mobility in the postbellum South and West.[5] I begin by considering Chinese, Indian, and white vagabonds in several of the novel's source texts in order to establish a comparative racial context for understanding Huck and Jim's divergent experiences of mobility and imprisonment as they travel downriver. Next, I consider how Jim's sufferings and captivity in the concluding chapters of *Huckleberry Finn* resonate with the racially stratified vagrancy laws that helped to re-bind "emancipated" black Southerners to the land as either sharecroppers or convict laborers. In addition to illuminating the novel's ending, this link between vagrancy and institutions of captive labor (which Joan Dayan has described in terms of "civil death")[6] also provides a historical context for interpreting the novel's morbid interest in the unburied dead.[7] This chapter concludes by turning westward to the aftermaths of Chinese purges and Indian massacres dramatized in Harte's little-known rewriting of *Huckleberry Finn*, "Three Vagabonds of Trinidad"—a story that bears witness to both the importation of Jim Crow tactics into California race relations and the fragile alliances formed, both historically and in antiracist literary imagination, between members of differently dispossessed groups. Attending to legal and cultural connections between vagrancy and racialization highlights the ways in which the relative immobilization of Chinese, Native American, and black bodies underwrote the romanticized white vagabondage at the heart of *Huckleberry Finn* and its intertexts.

I. Vagrant Sources

While critics often frame *Huckleberry Finn* as a return to the Southern scenes of Twain's childhood, the novel's setting at the western edge of the South retains significant ties to the multiracial western locations—such as Hawaii, Virginia City, San Francisco, and Calaveras County—in which the author established his career. In two earlier texts—"Goldsmith's Friend Abroad Again" (1870–1871) and *The Adventures of Tom Sawyer* (1876)—Twain began to explore the forms of racialized mobility, incarceration, and labor that would later become prominent themes in *Huckleberry Finn*. These texts establish metaphorical connections between death and criminalized vagrancy that help us better understand the motif of the walking dead throughout *Huckleberry Finn*, and particularly in Pap's maddening nightmare about dead tramps.

"Goldsmith's Friend"—an early experiment in the naïve first-person narration so central to *Huckleberry Finn* and one of Twain's more frequently reprinted stories in China[8]—is an epistolary narrative told through the letters of a Chinese migrant named Ah Song Hi addressed to a friend in China. The story's title alludes to Oliver Goldsmith's *The Citizen of the World (1760–61)*,[9] a series of observations about English society purportedly written by a self-exiled Chinese philosopher. While both these texts satirize Western customs and institutions, Twain's text features a working-class traveler whose movements are much more constrained than those of Goldsmith's Chinese cosmopolitan. Ah Song Hi's experience of the United States reflects a context in which the prohibition on testimony, the Foreign Miners' Tax, and widespread anti-Chinese discourses made public space particularly perilous for Chinese immigrants: they were frequently displaced and, thus, frequently treated as vagrants. Initially naïve, the tone of the letters becomes increasingly puzzled and then embittered as Ah Song Hi describes his passage in the steerage of a steamship, his harassment and arbitrary arrest on the streets of San Francisco, encounters with fellow inmates in the city prison, and his dismal journey through the U.S. legal system. The protagonist is cheated, crowded, and intentionally scalded with hot steam during his transpacific passage and subsequently set loose in California when his employer's plans to hire out indentured workers to Southern plantations fall through. Still, he must repay his loan for the transpacific voyage (plus interest) to his employer, who has secured Ah Song Hi's wife, son, and two daughters in China as collateral. Yet the protagonist remains optimistic about America until his prolonged encounter with the nation's penal system, whose very existence baffles him ("I had long had an idea that Americans, being free, had no need of prisons, which are a contrivance of despots for keeping restless patriots out of mischief" ["GF," 461]). Awaiting trial in the city prison, Ah Song Hi is beaten by two Irish women imprisoned in an adjacent cell—habitual layabouts who, upon discovering that he is a "Chinaman," berate him as "a bloody interlopin' loafer." Only then does he begin to become disillusioned with the racial organization of the United States, laconically remarking that "'Loafer' means one who will not work" ("GF," 463). In the prison, "loafer" denotes both the idleness of unemployed vagrants and the specifically racialized status of the "Chinaman." For the latter, loafing is declared to be an essentialized, biologically heritable ("bloody" in the sense of "in the blood") characteristic that has nothing to do with being unemployed. Indeed, it is only to the extent that Chinese immigrants might *be* employed at the expense of white workers that they were stereotyped as "interlopin'" coolies who devalued white labor.[10] Although the figure of the brutishly hard working "coolie" appears to be antithetical to the "loafer," it was precisely the threat posed by Chinese workers able to move about and freely contract their labor that led to their restricted mobility. In turn, the policing of Chinese access to public space through categories such as "vagrancy" confined them to the status of unfree laborers who could not freely seek out work. The contradiction between "interlopin'" (or employable) and "loafer" (which entails idleness) indicates that Ah Song Hi's Irish cellmates are projecting their own status as landless, unemployed "loafers" onto him, rather than acknowledging the extent to which the large-scale incorporation of mining, agriculture, and construction was rendering workers of all races increasingly expendable.[11] After recounting Ah Song Hi's summary trial (he is sentenced with "five dollars or ten days"), "Goldsmith's Friend" breaks off with the remark that the newspaper reporter "would praise all the policemen indiscriminately and abuse the Chinamen and dead people"—those who are either legally or biologically barred from bearing witness ("GF," 470).

Twain returns to the intersecting themes of vagrancy, race, and "dead people" with the character of Injun Joe in *Tom Sawyer*—a more proximate antecedent for the figure of Jim in *Huckleberry Finn*. Injun Joe first appears at the scene of a grave robbing, where his gang is exhuming a cadaver of unspecified race (disproportionately likely to be black)[12] for Doctor Robinson, who reminds Joe that he has paid in advance for the specimen. But the transaction turns out to be a trap, as Joe explains to the doctor:

Five years ago you drove me away from your father's kitchen one night, when I come to ask for something to eat, and you said I warn't there for any good; and when I swore I'd get even with you if it took a hundred years, your father had me jailed for a vagrant. Did you think I'd forget? The Injun blood ain't in me for nothing. And now I've *got* you, and you got to *settle*, you know![13]

Joe's race, destitution, and lack of domicile rendered him vulnerable to an arbitrary imprisonment that allegorizes the history of Native Americans throughout the U.S. West, who were first displaced from their ancestral lands and subsequently targeted by vagrancy laws. Joe's own traumatic history of being "jailed for a vagrant" not only references the history of violent Indian removals that left many vulnerable to allegations of vagrancy but may also be read as a commentary on specific statutes such as California's "Act for the Government and Protection of Indians" (1850), which empowered white "proprietors" to remove Native Americans from some of their domiciles and lands. According to the historian Shirley Ann Wilson Moore, "The new California law controlled Indian labor. . . . On the word of any white person, any Indian deemed to be 'loitering or strolling about' could be arrested and sold to the highest bidder to labor for a period of four months."[14] Joe's declaration of revenge ironically puns on the word *settle*, which denotes not only the monetary exchange for goods delivered that the doctor hoped for in this cadaver sale, nor merely the actions of white settler colonists who expropriated Native Americans, but also the act of racial retribution represented by Joe's killing of the doctor, which proceeds more or less as planned.

Nor was the doctor's offense an isolated incident. Joe's status as a half-Indian "vagrant" left him vulnerable to repeated, ritual punishments and accounts for much of his animus in Twain's novel. Later in *Tom Sawyer*, Huck Finn overhears Joe plotting to mutilate the Widow Douglass, because "her husband was rough on me—many times he was rough on me—and mainly he was the justice of the peace that jugged me for a vagrant. And that ain't all. It ain't a millionth part of it! He had me *horsewhipped*!—horsewhipped in front of the jail, like a nigger!—with all the town looking on! horsewhipped!–do you understand?" (*TS*, 223). Being publicly whipped before the entire town racially marks Joe's flesh: along with "many" other acts of roughness, horsewhipping and arbitrary imprisonment reduce Joe to the condition of a beast or "nigger." As with the Irish "loafers" in "Goldsmith's Friend," however, Joe's very outrage at being treated "like a nigger" registers his repulsion to blackness and calls attention to the divergent forms of vagabondage that are joined in the single body of the "half-breed." Joe does not object to *being* a vagrant but to being "jailed for a vagrant," "jugged . . . for a vagrant," and violently *racialized* as a vagrant in a public ritual of whipping. (By contrast, Tom Sawyer's own public flogging at school affirms his masculinity and whiteness insofar as he undergoes it voluntarily in order to protect Becky's white femininity from the lasciviousness associated with the schoolmaster's graphic medical anatomy book [*TS*, 162–165]).

Although Huck claims that it "ain't no matter" whether or not his readers have read Twain's earlier novel, Injun Joe haunts the plot of *Huckleberry Finn*. For it is Huck's share of Joe's treasure that furnishes the monetary impetus for the plot by giving Pap incentive to reclaim his son, thus driving Huck to go on the tramp with Jim. More significantly, Tom's narrow escape from Injun Joe in the concluding chapters of *Tom Sawyer* may be read as an inspiration for his perverse interest in constructing a sublimated "play" around Jim's incarceration in the final chapters of *Huckleberry Finn*. If Injun Joe's initial appearance looks forward to *Huckleberry Finn*'s overarching concern with intersections between race and vagrancy, his eventual demise gruesomely anticipates Jim's farcical captivity at the hands of Tom Sawyer.

Two weeks after Tom and Becky Thatcher find their way out of the labyrinthine cave where they are described as starving "captives" and "prisoners," Tom is shocked to learn that the judge has taken measures to protect others from getting lost in the cave: "Nobody will get lost in that cave any more [b]ecause I had its big door sheathed with boiler iron two weeks ago, and triple-locked" (*TS*, 251). Tom, in response, "turn[s] as white as a sheet" and reveals that he had run into Injun Joe while exploring the cave, and so the Indian must have been locked inside. Tom's enhanced whiteness is a direct result of the unthinkable sufferings of his "Injun" nemesis, whose death in captivity gives rise to mixed feelings of pity, dread, and relief:[15]

> When the cave door was unlocked, a sorrowful sight presented itself in the dim twilight of the place. Injun Joe lay stretched upon the ground,

dead, with his face close to the crack of the door, as if his longing eyes had been fixed, to the latest moment, upon the light and the cheer of the free world outside. Tom was touched. . . . His pity was moved, but nevertheless he felt an abounding sense of relief and security. (*TS*, 252–253)

Twain explains that this unexpected imprisonment and unintended death interrupted a pending petition that the governor pardon Joe, who has been convicted of murder on the basis of Tom's testimony. Instead of carrying out Joe's death sentence in accordance with due process, Judge Thatcher carries it out unwittingly, and innocently, through an act of benevolent "triple-lock[ing]" intended to protect white children from straying—or to make their straying safer. Like the notion of race as an "accident of birth"—which Twain later explored in the infant-swapping plot of *Pudd'nhead Wilson* (1894)—this sentimentalized *accident of death* apparently absolves the law of any intention to harm Joe, despite the fact that the uneven and arbitrary criminalization of vagrancy had rendered him "dead in law" long before the judge literalized his death.[16]

While scholars have long noted Twain's claim that Injun Joe was based on a real resident ("more loafer than villain," as John Gerber puts it)[17] of Hannibal, Missouri, and while Twain's *Autobiography* includes a striking memory of the night when the "real" Injun Joe died, Twain's staging of the character's death in *Tom Sawyer* was influenced by an accident that Twain reported on in Gold Hill, Nevada. In an April 16–18, 1863, *Virginia City Territorial Enterprise* article entitled "Horrible Affair," Twain writes that, when "a noted desperado" was believed to have fled into a tunnel near Gold Hill, a group of citizens "stopped up the mouth of the tunnel" in order to prevent his escape. "The next day," Twain continues,

> a strong posse went up, rolled away the stones from the mouth of the sepulcher, went in and found five dead Indians!—three men, one squaw and one child, who had gone in there to sleep, perhaps, and been smothered by the foul atmosphere after the tunnel had been closed up. . . . The intention of the citizens was good, but the result was most unfortunate. To shut up a murderer in a tunnel was well enough, but to leave him there all night was calculated to impair his chances for a fair trial.[18]

After shifting its attention from a manhunt to the spectacle of suffocated Native American bodies, "Horrible Affair" abruptly returns to the question of a "fair trial" for the criminal. Like the judge's unintentional killing of Injun Joe, the sketch's incongruous concern with the desperado's "fair trial" draws attention to how legal institutions can obscure the structural injustices that render indigenous populations vulnerable to accidental and barely noticed deaths. Injun Joe's death scene simplifies this earlier report by reducing the party of Native Americans and the "noted desperado" into a single person, and thus rendering the act of unintended imprisonment and killing less horrific. If Twain minimizes the horror of this scenario by replacing the five presumably innocent victims with the corpse of a vindictive murderer, he also aligns Injun Joe's former experiences of being punished as a "vagrant" with the plight of five displaced Native American men, women, and children in search of shelter.

Twain's treatments of racially divergent forms of vagrancy in "Goldsmith's Friend" and *Tom Sawyer* help account for *Huckleberry Finn*'s most haunting scene of vagabondage, or "tramping," which occurs during the last night Huck spends with his drunk, abusive father. Shortly after his tirades against the "govment" that would entitle a "free nigger" to education and suffrage, Pap has nightmares about snakes and tramps—nightmares so vivid that he chases Huck around the cabin with a clasp-knife.

> He was laying over by the corner. By-and-by he raised up, part way, and listened, with his head to one side. He says very low:
> "Tramp—tramp—tramp; that's the dead; tramp—tramp—tramp; they're coming after me; but I won't go—Oh, they're here! don't touch me—don't! hands off—they're cold; let go—Oh, let a poor devil alone!"[19]

Pap's nightmarish encounter with the walking dead, which so closely follows on the heels of his complaints about the enfranchisement of "free niggers," expresses his own anxieties about class and race. If emancipated (though landless) blacks could educate themselves and vote, then where did he stand as a "poor," unemployed white "tramp"?[20] Twain's concern with racialized vagrancy dramatizes the resolution to this problem, whereby nonwhite vagabonds were intimidated (often by poor whites), disciplined, and rebound to the land, while white tramps were relatively free to move throughout, and beyond, the South. Twain's description of Pap's nightmare incorporates both these divergent tendencies: contrasting the disciplinary tempo marked by the refrain ("Tramp—tramp—tramp") with a vagrant and undisciplined patchwork of observations, wayward exclamations, sharp intakes of breath ("Oh") and entreaties that do not interrupt so much as they constitute this play-by-play description of Pap's waking dream. In Pap's dream, the onomatopoeic advent of disciplinary time simultaneously, and paradoxically, denotes—over and over again—the *proliferation* of "tramps" whose very bodies were imagined in opposition to discipline and progress. Although its description may appear out of place in the development of Twain's plot, Pap's dream of the walking dead exemplifies the intertwining of picaresque and Gothic incidents that characterizes the novel as a whole.

"Tramp—tramp—tramp" does more than simply invoke the homogenization of time embodied in the tread of regular, disciplined footsteps. For the refrain of Pap's dream would have been immediately recognizable to readers who had lived through the 1860s as the title of one of the most popular Civil War songs—a prisoner's song that was adapted as a marching song, cheaply reprinted, and distributed to homes where it was sung to the accompaniment of a piano, guitar, or other musical instrument (Figure 2.1).[21] Composed by the popular Civil War songwriter George Root, "Tramp, Tramp, Tramp" sold almost 100,000 copies within six months and was reported to have sold 150,000 by the end of 1865.[22] Its hopeful yet plaintive verses, voiced by a captured Union soldier waiting "within the prison cell" for his redemption, often return to the scenario expressed by the song's subtitle, "The Prisoner's Hope."[23] The chorus responds with the emphatic, upbeat force that made "Tramp!" a popular marching song:

> Tramp, tramp, tramp, the boys are marching,
> Cheer up comrades they will come.
> And beneath the starry flag
> We shall breathe the air again
> Of the free land in our own beloved home.[24]

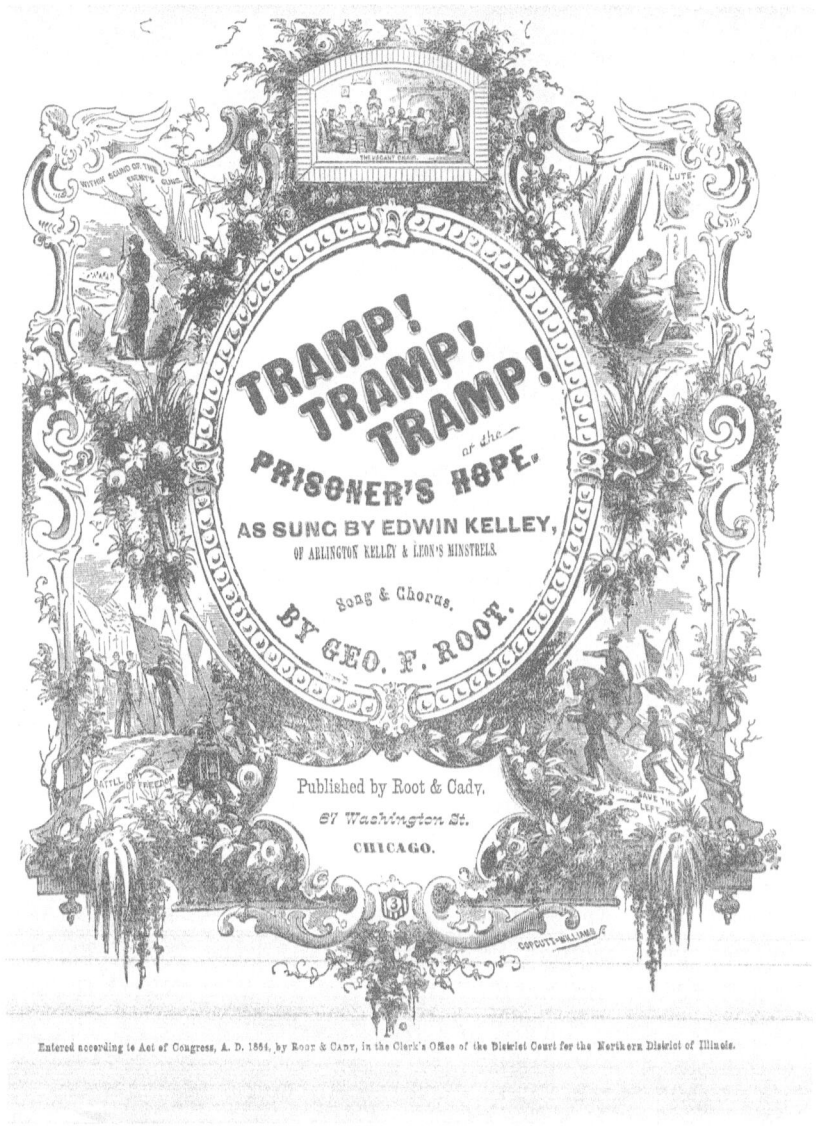

Figure 2.1: George Root, "Tramp! Tramp! Tramp! or the Prisoner's Hope." Chicago: Root & Cady, 1864. Courtesy of William L. Clements Library, University of Michigan at Ann Arbor.

In Pap's dream, Twain's readers would have heard anachronistic echoes of the steadily approaching footsteps of the Union victory and, with it, the promise of an Emancipation that would make the United States a "free land" for both war prisoners and slaves. By associating the sound of tramping feet with "the starry flag," "Tramp, tramp, tramp" links the time of military discipline with the future-oriented time of the nation-state. Yet beneath the song's often manic tune and upbeat *tempo di marcia* rhythm lie the darkness and terror of a Confederate prison cell. The song confronts listeners with the problem of how to reconcile its martial tempo with the time of imprisonment: an empty and only obliquely represented time whose subjects continually hope for their future reincorporation into the forward marching time of freedom and nation. The captive speaker of Root's lyrics plaintively describes the marching he cannot presently perform, and the home, flag, and nation from which he has been indefinitely removed.

The carceral setting of Root's song returns us to the post-Reconstruction context in which Twain used it to invoke dead tramps. For in addition to recognizing Root's song in Pap's dream, many of Twain's readers in 1884 would have associated the repeated word "tramp" with sensationalistic accounts of tramps in journalism and pulp literature,[25] as well as disciplinary practices that led to the disproportionate immobilization or imprisonment of black vagrants. Among other things, Twain's invocation of "Tramp, Tramp, Tramp" reminds us that Pap himself has already appeared as a vagabond both in his wandering predisposition (after all, he appears first to Huck in the form of his tracks) and in his day-to-day routines: "Every time he got money he got drunk; and every time he got drunk he raised Cain around town; and every time he raised Cain he got jailed" (*HF*, 36). (Note that, unlike Ah Song Hi and Injun Joe, Pap is jailed for the action of "rais[ing] Cain," not simply "for a vagrant.") The juxtaposition of romantic vagabonds and disciplinary state violence (tramping soldiers or prisons) in Pap's dream draws attention to the dynamics of racialization that I discuss in the following section: on the one hand, the uncomfortable proximity of class and status between white and nonwhite vagrants; on the other hand, the legal and customary practices designed to obfuscate that proximity.

II. Vagrancy and Civil Death in Huckleberry Finn

Pap is not the only tramp in *Huckleberry Finn*, nor are the novel's only animated corpses those who tramp through this waking dream. At times, Huck's own references to death recur with an almost mechanical regularity: "I felt so lonesome I most wished I was dead.... I heard an owl, away off, who-whooing about somebody that was dead, and a whippowill and a dog crying about somebody that was going to die" (*HF*, 16). After Pap's nightmare and the domestic violence it precipitates, Huck finalizes his plans to "just tramp right across the country, mostly night times, and hunt and fish to keep alive" (*HF*, 39). Huck stages his own bloody death, paddles over to Jackson's Island, and slips into the chronotope[26] of vagabondage that T. S. Eliot calls "nowhere." Thereafter, he is provisionally and voluntarily dead to law and "sivilization," slipping into new identities every time he steps on land and slipping out of them just as easily whenever he jumps off a raft, survives a collision with a steamboat, witnesses a feud ("they'll think I've been killed, and floated down the river"), or lights out for the territory (*HF*, 134). As a vagabond, Huck seems equally ready to embrace the healing potential of pastoral, Jim's homosocial charm, or the voyeuristic pleasure of an unseen eavesdropper. For Huck, "Other places do seem so cramped up and smothery, but . . . you feel mighty free and easy and comfortable on a raft" (ibid.). Since Huck's experience as a "dead" tramp seems refulgent with life and freedom, we're left wondering where the immobilizing and terrifying aspects of Pap's walking dead come into play in *Huckleberry Finn*. For even Pap is empowered by the law (able to sue and testify in court, for example), and his nightmare only reflects his anxieties that the enfranchisement of free blacks might somehow render him more proximate to death. This section explores two different ways in which "sivilized" life is negated in the novel's dramatizations of black and white vagrancy: on the one hand, Huck often enjoys the idyllic liberties of "uncivilized" life on Jackson's Island and the river; on the other hand, Jim experiences the same geographical locations that Huck traverses from the subject position of *civil death*.

Legal codes and customs pertaining to black and white travelers in the postbellum period highlight two distinct contexts for the picaresque downriver chapters of Twain's novel. Huck experiences a freedom that is alternately exhilarating, disillusioning, and edifying as he experiments with boundaries of race, class, and gender while shuttling between river and shore. Huck's own liberties along the river are echoed in the king and duke, corrupt "tramps" who for a time abuse the fluidity of identity and location afforded to white travelers with relative impunity. By contrast, Jim's travels occur in hiding under the guise of captivity; his spatial progress (or regress) down the river paradoxically requires that he remain immobile, concealed in a cave, secluded in a swamp, posing as a captured runaway tied up in the wigwam on the raft, or painted blue and disguised as a "Sick Arab" who "didn't only look like he was dead, he looked considerably more than that" (HF, 171).

As Axel Nissen has shown, Huck's status as a vagabond reflects the emergence of a wandering class of expropriated "tramps" in the 1870s and 1880s and the sensationalistic literature that accompanied them. When read in light of an anxious and sometimes violent public discourse surrounding tramps and the series of tramp acts[27] enacted during these decades, Huck's indulgent experimentation with "the independence of the vagabond" turns out to be less exhilarating than T. S. Eliot suggests. As Michael Denning explains, "The 'tramp' is no myth or symbol in the 'American mind,' no eternal archetype of 'America.' It was a category constructed in the wake of the 1873 depression and the 1877 railroad strikes to designate migratory and unemployed workers; indeed it was [the] ideological naming of the new phenomenon of unemployment."[28] These unemployed migrants were often met with antipathy, as in an 1877 article in the *Chicago Tribune* that facetiously advises neighborhoods interested in protecting their "portable property" to "put a little ... arsenic in the meat and other supplies furnished [for] the tramp."[29] Such antitramp writings spread anxieties about hordes of vagabonds—often associated with socialism and sexual deviance—who threatened to freeload, pillage the countryside, or seduce local women.

Yet tramps represented freedom and adventure no less than they evoked the dangers of idleness and crime. *The Tramp: His Tricks, Tallies, and Tell-Tales* (1878), a pamphlet illustrated and "edited" by Frank Bellew and purportedly authored by an "ex-tramp," presents a picaresque, comedic account of the tramp's adventures among farmers' daughters, vicious dogs, and a nationwide secret society of tramps.

Figure 2.2: Colophon image from Frank Bellew, *The Tramp: His Tricks, Tallies, and Tell-Tales, With All His Signs, Countersigns, Grips, Pass-Words, and Villainies Exposed* (New York: Dick & Fitzgerald, 1878), 12. Courtesy of the University of California, Berkeley Library.

While it occasionally lapses into sensationalistic, vaguely revolutionary warnings that "the Tramps are a fearful power in this country," the narrative more often humanizes the figure of the tramp.[30] Even the text's most ghastly illustration—in which the narrator is depicted as a decapitated body (Figure 2.2)—is glossed in a way that emphasizes the tramp's resemblance to the forward-looking spirit of speculation and progress:

> So commenced my new march in the bloody campaign of life, which has so many defeats, and so few victories. March, march, march. My thoughts were marching faster than my feet; my fears outmarched my hopes, and got leagues and leagues ahead of them, making everything a howling wilderness in their path; then my hopes made a spurt and got ahead of my fears. So I found my mind in California, deep in the gold mines, by the time my legs reached Middletown.[31]

War and decapitation here serve as comic metaphors for the attitude of a man who plans not too little, but too far ahead—who is pulled forward by his desires, rather than pursued by the law. Like the tramps described in Bellew's book, Huck, the king, and the duke are relatively at liberty to enter and traverse a range of Southern spaces; even when he is mistakenly identified as a "runaway 'prentice" bound by the law to a "mean old farmer," Huck is treated kindly, rather than returned to his supposed servitude (*HF*, 70). These divergent attitudes toward tramps—viewed as either subversive bodies who should be violently disciplined or figures of restless freedom and possibility—were often structured by racial difference, since racialized groups were often associated with stereotypes of dysfunctional domesticity, idleness, irresponsibility, and lack of domicile in this era. Even Bellew's illustration registers the uncomfortable proximity between the presumably white narrator "marching" through life and the black vagrants stigmatized throughout the postbellum South by blurring conventional markers of race—depicting a tramp with dark skin, exaggeratedly white eyeballs, and somewhat curly hair. Antiblack and anti-Chinese violence in the South and throughout California were often motivated by a need to reestablish racial distinctions between white and nonwhite subjects similarly threatened by trends toward displacement, unemployment, and devalued labor in an era of capitalist consolidation.

For many emancipated blacks, mobility offered a promise of an as yet unrealized freedom. As Saidiya Hartman writes, "The sheer capacity to move, as demonstrated by the mass movement off the plantation, rather than the gains or loss experienced at one's destination, provided the only palpable evidence of freedom."[32] However, the postbellum period also saw the rise of new codes, laws, and racist customs that outlawed black mobility (constructed as "idleness"), privatized public spaces, and precluded subsistence activities such as hunting, fishing, squatting, and moving about.[33] Under such conditions, black vagrants were much more susceptible to persecution, capture, and punishment than the armies of white loafers who inspired the "tramp scare." "Without the right to move on their own terms," writes Todd DePastino, "African Americans were effectively barred from the privileges of tramping.... The black aversion to tramping is attributable not only to outright racial discrimination in public assistance, but also to the hostility and violence that blacks could expect to encounter on the road itself. Simply put, black migrants could not count on the already haphazard kindness of strangers—not to mention railroads, missions, and municipal authorities—upon which the transient homeless so often depended."[34] Southern black codes—which were themselves modeled on California vagrancy statutes such as the 1850 "Act for the Government and Protection of Indians" and the 1855 Vagrancy Act that specifically restricted the mobility and liberties of "all persons who are commonly known as 'Greasers'"[35]—included vagrancy and apprentice clauses to constrain the mobility of blacks and to bind their bodies and labor to the land. Both before and after the war, free blacks were often barred from owning and working their own land[36] (if not driven from their homes by extralegal terror) and subsequently arrested as landless "vagrants." Tracing the United States' contemporary system of racially targeted incarceration to this period, Michelle Alexander notes in *The New Jim Crow: Mass Incarceration in the Age of Colorblindness* that, in the wake of Emancipation,

> nine southern states adopted vagrancy laws—which essentially made it a criminal offense not to work and were applied selectively to blacks—and eight of those states enacted convict laws allowing for the hiring-out of county prisoners to plantation owners and private companies. Prisoners were forced to work for little or no pay. One vagrancy act

specifically provided that 'all free negroes and mulattoes over the age of eighteen' must have written proof of a job at the beginning of every year. Those found with no lawful employment were deemed vagrants and convicted.[37]

In Mississippi, "An Act to Amend the Vagrant Laws of the State" (1865) considerably broadened the definition of "vagrant" to include a catalogue of undesirables and "all other idle and disorderly persons"; moreover, it introduced a second category of vagrancy targeting "idle Negroes and white persons associating with them 'on terms of equality' or guilty of sexual relations with them."[38] The Mississippi Black Code denied due process to those charged with vagrancy and left black "vagrants" particularly vulnerable to being "hired out at auction for whatever term was necessary to pay [their] fine and costs."[39] While vagrancy laws—which often led to the imprisonment or forced apprenticeship of those found guilty—did not always so explicitly target black Southerners,[40] their discriminatory enforcement led to a well-documented process of virtual re-enslavement: as W. E. B. Du Bois put it, "No open-minded student can read [the black codes] without being convinced they meant nothing more nor less than slavery in daily toil."[41] Vagrancy, like race, was a matter of status rather than act: it criminalized and degraded persons for what they were, not for illegal actions performed or intended.[42] The discursive correlation of vagrancy with blackness, writes Bryan Wagner, assigned to "so-called black vagrants . . . an array of emblematic habits (loafing and stealing), inclinations (shiftlessness and intemperance), and attributes (dirtiness and disease) that left them vulnerable to legal prosecution. With characteristics that would have been recognizable from blackface entertainments and narrative representations of fugitive slaves and free blacks, the vagrant became the subject of intense scrutiny in public debates about the meaning and impact of slave emancipation in the United States."[43]

As historians have shown, the postbellum period of "southern enclosure" characterized by intensified industrial production and large monocrop plantations gave rise to a new peculiar institution of involuntary, indebted, or cheap racialized labor. "The vast majority of southern convicts were black; punishment and rehabilitation were distinctly subordinated to labor exploitation; and prisoners were leased as laborers to the region's capitalists, or worked as state slaves on the chain gang."[44] Bolstered by the "punishment for crime" exception to the Thirteenth Amendment and the *Ruffin v. Commonwealth* case, which defined the status of convicts as "slaves of the state," the convict lease system constructed imprisonment as a legal status characterized by underremunerated labor, not as a physical location within a penitentiary.[45] The Southern penal system was organized for profit rather than for rehabilitation, so that even where state penitentiaries existed—as in Huck's home state of Missouri—outside corporations were allowed to set up factories within the walls of the state penitentiary to exploit the labor of thousands of convicts.[46] Twain wrote *Huckleberry Finn* in the years following the end of Reconstruction—during what Alexander calls "the nation's first prison boom," when a disproportionately black and increasingly young convict population serving increasingly long sentences "grew ten times faster than the general population."[47]

Relatively lacking in resources, land, education, and capital, as well as positive entitlements or protection from the state, emancipated blacks were often subjected to imprisonment and coerced labor as "slaves of the state."[48] Black vagrants were especially vulnerable to the legal status that Dayan describes as "civil death" or "the state of a person who, though possessing *natural life,* has lost all *civil rights.*"[49] By focusing on "the sorcery of law" that creates populations of the living dead, Dayan traces an unnerving continuity between the suspended rights of post-Reconstruction convicts and the "social death" imposed upon antebellum slaves—a continuity established by legal metaphors grounded in supernatural categories of tainted blood, "negative personhood," and subjects "dead in law."[50] The criminalization and civil death of convicted black vagrants guaranteed the immobilization of ostensibly "free" black laborers throughout the plantations of the post-Reconstruction South. In Twain's novel, this partial, negated form of personhood underlies Huck's notorious, nonchalant response to being asked whether anybody was hurt in a steamboat accident: "No'm. Killed a nigger" (*HF,* 230). More broadly, it provides a postbellum context for understanding why, in contrast to Huck's adventurous mobility in the picaresque chapters of Twain's novel, Jim's mobility depends wholly on his willingness to travel hidden away, shut in, or bound hand and foot. Indeed, *Huckleberry Finn* so consistently represents Jim in the attitudes and "close place[s]" (to literalize Huck's metaphor) of captivity that the final, farcical prolongation of Jim's imprisonment should come as no surprise (*HF*, 223).

The racially uneven imposition of "civil death" sheds sober light on one of *Huckleberry Finn*'s funniest passages, in which Huck misquotes a soliloquy from *Hamlet*. While critics generally view this scene as a satire on middlebrow Americans' fascination with Shakespeare, Twain's rewritten version of the soliloquy opens with lines ("calamity of so long life" and "the fear of something after death") that resonate with the situation of slaves and vagrants as "dead in law." The passage's central lines cry out to be read in light of both antebellum and post-Reconstruction assaults on the very temporality of black lives: "For who would bear the whips and scorns of time, / The oppressor's wrong, the proud man's contumely, / The law's delay . . . " (*HF*, 152). This cluster of images— whips, oppressors, and the language of status associated with pride and contumely—subtly revises Shakespeare to suit the context of U.S. race relations. Twain redeploys "the law's delay" in the context of Jim Crow vigilantism, where the discriminatory suspension of law both precipitates and neglects to punish racially motivated lynchings.[51] Moreover, "the law's delay" eloquently describes the ironic anachronisms brought about by the postbellum recapture of freedmen's labor, as well as Jim's prolonged captivity at the hands of Tom and Huck.[52]

The whips of time, the law's delay: temporality itself is inflicted upon Jim as both hurry and delay, both driver's lash and prison cell, both wage labor's clock time and the empty time of enforced idleness. Penitentiaries and convict gangs arrest the "tramping" of the romanticized vagabond, replacing the carefree time of loafing with the time of imprisonment and coerced labor. Postbellum institutions thus reinscribed a familiar temporal regime: "In antebellum America, it was the deprivation of time in the life of the slave that first signaled his or her status as a piece of property. . . . A 'slave' was he or she who, most literally, stood outside of time."[53] Jim inhabits a time excluded from progress and futurity long before his incarceration at the Phelps plantation among spiders, snakes, rats, and other inventions of Tom's medieval imagination. Even on the raft, when Huck sees Jim mourning in the very pose of captivity ("he was setting there with his head down betwixt his knees, moaning and mourning to himself"), Huck notes that "I knowed what it was about. He was thinking about his wife and his children" (*HF*,

170). The implication is that Jim sat like this often—huddled and hurting in a condition akin to the "interminable awaiting" left in slavery's wake.⁵⁴ Jim's tears—often unacknowledged or even mocked (as when Huck first sees him sleeping, head between knees, on the raft)—appear as the by-product of an escape plan gone awry, a fugitive slave trajectory commandeered by three white tramps seeking profit and adventure. Ironically, it is Tom who invents the emblem for this extraction of enjoyment from the black captive's time and grief: a stalk of "mullen" that Jim, re-enacting the rituals of European romance, is to water with his own tears.

Twain's interest in race, vagrancy, and incarceration was not restricted to *Huckleberry Finn* and the condition of southern blacks: as early as 1866 he devotes a passage in *Mark Twain's Letters from Hawaii* to describing a mysterious black prisoner named General George Washington;⁵⁵ in *Roughing It*, he mentions a pair of "vagrant Mexicans" (whom he also calls "Greasers") who made a fortune in gold;⁵⁶ in *A Tramp Abroad* (1880), written during the hiatus in the composition of *Huckleberry Finn*, he playfully identifies himself with tramp culture; and he depicts medieval dungeons in *The Prince and the Pauper* (1881), where Miles is imprisoned as a "sturdy vagabond."⁵⁷ *Pudd'nhead Wilson* alludes to the relative mobility accorded to white tramps when Tom Driscoll puts on a "disguise proper for a tramp" to escape the murder scene (*PW*, 101). Twain returned to the brutal conditions of medieval dungeons in his allegory of the anachronistic South, *A Connecticut Yankee in King Arthur's Court* (1889), and attempted to speak for the colonial captives of U.S. imperialism in "To the Person Sitting in Darkness" (1901); in 1902, he donated a set of his books to the federal prison in Atlanta; in 1905, he used the microorganisms in the body of a "mouldering old bald-headed tramp" named Blitzowski to produce a satirical allegory about immigration, national identity, and U.S. empire.⁵⁸

In the concluding section of this chapter, however, I focus on "Three Vagabonds of Trinidad," a little-known recasting of *Huckleberry Finn* by Bret Harte that explicitly connects vagrancy and comparative racialization by returning from that novel's southern settings to the more recognizably western or "frontier" predicaments dramatized in Twain's earlier treatments of Ah Song Hi and Injun Joe.⁵⁹

III. Huck in Trinidad

Shortly after setting aside the manuscript of *Huckleberry Finn* in 1876, Twain collaborated on *Ah Sin* with his friend Bret Harte. Although the play's lukewarm reception precipitated a permanent break in their friendship, Harte may have learned a few things from Twain's unfinished draft of *Huckleberry Finn* when he visited Twain in Hartford in 1876 to work on *Ah Sin*. Perhaps Twain discussed the manuscript with him, or asked him to read it over, as he had done with *The Innocents Abroad* (1869). Or Harte may have simply read Twain's novel when it was published eight years later. In any case, Harte's "Three Vagabonds of Trinidad" (1900) strongly echoes the first, idyllic section of *Huckleberry Finn*, when Huck and Jim become better acquainted on Jackson's Island and start traveling upriver.[60] Harte's reworking of Twain's themes yields an expanded picture of how racialized constructions of vagrancy and mobility were imposed, in different but connected ways, upon other racial groups in the American West. Reading "Three Vagabonds" with Twain's writings shows how diverse practices of racial violence such as lynchings, chain gangs, Indian wars, the reservation system, purges, and Chinese Exclusion created uneven conditions that were then reproduced—or intensified—by vagrancy laws. Articulated with such forms of legal and extralegal racism, even vagrancy laws that make no direct reference to race produced racially differentiated forms of mobility and immobilization throughout the nation's southern and western regions.

"Three Vagabonds" reworks Twain's motifs of childhood, vagrancy, pastoral, and racial subjection into a dark commentary on racialization both in the story's immediate setting (an antebellum frontier settlement) and within the broader imperial context of the turn of the century, when the United States was at war with the Philippines and consolidating its new overseas holdings in the Caribbean and the Pacific. By setting the story in the antebellum town of Trinidad, California—and partly on an apparently uninhabited offshore island located amid "the thunders of the distant Pacific"—Harte links the pre-Emancipation era of 1860 with more recent instances of U.S. imperialism, such as the annexation of Hawai'i and the War of 1898.[61] In addition to naming a town located in the midst of Humboldt County's anti-Indian and anti-Chinese violence, "Trinidad" also points towards the Caribbean island where British planters were, in the 1850s and 1860s, importing indentured Chinese workers to supplement the labor of recently emancipated slaves.

These sites of slavery, indenture, and overseas imperialism extend the story's more explicit references to nativist and expansionist sentiments. At one point, Harte's narrator quotes the racist remarks of "a prominent citizen" named Mr. Skinner in order to convey the extent of racial animus "in an ordinary American frontier town which did not then dream of Expansion and Empire!" ("TVT," 159–160). Skinner's remarks reveal an inadequate—or perhaps repressed—understanding of the relations between race and class: "The nigger of every description—yeller, brown, or black, call him 'Chinese,' 'Injin,' or 'Kanaka,' or what you like—hez to clar off of God's footstool when the Anglo-Saxon gets started! It stands to reason that they can't live alongside o' printin' presses, M'Cormick's reapers, and the Bible!" ("TVT," 159). The very indeterminacy of the category "nigger of every description"—as well as its shifting definition as the negation of "Anglo-Saxon," print culture, mechanized agriculture, and Christianity—registers numerous ways in which uneducated, landless, working-class white men might be seen as proximate to "niggers." Farming technologies such as the reaper, after all, threatened to devalue and displace white rural laborers no less than other groups. Moreover, the speaker's dialect and hostility clearly mark him as marginal to both "printin' presses . . . and the Bible"—which may be why, as his name indicates, Skinner insists on biologically essentialist delineations of race.

The story opens with a benevolent white Editor attempting to place his protégé and employee—"a waif from a Chinese wash-house" named Li Tee—in the household of a farmer's wife. Mrs. Martin's attempts at civilizing Li Tee fail, and the boy repeatedly runs away to join his only companion in the settlement of Trinidad: "'Jim,' a well-known drunken Indian vagrant of the settlement" ("TVT," 157). Described as "equal outcasts of civilization," the Chinese boy and "Injin Jim" retreat to an island in the bay, where they are eventually joined by an adventurous white boy, Master Bob Skinner, who goes to the island with his father's gun and a plan to "either capture Li Tee and Jim, or join them in their lawless existence" ("TVT," 158). Quickly setting aside "his plan of a stealthy invasion," Bob ends up spending an idyllic day with the two "equal vagabonds," reveling in the island's isolation from the town's conventionality:

They fished together, gathered cranberries on the marsh, shot a wild duck and two plovers, and when Master Skinner assisted in the cooking of their fish in a conical basket sunk in the ground . . . the boy's felicity was supreme. And what an afternoon! To lie, after this feast, on their bellies in the grass, replete like animals, hidden from everything by the sunshine above them; so quiet that gray clouds of sandpipers settled fearlessly around them, and a shining brown muskrat slipped from the ooze within a few feet of their faces—was to feel themselves a part of the wild life in earth and sky. ("TVT," 161)

After they all sleep "pigged together" in a wigwam, Bob returns to his family with a story about having lost his gun when his canoe overturned. But, instead of returning with supplies as promised, Bob betrays Li Tee and Jim, who both end up dead—the former starved, the latter shot. Like Huck, Bob enjoys only the freedom and pastoralism associated with "lawless existence" without being touched by the diverse laws, regulations, and extralegal violence that constrained the movements of black, Chinese, and Native American workers while racializing access to "public" space.

"Three Vagabonds" extends Twain's account of Huck and Jim on Jackson's Island into western contexts of comparative racialization. Historically, the parallels between forms of racialization treated in these two texts (characterized by a lack of positive legal protections, stereotypes about vagabond morals and bad hygiene, and the constant threat of extralegal violence) can be explained by the westward circulation of southern Democrats and their tactics during and after the years of Radical Reconstruction: as the historian Jean Pfaelzer writes, "By 1867 Democrats had swept elections across California by opposing black male suffrage and the ratification of the Fifteenth Amendment. As the party took over California . . . southern traditions of lynching, racial violence, Black Codes, arson, and policies denying land ownership to racial minorities surfaced in California, Oregon, and the Washington Territory."[62] The blanket racism expressed by Bob Skinner's father, directed against "the nigger of every description," thus gave rise to "a racial overlay . . . that treated Indians, African Americans, and Chinese in the west with similar brutality in legislation, in land policy, and in labor practices," denying them citizenship and a range of civil rights.

At the same time, new laws also imposed upon the Chinese a system of debt peonage, backed by the threat of eviction and the prohibition of land ownership, that paralleled the situation of Southern freedmen.[63] While it is important to bear in mind the discrepancies between differently racialized groups,[64] "Three Vagabonds" also recalls commonalities such as those imposed by the California Supreme Court's decision in *People v. Hall* (1854), in which Chinese witnesses were barred from testifying against white men because "the words 'black person' [in the California Constitution] must be taken as contradistinguished from white, and necessarily excludes all races other than the Caucasian."[65] The 1879 California Constitution even adapted the "punishment for crime" exception to the Thirteenth Amendment's abolition of involuntary servitude, declaring that "no Chinese shall be employed in any state, county, municipal, or other public work, except in punishment for crime."[66] As the historian Najia Aarim Heriot explains in *Chinese Immigrants, African Americans, and Racial Anxiety in the United States, 1848–82*, the anti-Chinese movement in the U.S. West derived from "the antebellum legislation that aimed to restrict the right of free blacks to the liberties accorded all white Americans and European immigrants, to come and go and to dispose of their person as they pleased."[67]

Yet Harte's story also includes significant digressions that limn the historically disparate processes by which Li Tee and Jim have been produced as "equal vagabonds" ("TVT," 165). Li Tee's situation, for example, evokes both the lack of legal protections for Chinese immigrants and the gendered asymmetry of immigration laws that effectively prohibited working-class Chinese women from entering the country and thus outlawed the establishment of monogamous families (and the socially legitimized work of social reproduction that such families performed) among Chinese laborers. "A waif from a Chinese wash-house," Li Tee

> was impounded by some indignant miners for bringing home a highly imperfect and insufficient washing, and kept as hostage for a more proper return of the garments. Unfortunately, another gang of miners, equally aggrieved, had at the same time looted the wash-house and driven off the occupants, so that Li Tee remained unclaimed. ("TVT," 156)

In addition to performing the outsourced domestic labor of washing that supported white miners, Trinidad's Chinese laundrymen had no legally protected claim to either property in their washhouse or custody of their "waif." Detained at will by miners, Li Tee ends up being denied access not only to public schools and the Christian Sabbath school but also to most of Trinidad's public spaces: the Editor warns him to "mind you keep clear of the schoolhouse. Don't go by the Flat either if the men are at work, and don't, if you value your skin, pass Flanigan's shanty.... Look out for Barker's dog at the crossing, and keep off the main road if the tunnel men are coming over the hill" ("TVT," 156). Included in the settlement for the sake of his labor, yet subject to persecution (apparently as potential competition) by schoolchildren, Irishmen like Flanigan, and railroad workers, Li Tee is rendered a "vagabond" by the peculiar combination of laws, prejudices, and economic forces that installed Chinese laborers in the western United States as undomesticated, unassimilable, and effectively stateless "aliens."

Humboldt County, the story's setting, was an epicenter of the nearly two hundred purges of Chinese residents from California settlements that are documented in Pfaelzer's *Driven Out: The Forgotten War against Chinese Americans*. In 1885, the town of Eureka gave its entire Chinese population two days to leave town; the following year, "Eureka's Committee of Fifteen bullied the tiny fishing village of Trinidad to expel its one Chinese man, a hotel worker."[68] Blaming Chinese laborers for low wages, poor working conditions, and their own lack of employment, unemployed (or "vagrant") white men played a key role in such expulsions. Through a combination of protest, intimidation, looting, arson, and lynching, working-class whites projected and transferred their own most denigrated traits onto the Chinese. Although vagrancy laws were not often deployed in these roundups or their aftermaths, laws that prohibited Chinese land ownership and rendered existing working and living spaces (wooden laundry houses and crowded dormitories) illegal for reasons of "hygiene" collaborated with actual purges to deprive the Chinese of domicile. San Francisco's 1870 Cubic Air Ordinance, for example, required at least five hundred cubic feet of living space for each adult and led to a raid on Chinatown tenements in which "police ... made mass arrests, hauling a hundred Chinese men to jail and filling the county prison."[69] In 1892, the Geary Act effectively criminalized all Chinese laborers in the United States by requiring them to register and carry photographic identification cards proving they were legal residents. When thousands of Chinese immigrants refused to obey this "Dog Tag Law" in an act of collective civil disobedience, a surge of citizens' arrests filled local jails with hundreds of unregistered Chinese waiting to be deported and caused thousands of others to flee their California homes.[70] The history of these purges, dislocations, arrests, and detentions lends a chilling (if anachronistic) undertone to the offhand remark of the Editor in Harte's story, who tells Li Tee, affectionately, "I don't suppose there's another imp like you in all Trinidad County" ("TVT," 155).

Jim, however, is paradoxically introduced as "a well-known drunken Indian vagrant of the settlement"—a vagrant who doesn't seem to ever wander far. Harte's narrator explains that Jim was "tied to [the settlement's] civilization by the single link of 'fire water,' for which he forsook equally the Reservation where it was forbidden and his own camps where it was unknown" ("TVT," 157). While this characterization of Jim's alcoholism seems exaggerated, it nevertheless makes a distinction between the Reservation established for displaced Indians and Jim's "own camps"—a distinction that quietly acknowledges the history of settler colonialism and Indian removal that, in Trinidad, led to the displacement of Yurok Indians from their land in 1855.[71] Harte's island setting points to another incident that he had reported when writing for the *Northern Californian* in February 1860—the year in which "Three Vagabonds" is set. Harte's outraged article, "Indiscriminate Massacre of Indians, Women and Children Butchered," not only documented the violent removal of Wiyot Indians from a village on Indian Island in Humboldt Bay—it also led to the author's own flight from the region, when local whites threatened to lynch him.[72] In Harte's own historical moment, the Dawes Act (1887) was atomizing ties to tribal lands and traditional kinship networks while displacing many Native Americans from their homes in a process that accounts for the story's distinction between the Reservation and Jim's "own camps." Such removals rendered Native Americans increasingly susceptible to being perceived—and disciplined—as vagrants: "Driven out of the mining areas, often unemployed as a consequence of the part-time hiring policies of most *rancheros*, and increasingly desperate for food and clothing, Native Americans in California often appeared as vagrants."[73] Jim's status as a "vagrant" is determined by this history of violent dislocations, as well as by firearms prohibitions that impede his ability to sustain himself by hunting. Whereas Harte notes that Bob's brash approach to hunting makes animals too skittish to catch by hand, Jim's attempt to adapt to white hunting techniques leads to his death after he commits the simple (but, for an Indian, illegal) act of shooting a gun in the woods. For he is seen by a frontiersman who cannot bear the thought of "An Indian with a weapon that made him the equal of the white!" ("TVT," 163). These historical developments, whose effects were as palpable in 1900 as they had been forty years earlier, underwrite Jim's vagabond status and eventual death in a killing that—like the death of Injun Joe—would not count as murder.

The agents and casualties of mobility featured in *Huckleberry Finn* and its intertexts make visible the long, comparative genealogy of the whiteness of the free vagabond. Even as indentured Chinese laborers, chain gangs, and nominally free workers of all races built railroads, bridges, roads, and other infrastructure for what Marx called "the annihilation of space,"[74] the enjoyment of free mobility and adventure was enforced as white. As Bruce Braun puts it in a discussion of outdoor risk culture that eloquently captures Huck's final "lighting out for the territory," "In these stories of space, race, and risk only white subjects move. All others are spatially incarcerated—fixed in place within a social imaginary that assumes the whiteness of the adventurous individual."[75]

But even as they highlight legal practices designed to outlaw, displace, and discipline nonwhites seeking to express or realize freedom in "the sheer capacity to move,"[76] these texts also establish the groundwork for interracial solidarities that might redress the different forms of spatial constraint they represent. Despite its morbid ending, even "Three Vagabonds" can be read as an allegory of the sparsely documented contacts between dislocated Chinese and Indians in California: for example, some Chinese who had been purged from Northern California towns continued to live on Karuk and Hoopa land and intermarried with Native American women.[77] And in "Goldsmith's Friend," Ah Song Hi has a brief vision of San Francisco's assembled inmates as an international, multiracial, vagabond collective when describing the criminal court: "We were all marched out into the dungeon and joined there by all manner of vagrants and vagabonds, of all shades and colours and nationalities, from the other cells and cages of the place; and pretty soon our whole menagerie was marched up-stairs and locked fast behind a high railing in a dirty room with a dirty audience in it" ("GF," 466). In the momentary respite from state repression that occurs between being caged in prison and being "locked fast" in court, these heterogeneous "vagrants and vagabonds" embody an unrealized collective sundered by the multiple, uneven, and often competitive histories of racialization. Though differentiated by historical conditions and racial stereotypes, this multitude of vagabonds is unified by their marginalization with respect to public space and forms of mobility. Whereas differential access to space and mobility represents an instance of cross-racial convergence (as different histories of displacement converge in the apparently race-blind designation of "vagrancy"), the following chapter considers how the figure of deindividualized "coolie" masses, with its misleading analogy between Chinese laborers and antebellum slaves, served to differentiate Chinese immigrants from African Americans in arguments for Chinese Exclusion.

3

"Coolies" and Corporate Personhood in *Those Extraordinary Twins*

In an uncharacteristically solemn scene of *The Comedy of Those Extraordinary Twins* (1894), Judge Robinson berates the jury for allowing an assault to go unpunished because it could not determine which of the conjoined twins, Luigi and Angelo Cappello, was responsible for the act:

> In all my experience on the bench, I have not seen Justice bow her head in shame in this court until this day. You little realize what far-reaching harm has just been wrought here under the fickle forms of law. Imitation is the bane of courts . . . and in no long time you will see the fatal work of this hour seized upon by profligate so-called guardians of justice in all the wide circumstance of this planet and perpetuated in their pernicious decisions. I wash my hands of this iniquity. . . . What have you accomplished this day? Do you realize it? You have set adrift, unadmonished, in this community, two men endowed with an awful and mysterious gift, a hidden and grisly power for evil—a power by which each in his turn may commit crime after crime of the most heinous character, and no man be able to tell which is the guilty or which the innocent party in any case of them all. Look to your homes—look to your property—look to your lives—for you have need![1]

Because the intention and responsibility underlying the twins' actions cannot be reduced to an individual person, the judge perceives the conjoined twins as a "grisly power" that exceeds the "forms of law" premised upon liberal individualism. Three terms applied to the Cappello twins in Twain's narrative—"combination," "corporation," and "foreigners"—provide historical context for this anxious outburst. Whereas

Those Extraordinary Twins and its companion novel, *The Tragedy of Pudd'nhead Wilson* (1893–1884), have frequently been read as fictional meditations on such themes as identity, racial "passing," miscegenation, and disability, Brook Thomas and Robin Blyn have noted that the conjoined twins win in court "by relying on the confusion of identity caused by merging two people into a corporate body."[2] For Thomas, *Twins* raises questions about whether and how "a legal system that assigns guilt and blame on an individual basis" should be modified to hold corporations and their members responsible for their actions. Yet, according to Thomas, *Twins* and other classic realist novels fail to follow through on these questions about corporate responsibility: "Twain does not develop that possibility. Milking his scene, instead, for its humorous possibilities, he suggests that link between the twins' act and that of corporations only through an offhand remark by the judge."[3]

This chapter follows through on Twain's farcical treatment of the twins' corporate personhood by showing how it connects *Pudd'nhead Wilson*'s interest in the legal fiction of race with other legal fictions ("coolies" and "corporate personhood") central to the broader economic transformations of the Gilded Age. Unsuccessfully prosecuted "as a corporation" (*ET*, 157), the conjoined twins embody postwar disruptions precipitated by industrialization, monopoly capitalism, and the increasing prominence of immigrants as both a labor source and a means of dividing and controlling the U.S. working class.

Drawing on legal cases, popular cartoons, and anti-Chinese documents, I situate the slaveholding southern town satirized in *Pudd'nhead* and *Those Extraordinary Twins* amid broader postbellum responses to immigrant labor, finance capital, and what Alan Trachtenberg describes as "the incorporation of America."[4] Twain composed these texts in 1892—not only the year that Homer Plessy boarded a whites-only car on a Louisiana train and "the year when the most lynchings occurred in the United States,"[5] but also the year in which the Geary Act renewed and intensified the 1882 Chinese Exclusion Act by stipulating that all Chinese residents carry certificates of residency that included identification photographs. Public debates about corporate personhood and Chinese immigration in the post-Reconstruction period do not just highlight how Twain's conjoined twins index corporate abuses of legal protections or the masses of underpaid workers often associated with (or aggressively dissociated from) Chinese "coolie" labor—they also illuminate the intricate connections between Twain's farce about conjoined twins and his tragedy about racial passing.

The textual history of *Pudd'nhead* and *Those Extraordinary Twins* reveals a series of comparisons between immigrants and slaves, corporations and free black southerners, social upheaval and the specter of the Chinese "coolie"—comparisons that were largely suppressed when Twain separated his narrative into two nearly distinct texts. The Morgan Library's manuscript of *Pudd'nhead Wilson*—an early 1892 draft that combined the tragedy and the farce—juxtaposes the problems of immigration, corporate bodies, slavery, and racial identification by treating the conjoined twins and Tom Driscoll's experience of racial "passing" in the same narrative. Leslie Fiedler argues that Twain's separation of the combined plots of infant swapping and conjoined twins was an aesthetic mistake: "He fumbled the really great and monstrous poem on duplicity that was within his grasp. The principle of analogy which suggested to him linking the story of Siamese Twins, one a teetotaler, the other a drunk; Jekyll and Hyde inside a single burlesque skin—to a tale of a Negro and white baby switched in the cradle finally seemed to him insufficient."[6] While I share Fiedler's interest in the "monstrous" text of duplicity that would have associated conjoined twins with "a Negro and white baby switched in the cradle," I argue that this association takes the form of differential racialization rather than "analogy," that it concerns corporations and postbellum labor politics rather than the universal theme of "duplicity," and that the joint publication of *Pudd'nhead* and *Twins* as two not-quite-distinct texts highlights the intersecting but divergent practices deployed to categorize and discipline European, free black, and Chinese laborers in these decades.

I. Twain's Twins

Recounting the origins of both *Pudd'nhead* and *Twins*, Twain wrote, "Originally the story was called 'Those Extraordinary Twins.' I meant to make it very short. I had seen a picture of a youthful Italian 'freak'—or 'freaks'—which was—or which were—on exhibition in our cities—a combination consisting of two heads and four arms joined to a single body and a single pair of legs—and I thought I would write an extravagantly fantastic little story with this freak of nature for hero—or heroes—a silly young miss for heroine, and two old ladies and two boys for the minor parts" (*ET*, 126). With their appositional stutters and enumeration of body parts, these lines anticipate one of his farce's central themes: the blurring of singular and plural. When he separated his two works in an effort to emphasize the murder plot at the core of *Pudd'nhead Wilson*, Twain effectively turned the tragedy and farce into twins that appeared distinct but remained connected by ghostly ligatures—for example, in *Pudd'nhead* the nonconjoined twins still talk of being exhibited for money as children, and the lynching of one conjoined twin at the end of *Twins* renders literal Wilson's ill-fated joke, in *Pudd'nhead*, about killing his half of a dog.[7]

The plot of *Twins*—a tale that Twain extracted from the longer combined manuscript through a "literary Caesarean operation" (*ET*, 129)—consists of a series of episodes designed to showcase the twins' conjoined bodies and opposed personalities. The trouble begins when Aunt Patsy Cooper and her daughter Rowena learn that their new boarders are the "conglomerate twins" Luigi (who is passionate and "dark-complected") and Angelo (who is prudish and lighter-skinned; *ET*, 129, 138). The twins tell their story, explain how they share the maintenance and control of their body, perform a duet, and bicker about temperance and religion. After Tom Driscoll insults them, Luigi kicks him at a meeting of the anti-temperance Sons of Liberty; Tom then takes the twins to court, where Pudd'nhead Wilson successfully defends them by challenging the witnesses to decide which of the twins was responsible for the kick. Luigi then agrees to fight a duel with Judge Driscoll to settle the matter, but Angelo gains control of their legs at midnight and runs away. Finally, when Luigi is elected to the board of aldermen, the city government is stalled because he cannot take his seat (since Angelo, who was not a member, was not allowed there); the people decide to resolve the situation by lynching Luigi.

Contemporary reviews of Twain's volume followed the author's lead in framing *Twins* as a humorous and inconsequential supplement to *Pudd'nhead*'s more serious exploration of racial inequality. Among the reviewers who mentioned *Twins* at all, most commented on Twain's preface and noted how the text provides a glimpse of Twain's "jack-leg" (*ET*, 125) process of composition and revision. A review in the *Hartford*

Times, for example, called *Twins* "the roaring comedy which follows what [Twain] considers the tragedy of the longer story" and appreciated the "frank and funny revelation of the way in which *Pudd'nhead* came to be written."[8] Others passed over the comedy as a "spirited farce," a series of "grotesque drolleries" that are "of no great consequence," a "preposterous sketch" whose "drivel [mars] the unity" of *Pudd'nhead*, and an "extravaganza run mad without sufficient base."[9] In another frustrated response to Twain's "absurd extravaganza," a reviewer for *Critic* commented: "One is amused and laughs unrestrainedly but then the irksome question comes up: What is this? is it literature? is Mr. Clemens a 'writer' at all? must he not after all be described as an admirable after-dinner storyteller—humorous, imaginative, dramatic, like Dickens—who in an evil moment, urged by admiring friends, has put pen to paper and written down his stories?"[10]

Later critics have attempted to take *Twins* more seriously both as an exploration of conjoined embodiment and as a semidetached narrative that provides clues to understanding *Pudd'nhead* and Twain's other writings. In *The Ordeal of Mark Twain*, Van Wyck Brooks frames *Twins* as a dark exploration of one of Twain's most frequent themes: "a pair of incompatibles bound together in one flesh."[11] Fiedler proclaims that, had they not been separated, *Pudd'nhead*, *Twins*, and Pudd'nhead Wilson's largely expurgated calendar would have constituted "the most extraordinary book in American literature"—a "great and monstrous poem on duplicity."[12] More recently, Nancy Fredricks shows how *Pudd'nhead*'s persistent and indelible references to conjoined twins echo the twins' challenges to law and order in *Twins*,[13] Emily Russell draws on disability studies to argue that the twins' anomalous bodies are eventually contained by freak show conventions and Twain's decision to separate the two texts,[14] and Elizabeth Maddock Dillon juxtaposes *Pudd'nhead* with *Twins*' conjoinment plot, arguing that "this second narrative of subject formation reveals not just the problems of race that beset the nation in the era of Jim Crow, but the extent to which racialization is itself embedded in the formation of a coherent liberal subject."[15] While readings of *Twins* tend to view conjoined bodies as analogues of racially differentiated black and white bodies,[16] I read *Twins* in the expanded context of antimodern, anticorporate, and nativist movements that converged on the issue of Chinese Exclusion in this period. The thematization of numerical confusion (i.e., the ways in which the uncountable "Counts," Luigi and Angelo, blur singular and plural) in *Twins* reflects how industrial capitalism unsettled the Jacksonian individualism of the antebellum era. "For those who pitted the forces of individualism against the forces of collectivism," writes Brook Thomas, "corporations were on the side of socialism against a virtuous capitalist republicanism based on the responsible actions of autonomous individuals."[17]

Twain's fascination with notions of doubling and duplicity extended from his literary plots about exchanged and conjoined identities to his pen name and his public performances. As a humorist and entertainer, he was especially drawn to conjoined twins: in 1869, he published a sketch about Chang and Eng Bunker, "Personal Habits of the Siamese Twins," in *Packard's Monthly*; his 1884–1885 lecture tour with George Washington Cable was entitled "Twins of Genius"; in 1888, he introduced the lyceum lecturers James Whitcomb Riley and Bill Nye as the conjoined pair "Mr. Chang Riley" and "Mr. Eng Nye" ("The sympathy existing between the two was most extraordinary; it was so fine, so strong, so subtle, that what the one ate the other digested, when one slept the other snored, if one sold a thing the other scooped the usufruct.")[18] At a New Year's Party in 1906, Twain and an associate named Brynner dressed up as conjoined twins joined by a pink ribbon: Twain began lecturing on temperance but became increasingly inebriated as his "Siamese brother" surreptitiously imbibed from a flask.[19] In the unpublished manuscript of *No. 44, The Mysterious Stranger*, Forty-Four puts to work "Duplicates" of the print shop's workers, conflating the theme of doubling with labor exploitation.[20] In addition to enabling comic scenes involving handshakes, piano duets, a kick, a duel, and a hanging, the conjoined Cappello twins continually present readers with a physical challenge to the assumptions of liberal individualism. In *One of Us: Conjoined Twins and the Future of the Normal*, Alice Domurat Dreger writes,

> In the United States, conjoinment might be especially challenging because American culture equates individualism with independence, and interdependence with weakness. . . . To be true to yourself as an American, you must show yourself to be different, separate, distinguishable from all others. Being an individual in the United States does not

mean being an integrated member of a community, as it does in some cultures—cultures where conjoinment might be easier to live with for precisely this reason.[21]

Whereas doubles and swapped identities—as in *The Prince and the Pauper* (1881) and the case of Tom Driscoll and Valet de Chambre in *Pudd'nhead*—highlight analogies and relations of substitution between two individuals, conjoined bodies undercut the very notion of independent individuals, raising questions about interdependence, contiguity, and modes of articulation "in which things are related, as much through their differences as through their similarities."[22] Several scenes in *Twins*—such as the court that cannot decide which twin performed the kick, the abortive duel between Judge Driscoll and Luigi (proxy for the unwilling Angelo), and the people's decision to lynch just one of the two twins—satirize the incommensurability between conjoinment and Western models of justice.

Twins returns to themes and comic devices that Twain first explored decades earlier in "Personal Habits of the Siamese Twins."[23] That sketch features the conjoined celebrities Chang and Eng—ethnically Chinese twins who were born in Siam, taken on a world tour, exhibited by P. T. Barnum, and eventually naturalized as U.S. citizens after moving to Wilkesboro, North Carolina. Drawing on earlier accounts of personal differences between the twins and alluding to the title of a pamphlet by Judge J. N. Moreheid entitled *Lives, Adventures, Anecdotes, Amusements, and Domestic Habits of the Siamese Twins* (1850), "Personal Habits" humorously details the radically different personalities of its (fictionalized) twins: Chang is a Roman Catholic and a temperance man who fought for the Union; Eng is a Baptist drinker who fought on the Confederate side; when they took each other prisoner during the war, a general army court decided they should be exchanged.[24] Cynthia Wu observes that this sketch bears "striking similarities" to the treatment of the Cappello twins in *Pudd'nhead* and *Twins*: "All three texts convey concerns about the inseparability of self and other that ultimately raise questions about how difference can be reconciled, be it with violence or with negotiation."[25] Noting that Twain's sketch—like many other nineteenth-century treatments of "Siamese twins" (a term that was generalized from the Bunkers to refer to all conjoined twins)—deployed

Chang and Eng as metaphors while de-emphasizing the twins' Chinese ethnicity, Wu argues that, "under the punchy veneer of deadpan humor emblematic of Twain's style, the essay acknowledges the existence of ongoing sectional strife in the wake of the Civil War and reveals ambivalent feelings toward the phenomenon of Asian migration to the American continent during this time, making a crucial link between sectional reconciliation along the Eastern seaboard and the influx of noncitizen labor exploited on the California coast during this period."[26] To the extent that Twain's twins in the 1890s recall his 1869 sketch about Chang and Eng, they echo these earlier connections between Asiatic migrant labor in the western states and post-Reconstruction policies that introduced Jim Crow legislation in the interest of sectional reconciliation.

However, the Italian Tocci brothers were a more immediate source for Twain's Italian twins. Four factors may have motivated Twain to base Luigi and Angelo on the Tocci twins: the fact that, unlike the Bunker twins, Giovanni and Giacomo Tocci shared a single pair of legs and thus raised questions about corporeal control that are crucial to the plot of *Twins*;[27] sugar planters' hopes that Italians—along with other immigrants, including Chinese indentured workers—would reduce the South's reliance on African American plantation labor;[28] contemporary prejudices against Italian immigrant laborers in the 1880s and 1890s that had culminated in the lynching of eleven Italians in New Orleans;[29] and racial stereotypes that divergently associated Italians with European culture and dark skin. While the Italian twins introduce specific dynamics of immigration and racialization, xenophobic attitudes toward Italian immigrants intersected with populist rhetoric that associated Chinese and other immigrant laborers with the dehumanizing effects of industrial capitalism.

Before considering how Twain's conjoined twins articulate black-white relations with nativist discourses about Italian and Chinese immigrants, this chapter first examines another combined body that undercut the norms of liberal individualism: the corporation. "Within the age of the [individualist] robber barons," writes Trachtenberg, "another age and another form took shape, that of the giant corporate body."[30] In their coordinated actions and their limited liability before the law, Twain's combined twins allegorize the emergent legal fiction of corporate personhood that dramatically enhanced the power of big businesses by extending them equal protection under the Fourteenth Amendment. By associating the twins' corporate body with "an awful and mysterious gift, a hidden and grisly power for evil," *Twins* touches on a popular theme of the era's antimonopoly fiction: the threats to self-reliant Anglo-Saxon men posed by incorporation and the widespread employment of racialized and immigrant labor. For example, Frank Norris's fictionalization of the 1880 Mussel Slough incident—a violent conflict between settlers and agents of the Southern Pacific Railroad—would influentially depict the railroad corporation as an octopus that sucked the life out of struggling characters. Summarizing the suffering brought upon white families by the railroad in the closing lines of *The Octopus* (1901), he writes: "Men—motes in the sunshine—perished, were shot down in the very noon of life, hearts were broken, little children started in life lamentably handicapped; young girls were brought to a life of shame; old women died in the heart of life for lack of food. In that little, isolated group of human insects, misery, death, and anguish spun like a wheel of fire."[31]

II. Corporate Bodies

Twain and Charles Dudley Warner's co-authored novel, *The Gilded Age: A Tale of Today* (1873), gave a name to the speculation, political corruption, and materialism that characterized the decades following the Civil War. Historians of the Gilded Age have emphasized the social transformations brought about by unprecedented waves of immigration, urbanization, industrialization, and big business. In his groundbreaking study of figurative and literal processes of incorporation during this period—which he describes as the "seedtime of a new corporate order"—Trachtenberg argues "that economic incorporation wrenched American society from the moorings of familiar values, [and] that the process proceeded by contradiction and conflict."[32] The corporate form provided the impetus for large-scale projects ranging from railroads and skyscrapers to oil refineries and manufacturing by enabling officers and shareholders to leverage massive pools of capital with limited liability. Twain was ambivalent about corporations: whereas *The Gilded Age* satirizes an "Incorporatorship" scheme and comments on the futility of suing a railroad corporation, "Concerning the Jews" notes that "in our days we have learned the value of combination. We apply it everywhere—in railway systems, in trusts, in trade unions, in Salvation Armies, in minor politics, in major politics, in European Concerts. Whatever our strength may be, big or little, we organize it. We have found out that that is the only way to get the most out of it that is in it."[33] Whereas "To the Person Sitting in Darkness" critiques imperialism by denouncing the corporate "Blessings-of-Civilization Trust," by 1908 Twain would become the first author to incorporate his own name.[34]

Beneath the "freak show conventions"[35] with which Twain frames the twins, Luigi and Angelo present readers with a spectacle of economy and Taylorist efficiency: "They . . . carved the beef steak with one set of their hands while they distributed at the same time with the other set." The servant is amazed to see "the commingling arms feed potatoes into one mouth and coffee into the other at the same time," and the twins explain that "we are always helping each other that way. It is a great economy for us both; it saves time and labor" (*ET*, 137–138). They go on to explain that the work of their coordinated arms is "often of the extremest value," as when eating in alternate shifts on riverboats: "Neither of us eats anything at the other's table, but just simply works—works. Thus, you see, there are four hands to feed Angelo, and the same four to feed me. Each of us eats two meals" (*ET*, 139). Their conjoined bodies provide the twins with various opportunities to be "practical . . . and economical" by paying for only one train seat, hotel bed, theater ticket, or bath (*ET*, 139).[36] Even the twins' mysterious alteration of "utter and indisputable command of our body" (*ET*, 147) is so punctual that it regulates clocks—and thus modern institutions and "time-discipline"[37]—across the globe: "So exactly to the instant does the change come, that during our stay in many of the great cities of the world, the public clocks were regulated by it; and as hundreds of thousands of private clocks and watches were set and corrected in accordance with the public clocks, we really furnished the standard time for the entire city" (*ET*, 147).

Their efficiency and punctuality link the twins to the other representative of modern capitalism in Dawson's Landing: the Yankee lawyer, surveyor, and accountant David "Pudd'nhead" Wilson, with his urbane wit and his penchant for methodical activities such as writing calendars and taking fingerprints. Wilson and the Italian twins become involved in the profound social transformation that Dawson's Landing undergoes when it incorporates as a city and holds its first elections for city government during the course of Twain's narratives. If their urban, cosmopolitan, and eminently practical outsider status marginalizes Wilson and the Italians, it also helps explain their political empowerment when, shortly after "the village had just been converted into a city by charter," Wilson is asked to run for mayor and Luigi is elected onto the new board of aldermen (*ET*, 164–165). The town's incorporation—which Twain mentions immediately after Wilson successfully defends the twins in court—marks a shift from small-scale community and economy to "the city as a social force whose fusion of factory, marketplace, and home in a process of incorporation reshaped the entire society and its culture. That process altered relations, defied inherited values, transformed instruments of perception and communication, even as it transformed the perceptible social world."[38]

John Carlos Rowe reads *Pudd'nhead* as a satire of another aspect of Gilded Age capitalism: the unprecedented financial speculations that provided impetus for corporate enterprise. Rowe situates the pivotal role of speculative plot elements in *Pudd'nhead*—including slaveholders' speculations on their slaves' lives, Percy Driscoll's land speculations, Tom Driscoll's gambling, Roxy's bank failure, and David Wilson's decision to seek his fortune in Dawson's Landing—amid "the economic 'failures' that punctuated the American economy from the Panic of 1837 to the Panics of 1873 and 1893."[39] The last of these financial crises led to the failure of Twain's own speculative investments in the Paige Typesetter and in his publishing venture, Charles L. Webster & Co., during the years he was writing and revising *Pudd'nhead* and *Twins*.[40] According to Rowe, the failed promise of speculative capitalism connects Twain's own financial ruin to those of his characters, culminating in Tom Driscoll's re-enslavement and sale at the end of the novel in a plot twist that blurs the boundaries between antebellum slavery and the forms of "new economic servitude"[41] that arose in the wake of Reconstruction.

The rampant speculations of the Gilded Age were enabled by the corporation, a legal entity that permitted stockholders to acquire speculative gains by investing in companies controlled by a small group of managers. Between the antebellum period and the end of the nineteenth century, U.S. laws shifted from a system in which corporate charters were granted only to businesses that "had a quasi-public character and pursued public purposes" to one that allowed private businesses the right "to incorporate freely."[42] Twain demonstrated a nuanced understanding of the corporate form (and its abuses) when he deployed it as a metaphor for a corrupt government in *A Connecticut Yankee*: "So to speak, I was become a stockholder in a corporation where nine hundred and ninety-four of the members furnished all the money and did all the work, and the other six elected themselves a permanent board of direction and took all the dividends."[43] While the division between the corporation's relatively few directors and its potentially vast number of stockholders and employees does not exactly correspond to the corporeal dynamics of Twain's conjoined twins, it resonates with Luigi and Angelo's system of alternating control when eating with four hands ("Neither of us eats anything at the other's table, but just simply works—works") and with the fact that, at any given time, only one of them is in control of their shared legs. Moreover, the judge's warning that the twins possess "an awful and mysterious gift, a hidden and grisly power for evil" echoes contemporaneous responses to the hidden, mysterious powers of corporations and trusts to regulate prices, corner markets, exploit workers, and cheat stockholders. Trachtenberg, for example, writes that, "with the corporate device as its chief instrument, business grew increasingly arcane and mysterious, spawning new roles intermediary between capital and labor, in middle management, accounting, legal departments, public relations, advertising, marketing, sales: the entire apparatus of twentieth-century corporate life was developed in these years and clouded the public perception of the typical acts of business."[44] In representing the "combined" life of conjoined twins, I argue, Twain's farce raises questions and problems associated with the profound social influence of the new corporate culture (*ET*, 144). *Those Extraordinary Twins* engages with the "subtle shifts in the meaning of prevalent ideas, ideas regarding the identity of the individual, the relation between public and private realms, and the character of the nation" that were introduced by the emergence of corporations as a dominant economic form.[45]

These cultural shifts were first registered in the legal cases that defined, refashioned, and (occasionally) regulated corporations. In *The Transformation of American Law, 1870–1960*, legal historian Morton

Horwitz reports that, "during the last quarter of the nineteenth century, the legal literature was filled with discussions of the nature of the corporation—whether, like a partnership, it is a mere aggregate of individuals or whether, instead, it is an entity separate from the individuals who compose it."[46] The U.S. Supreme Court reporter's headnote[47] in *Santa Clara County v. Southern Pacific Railroad* (1886) notoriously took for granted that Fourteenth Amendment protections of individual civil rights and due process applied to corporations: "The court does not wish to hear argument on the question whether the provision in the Fourteenth Amendment to the Constitution, which forbids a State to deny to any person within its jurisdiction the equal protection of the laws, applies to these corporations. We are all of the opinion that it does."[48] Although the court does not explain whether this opinion was intended to establish that corporations were to be treated as legal persons or simply to defend the rights and limited liability of individual corporate shareholders, *Santa Clara County v. Southern Pacific Railroad* would later be cited as the precedent for theories of corporate personhood that, according to Horwitz, were developed in response to "a crisis of legitimacy in liberal individualism arising from the recent emergence of powerful collective institutions."[49] In a unanimous decision, the court ruled in favor of the Southern Pacific Railroad Corporation's suit against new taxes imposed by California's 1879 constitution.

A pivotal scene in *Those Extraordinary Twins*—in which Luigi and Angelo are charged "as a corporation" with kicking Tom Driscoll, then absolved by a jury that cannot determine which twin dealt the blow— explores the legal and ethical perplexities involved in deliberating about corporate bodies. Wilson successfully defends the twins by asking each of the prosecution's witnesses, "Are you perfectly sure that you saw both of them kick him, or only one?" (*ET*, 153). The impossibility of distinguishing between an individual kick and a "mutual kick" (*ET*, 157) leaves the twins with a power of limited liability analogous to that of corporations. In Twain's earlier manuscript, Tom responds at greater length to the legal aporia precipitated by the twins' conjoinment: "Never once thought of their slipping out of it the way they did, with their vile double-action & single-action, interchangeable at will when they want to commit crime, & the original Satan himself not able to tell t'other from which when you want to fetch them to book."[50]

Twain may have drawn on popular anecdotes about Chang and Eng Bunker in fashioning this courtroom scene. Publicity materials for the Bunkers emphasized the shared agency and impulses that confound the legal system in *Those Extraordinary Twins*: "Although they stand so close together, yet they do not seem to be at all in each other's way, and whatever movement is made by one is responded to so immediately by the other, that it seems as if they were moved by the same impulse. They never thwart or oppose each other in any way."[51] The twins' biographers recount an anecdote in which Chang punched an aggressive spectator at an exhibition: "The magistrate, after studying the twins' connecting band, addressed the complainant. The judge agreed that Chang could be jailed for assault, but added that if Eng were also jailed it would amount to false arrest and the complainant himself would have to be prosecuted. Needless to say, the injured party dropped his charges."[52] Moreheid's *Lives, Adventures, Anecdotes, Amusements, and Domestic Habits of the Siamese Twins* also meditates on the twins' limited liability: "It must remain a mooted question, as to the liability of one of them to receive corporal punishment at the hands of the law for the acts of the other, which would be the case, if the punishment extended to the depriving either of them of life, as in that case, it must necessarily affect both alike."[53] To the extent that Twain's narrative revisits these issues of physical assault, legal liability, and corporal punishment, his Italian twins have origins in the ethnically Chinese Bunkers as well as the Tocci brothers.

The Chinese and Italian origins of Twain's conjoined twins point to another historical development connected to the rise of exploitative corporations: the emergence of an industrial working class fractured by ethnic and racial tensions. Commenting on the 13,259,469 recorded immigrants who entered the United States between 1866 and 1900, historian Roger Daniels writes that "these thirty-four years saw the entry of a larger number of persons, by far, than had come to the United States and the British North American colonies in the previous two and one-half centuries."[54] The majority of these were working-class men, and the growth of immigration from countries such as Italy (accounting for about 5.9% of all immigrants from 1881 to 1890) and China (accounting for 4.4% of all immigrants between 1871 and 1880, before Chinese Exclusion) fomented ethnic and class tensions.[55] "On every count," writes Trachtenberg, "labor seemed to represent a foreign culture, alien to American values epitomized by successful representatives of capital."[56] Although Twain noted that Luigi and Angelo Capello "had no occasion to have foreign names" (*ET*, 128) after he extricated *Twins* from *Pudd'nhead*, the critic Joseph Cosco has argued that the two texts dramatize debates about Italian immigration by presenting the Capellos in an ambivalent light: on the one hand, they enjoy popularity, begin the naturalization process, and are "asked to stand for seats in the forthcoming aldermanic board"; on the other hand, the community readily blames them for Tom's crimes and, in *Twins*, ends up lynching them (*PW*, 80).[57] Anti-Italian and anti-Chinese discourses intersected insofar as both were fueled by anxieties about the degradation of white labor under monopoly capitalism; however, while Pudd'nhead acknowledges that Italian immigrants were eligible for citizenship and public office, exclusion laws and the figure of the "coolie" positioned Chinese immigrants as inassimilable to norms of liberal individualism. If, as Dillon argues, "the contradiction of liberal subjectivity is played out by Twain in 1892 in racialized terms which equate whiteness with agency and blackness with property,"[58] *Those Extraordinary Twins* triangulates white individualism and black objecthood with the problem of corporate agency embodied by Chinese immigrant laborers.

III. "Coolies" and Monopoly Capitalism

Twain was familiar with the popular antimonopoly literature of his time: according to Alexander Saxton, *A Connecticut Yankee* "bears superficial resemblance to the anti-monopoly literature of the period."[59] Twain's publishing company, Charles L. Webster & Co., published four books by the antimonopoly political economist and advocate of Chinese Exclusion, Henry George.[60] Saxton notes that "the heart of [George's indictment of Chinese immigration] was that Chinese labor accentuated the trend toward monopoly. Was it not the great land engrossers, especially the Central Pacific Railroad, which organized and defended the importation of Chinese?"[61] To the extent that labor advocates viewed railroad corporations as the most extreme instances of monopoly capitalism, the Chinese immigrants whose labor helped sustain the railroads became figures—and convenient scapegoats—for the era's dramatic concentration of wealth and devaluation of labor.

The California Constitution of 1879 illustrates the extent to which public opinion conflated corporations and Chinese immigrant laborers. Article XIX, captioned "Chinese," "declared the presence of the Chinese to be dangerous to the well-being of the state and bade the legislature to do all in its power to discourage their immigration into California. It prohibited corporations from employing Chinese and forbade their employment on any public work—state, county, or municipal—except as a punishment for crime."[62] In February 1880, the legislature modified California's penal code, making it a misdemeanor punishable by fine or imprisonment in the county jail for any officer, director, or agent of a corporation to employ "any Chinese or Mongolian" in any capacity for any work whatever and "impos[ing] criminal liability on the corporation itself [such that] the corporation should forfeit its charter, its franchise, and all its corporate rights upon a second conviction."[63] Although this new legislation would soon be challenged in *In re Tiburcio Parrott* (1880), it was at first viewed as a decisive blow against the purportedly allied phenomena of monopoly capitalism and Chinese immigration. Since the railroad taxes contested in *Santa Clara County v. Southern Pacific Railroad* also originated in California's 1879 constitution,[64] the case that established the notion of "corporate personhood" can be traced back to antimonopoly, anti-Chinese sentiment in the U.S. West.

"The Mill Among the Mill-Hands" (Figure 3.1), a cartoon published on the cover of the February 20, 1880 issue of the *Wasp*, celebrates the new state constitution as a victory for the white working class by depicting the overthrow of mill corporations that supposedly degraded the value of white labor by employing underpaid Chinese laborers. Published just two years before Congress passed the Chinese Exclusion Act, this image metaphorically represents mills and other "corporations" as a number of caricatured Chinese bodies; the train crashing through the bodies presents an allegorical fantasy in which anti-Chinese violence stands in for anticorporate revolution. In addition to leveraging (and reproducing) an archive of racist images and assumptions that render Chinese bodies disproportionately subject to violence, this cartoon's depiction of the new constitution as a train willfully effaces the instrumental role of both Chinese migrant workers and railroad corporations in the construction of U.S. railroads. The cartoon's tautological image—in which a train riding on a track that would likely have been laid by Chinese workers hired by a railroad corporation

Figure 3.1: "The Mill Among the Mill-Hands," *Wasp* 4, no. 186 (February 21, 1880): cover. Courtesy of the Bancroft Library, University of California, Berkeley.

is shown running over corporations and Chinese workers—indicates how deeply rooted corporate projects and immigrant labor had become in everyday experience and hints that scapegoating Chinese immigrants would be an ineffectual method of resisting corporate expansion.

During the years leading up to the Chinese Exclusion Act, popular caricatures often associated the Chinese with various forms of monstrous and multiple embodiment. In the pages of the *Wasp* alone, the Chinese were represented as a volcanic eruption of disembodied heads, hordes of miniscule invaders, a swarm of famished grasshoppers, a gruesome giant labeled "Monopoly," one head of a hydra representing California's political problems, a hyperbolically efficient laborer with eleven arms, a "many-handed but soulless" devil, and a giant serpent whose scales are inscribed with phrases like "ruin to white labor," "smallpox," and "beneficial to corporations and monopolies."[65] These depictions of the Chinese were contemporaneous with caricatures depicting the corporation as a new economic monstrosity: several months before he drew "The Curse of California" (1882)[66]—the famous image of the railroad monopoly as an octopus squeezing life from stage lines, lumber dealers, miners, and farmers that popularized the metaphor for corrupt corporations—*Wasp* illustrator G. Frederick Keller published "The Ogre of Mussel Slough,"[67] which depicted the Mussel Slough massacre as a standoff between ordinary farmers and a two-headed giant. Bearing the heads of Leland Stanford and Charles Crocker, and with hands labeled "subsidy" and "land grab," this looming embodiment of corporate personhood approximates the form of conjoined twins. Just a week earlier, Keller had published another image that conflates singular and plural bodies: "What Shall We Do With Our Boys?" (1882) depicts a giant Chinese worker with eleven arms, labeled "chinese trade monopoly" (Figure 3.2). Juxtaposing this figure with a group of idling white boys (one of whom is being escorted toward a house of correction by a policeman), the cartoon attributes white unemployment to the employment of Chinese laborers in various branches of manufacture.[68]

Those Extraordinary Twins deploys similar images of monstrous multiple bodies and swarming arms. The twins first appear as "a stupefying apparition—a double-headed human creature with four arms, one body, and a single pair of legs!" (*ET*, 130). The ceaseless activity of their four arms confounds Aunt Patsy Cooper with an octopus-like vision of

Figure 3.2: G. Frederick Keller, "'What Shall We Do With Our Boys?'" *Wasp* 8, no. 292 (January–June 1882): 136–137. Courtesy of the Bancroft Library, University of California, Berkeley.

"a wormy squirming of arms in the air—seemed to be a couple of dozen of them, all writhing at once, and it just made me dizzy to see them go" (*ET*, 132). Twain's conjoined twins—referred to as "monsters," "foreigners," a "combination," and a "corporation"—resemble representations of "coolies" not only because racial and national "others" were frequently caricatured as monsters but also in their particular forms of monstrosity (swarming arms, combined bodies, undifferentiated masses) and in their shared association with increasingly influential corporations.

Colleen Lye's analysis of the figure of the "coolie" amid California's antimonopoly politics in this period helps explain the mass appeal of images depicting the monstrous bodies of Chinese laborers: "As the phantasmatically cheapening body capitalism strives to universalize, the coolie represents a biological impossibility and a numerical abstraction, whose social domination means that the robust American body will have disappeared."[69] Lye's reading of the coolie as "a figure of modernity's economic masses" also explains the frequency with which Chinese were represented as multiple, swarming, or grotesquely combined bodies, rather than as individual subjects: "There can be no such thing as a single coolie. Asiatic racial form is indissociably plural, and its affiliation with the urban multitude at the turn of the century is clearly connected to a contemporary sense of the general foreignness of the city."[70] Popular literature of the period bears this out: dozens of dystopian Chinese invasion narratives were "organized around the prospect of a horde of numberless, faceless Chinese pouring over American borders and bludgeoning a valiant nation into submission by degrees."[71] In Ignatius Donnelly's *Caesar's Column* (1890), for example, an industrial elite employing "vile hordes of Mongolian coolies" dominates white workers and farmers in the United States.[72] Even the common epithet "Chinaman" elides any aural distinction between the singular and plural, thus rendering the individuality of a Chinese immigrant as difficult to demarcate as that of a conjoined twin. Through the figure of the "coolie," corporate personhood—a legally recognized attribute of corporations—became metonymically associated with Chinese laborers.

If corporate subjectivity was projected onto Chinese laborers, it was also an attribute of corporations themselves. Several commentators invoked the Siamese twins as a figure for corporate structure:

> The facts which I have stated in this paper show that the Southern Pacific is in fact the Central Pacific, practically the same directory in both, the former operated under a lease to the latter; all the expenses charged in the account of the Central Pacific. While nominally two roads they are like the Siamese twins exhibited some years ago in this country, having two bodies, but after dissection it appears they had but a single heart.[73]

> This fiction [of legal personhood] may give rise to insolvable problems. For instance, a railroad company, whose road extends through two states, is organized under charters from both, each charter being the counterpart of the other. Is the result one or two "legal persons"? Since as much may be said on one side as the other, the problem is as insolvable as it is gratuitous. The question of real importance is: What are the rights and liabilities arising under these charters in respect of the corporate enterprise? And this question may be answered without reference to whether this railroad company is one or two "persons," or Siamese twins born of different mothers.[74]

In addition to highlighting the parallels between the corporate subjectivity attributed to corporations and to Chinese workers, the metaphor of "Siamese twins" functions as a condensed expression of intersecting Gilded Age anxieties about corporate capitalism, the mechanization of labor, and the integrity of racial and national borders.

As critics have noted, *Pudd'nhead Wilson*'s deployment of fingerprinting technology to establish both Tom's individual identity (as the murderer) and his race drew on numerous accounts of the effectiveness of fingerprints for policing racialized populations. In Twain's novel (and particularly in his earlier manuscript at the Morgan Library, whose final trial hinges upon distinguishing between Tom Driscoll's fingerprints and those of the conjoined twins), the appeal of fingerprints lies in their capacity to counteract the confusion presented by undifferentiated hordes of racialized bodies: "There is no duplicate of it among the swarming populations of the globe!" (*PW*, 114). The British eugenicist Sir Francis Galton—whose treatise *Finger Prints* inspired Twain's use of the technology in *Pudd'nhead* and whose writings on identical twins may have influenced the novel's changeling plot[75]—discusses the potential of fingerprints for identifying "Hindoos" and Chinese residents in British territories, "who to European eyes are still more alike than the Hindoos, and in whose names there is still less variety."[76] In colonial contexts, biometric identification enables the police to individuate bodies without having to distinguish between persons (faces, biographies, contexts) among "swarming populations": as Sarah Chinn writes in *Technology and the Logic of American Racism*, "Fingerprinting could thus achieve apparently opposite goals: unambiguously pinpointing individual indigenous people and depersonalizing native people as a group."[77] Twain, who had commented on the supposed difficulty of distinguishing between Chinese suspects in an early piece for the *Virginia City Territorial Enterprise*,[78] would have been struck by Galton's discussion of an early unsuccessful proposal by the San Francisco–based photographer Isaiah West Taber and several government officials to employ "the method of finger prints for the registration of Chinese, whose identification has always been a difficulty, and was giving a great deal of trouble at that particular time."[79] Taber, "who frequently photographed Chinatown scenes during the 1880s and 1890s,"[80] is credited with developing the method of taking prints with ink impressions and then enlarging them photographically for analysis—a method that Wilson approximates in Twain's novel by enlarging fingerprint impressions with the aid of a pantograph.

A more extensive description of Taber's work and the proposal to take Chinese residents' thumbprints appeared in the *San Francisco Daily Report* on September 19, 1885. Noting that there had been no effective way to stop the influx of Chinese immigrants passing as "prior residents" of the United States (and thus exempt from the Exclusion Act), the article explained that descriptions of physical characteristics such as height, hair color, complexion, and distinguishing marks on residency certificates are inadequate markers of identity: "Of the ordinary Chinese, in American eyes, the portrait of one will pass with little question for that of another."[81] The article's account of the proposed solution parallels Wilson's elaborate explanation of fingerprints in Twain's novel: "These curves are all different in different persons. Out of thousands of thumbs examined no two show the same lines or the same figures. But the same thumb always is marked the same. . . . No one can counterfeit it. It is his from early youth until the tissues are decayed."[82] Like *Pudd'nhead*, "Thumbs Down!" introduces fingerprinting and its associated vocabulary in the context of a fictionalized legal plot, in this case a speculative "Extract from Cross-Examination of the Future" in which a fingerprinting expert testifies that "The defendant's convolution turns to the right just 1-1600 part of an inch sooner than the plaintiff's."[83]

Although Galton never managed to find conclusive evidence that fingerprints varied by race[84] and that they could be used as a technology for discovering a biological basis for race, his recommendation that fingerprint identification be used extensively in colonial policing endorses the deployment of fingerprinting as a technology for producing racial difference: "In civil as well as in criminal cases, the need of some such system is shown to be greatly felt in many of our dependencies; where the features of the natives are distinguished with difficulty; where there is but little variety of surnames; where there are strong motives for prevarication, especially connected with land-tenure and pensions, and a proverbial prevalence of unveracity."[85] Assuming that evidence such as portraits, surnames, and testimony suffices among Anglo-Saxons, fingerprinting would be most useful among unruly, visually indistinguishable "natives." As the criminology scholar Simon Cole explains,

"Fingerprinting emerged as a solution to the problem of identification specifically in locales where perceived racial homogeneity was viewed as rendering individualization through Bertillonage technically unfeasible."[86] The proposal to take thumbprints of Chinese residents—like the 1892 Geary Act's widely resisted requirement that they register for residency certificates and have their photographs taken[87]—would racialize the Chinese by keeping records that could be used to incriminate them (or to incriminate other Chinese whose fingerprints did not match those of certified residents). Twain's deployment of fingerprints in *Pudd'nhead* further emphasizes the tension between individuation and racialization: by providing evidence of Tom's individual identity, his fingerprints simultaneously confirm his legal status as a "thing"—an item of inventory summarily sold off to repay his master's creditors.

Despite their apparent focus on individual identity rather than visual or racial characteristics, early proposals and implementations of fingerprinting in the United States focused on policing racialized groups. Noting several historical instances in which fingerprints were proposed "for the surveillance of racially marginalized populations rather than the identification of criminals," Cole observes that "much of the early history of fingerprint identification in the United States has the feel of playing out a script written by Twain in 1892."[88] Articulated with laws that criminalized, displaced, or excluded different racial groups, unevenly collected fingerprint records would serve to reinscribe racial differences throughout the United States and its colonies. *Pudd'nhead Wilson*'s finale—in which Wilson commands "Tom" (now revealed as the slave Valet de Chambre) to "make upon the window the fingerprints that will hang you!" (*PW*, 120)—illustrates how the apparently race-blind technology of fingerprinting can collude with slavery and, by extension, with other systems of racial inequality including segregation, colonial governance, and Chinese Exclusion. By reducing Tom Driscoll and Valet de Chambre's lives to a framework of formal equivalence ("We will call the children A and B. . . . Here are A's finger marks. . . . Here are B's"; *PW*, 116–117), Wilson reproduces racial hierarchy and re-enslaves Tom. Fingerprinting can only be imagined as a technology for establishing individual responsibility if it is abstracted from the social and legal conditions that dispossess, criminalize, and surveil entire populations. Although Twain's depiction of fingerprint technology in the antebellum South is anachronistic, it is also prescient in dramatizing how biometric surveillance would increasingly be deployed against people of color throughout the twentieth century.

Though Twain only mentions China once in *Pudd'nhead* and *Twins* (when Angelo reports that he and Luigi have travelled in India, China, and Japan), the foreign presences in Dawson's landing—fingerprints and the Italian twins—bear shadowy connections to Asia. The use of fingerprints for identification has origins in both China—where according to the *San Francisco Daily Report* they had "been used ... for centuries" to identify army deserters[89]—and Bengal, where the British raj used them to enforce contracts and identify criminals.[90] As Chinn has shown, *Pudd'nhead* draws an analogy between fingerprinting and the practice of palmistry—a technique for interpreting bodies that Count Angelo learned while traveling in "the Orient" (*PW*, 54).[91] The murder weapon in *Pudd'nhead*—an ornamented dagger "given to Luigi by a great Indian prince, the Gaikowar [*gaekwad*] of Baroda"—also has a South Asian provenance, and the twins' familiarity with the ruler of Baroda indicates that they acquired at least one powerful ally during their travels in Asia. While neither Twain nor Americans would have given much thought to the Philippines in the mid-1890s, one of the final references to the Cappellos in *Twins* refers to them as a "human phillipene" (*ET*, 184)—a distortion of the term "philopena" (a single almond with two kernels). Twain's unintentional invocation of the Philippines is prescient, for in just a few years later the United States would be waging war on Filipino nationalists and deploying surveillance technologies such as fingerprinting to secure possession of the islands.

Those Extraordinary Twins expresses the anxieties about southern industrialization and immigrant labor that Twain excised in order to streamline *Pudd'nhead*'s ambivalent narratives of biometric individuation and North-South reconciliation. Assuring his publisher that his revisions to the early, combined version of *Pudd'nhead* and *Twins* had successfully yielded a unified text, Twain wrote on July 30, 1893, "I have pulled the twins apart and made two individuals of them; I have sunk them out of sight, they are mere flitting shadows, now, and of no importance; their story has disappeared from the book."[92] Twain also revised the ending of *Pudd'nhead*, reporting that the rehabilitated twins (who run for city government positions in *Twins*) "straightway retired to Europe" after the trial (*PW*, 120).

In the earlier combined manuscript, however, the Cappello twins' departure for Europe is not a voluntary act. Instead, the conjoined twins run into trouble (as they do toward the end of the published version of *Twins*) when a series of courts decide that Luigi, having being elected to the board of aldermen, cannot bring his conjoined brother into its sessions. This dilemma paralyzes the city government until a "citizen" proposes that they hang Luigi (627). Whereas *Twins* concludes with the execution of Luigi (and, presumably, the concomitant death of Angelo), in Twain's draft the twins are presented with another option:

> So the town carried the halter to Luigi, explained its persuasions, & asked him to resign & go to Europe, & not stop anywhere this side.
> Luigi accepted the invitation, & took his brother along with him. They never returned. Then a new election was held, & the city got started right, this time.[93]

Given the choice of death or exile because the government cannot assimilate their conjoined agency, the twins choose what amounts to a coerced deportation. Twain's draft describes this outcome just before it abruptly disposes of other extraneous characters by having them fall down a well and only a few pages before it recounts how the man once known as Tom Driscoll was sold down the river. By placing the twins' coerced deportation in close proximity with the black man's sale into slavery, the Morgan Library manuscript of *Pudd'nhead Wilson* conveys both the similarity and the divergence of these characters' fates under legal constructions of immigration, slavery, and liberal individualism.

The acts of disarticulation (separating the narratives and separating the twins' bodies) associate Twain's revision process with the strategy of contrasting African Americans with Chinese immigrants evident in post-Reconstruction documents of reconciliation such as Henry Grady's address on "The South and Her Problems" (1887), which claimed that "the exclusion of the Chinese is the first step in the revolution that shall save liberty and law and religion to this land";[94] Booker T. Washington's "Atlanta Compromise" (1895) speech, which urged Southern blacks and whites to "cast down your bucket where you are" rather than emigrating northward or hiring immigrant laborers;[95] and Justice John Marshall Harlan's dissenting opinion in *Plessy v. Ferguson* (1896), which opposed segregation by comparing African Americans to the Chinese—"a race so different from our own" who are nevertheless permitted to ride in white coaches.[96] All these texts disentangle southern blacks from immigrant masses—and particularly the figure of excluded Chinese migrants—in order to foreground national reconciliation and local affiliations between black and white southerners. By publishing *Twins* as an appendix to *Pudd'nhead*, however, Twain dramatized the process by which a "monstrous" "foreign" "combination" must be "segregated" and made to (almost) disappear—reduced to "mere flitting shadows"—in order to suppress the glaring continuities between Wilson's re-enslavement of Tom Driscoll and modern techniques of "racial governmentality" unevenly brought to bear on immigrants, colonial subjects, and other racialized groups.[97] In *Following the Equator* (1897), Twain revisited these continuities by using Pudd'nhead Wilson's new calendar entries as chapter epigraphs: juxtaposed with Train's travelogue, Wilson's cynical wisdom connects the racial hierarchies of Dawson's Landing with global problems of migration, displacement, and racialized labor associated with British imperialism. Twain's later works of comparative antiracism and anti-imperialism—which I discuss in Chapter 5—extend this interrogation of the intersections between immigration, racialization, and the legacies of slavery in the wake of his 1895 lecture tour through the British Empire.

A Connecticut Yankee in the Court of Wu Chih Tien

Imperial Romance and Chinese Modernization

In a letter to William Dean Howells written on November 20, 1874, but playfully dated "1935," Twain indulges in an early instance of speculative fiction. Slipping into the popular genre of Chinese invasion narratives, the letter's fourth paragraph imagines a jarring encounter with a Chinese man and his "usual cargo" of missionaries during a flight:

> My air-ship was delayed by a collision with a fellow from China loaded with the usual cargo of jabbering, copper-colored missionaries, & so I was nearly an hour on my journey. But by the goodness of God thirteen of the missionaries were crippled & several killed, so I was content to lose the time.[1]

In the midst of a passage envisioning future technologies such as wireless telegraphy and airships, Twain inverts nineteenth-century transpacific relations by describing a situation in which China routinely sends missionaries to the United States. Twain's letter defamiliarizes both coolie discourse and the rhetoric of missionary uplift: here, the routine "cargo" of Chinese is not a shipload of indentured laborers but a group of missionaries intending to convert and civilize Americans.

Despite his letter's apparent scorn for these "jabbering, copper-colored missionaries" and his eagerness to see them crippled and killed, Twain would later reframe this apparently dystopian scenario as an instance of wishful thinking. His autobiographical dictation of September 12, 1908, offers a detailed commentary on this letter's predictions. There, he claims that the notion "that by 1935 we shall have Chinamen coming to us as missionaries" was not a prediction so much as a hope:

a hope that someday those excellent people would come here and teach us how to be at peace and bloodless for thousands of years without the brutal help of armies and navies. But that gentle dream is dead: we have taught them to adopt our sham civilisation and armies and navies to such other rotten assets as they may possess.[2]

In this account of his 1874 letter, Twain's hope is embodied in an alternative history of modernization and international relations—one in which China attains technological and cultural equality with (or supremacy over) Western nations and exports its culture to the United States. Twain's phrasing—"that gentle dream is dead"—aligns this vision of a modernized China with Hank Morgan's ill-fated "dream of a republic" in *A Connecticut Yankee in King Arthur's Court* (1889).[3] But whereas Hank Morgan's republic is premised upon Western technologies of war and governance, Twain's "gentle dream" identifies Chinese civilization as an antidote to Western warfare and, presumably, to its imperialist motives.

Whereas the preceding chapters have focused on Chinese immigrant laborers, this chapter expands upon Twain's imagined encounter with modernized Chinese missionaries to the United States by reading his writings alongside the antiracist and anti-imperialist discourses produced by two educated Chinese diasporic writers, Yung Wing and Wong Chin Foo. If, in the context of immigration policy, antimodern figurations of the "coolie" projected modernity's threats onto Chinese laborers, in the context of foreign relations imperialists framed China and other colonial arenas as premodern and uncivilized backdrops for vigorous Western intervention. Arguing that both China and Chinese immigrants were capable of reform, Yung and Wong emphatically differentiated middle-class Chinese intellectuals from working-class stereotypes. Their projects of Chinese and Chinese American modernization—which were linked to the controversial program of "Self-Strengthening" adapted by Chinese officials in this period—delineate a circumpacific context for reading Twain's relationships with prominent advocates of Chinese reform and his dramatization, in *A Connecticut Yankee*, of a modernization project gone awry.

China occupied an anomalous position among the field of non-Western nations viewed as potential arenas for imperialist conquest or other foreign interventions. For if some writers described "Oriental" cultures as innocent from the taints of industrial capitalism, others represented Chinese "coolies" as embodiments of modern capitalism's tendency to deprive workers of will and individuality. In a century characterized by massive demographic shifts, bloody wars, and struggles over reform, the Chinese were dramatically entangled in global processes of trade, diplomacy, labor migration, and technological modernization. Despite its recent defeats by Britain in the Opium Wars and the many concessions that it had made to foreign powers, China did not take a passive stance toward the West. In response to foreign incursions, its government initiated the "Self-Strengthening" movement in 1861—a program of education, technology transfer, and foreign diplomacy intended to modernize the country and enhance its military. In 1868, the Chinese sent Twain's friend Anson Burlingame[4]— previously the first U.S. minister to China—as their envoy extraordinary and minister plenipotentiary to the United States to negotiate a series of agreements concerning immigration, trade, and China's sovereignty. Twain praised the Burlingame Treaty—which protected the rights of Chinese immigrants to the United States, ensured reciprocal access to Chinese and U.S. public educational institutions, and granted China most-favored nation status—as a cosmopolitan step forward in human history: "It bridges the Pacific, it breaks down the Tartar wall, it inspires with fresh young blood the energies of the most venerable of the nations. It acquires a grand field for capital, labor, research, enterprise—it confers science, mechanics, social and political advancement, Christianity."[5] At this time, Twain expressed a keen interest in traveling to China: "[In 1866] Burlingame invited Twain to visit him in Peking next winter, promising to provide him with information about China."[6] In 1868, Twain mentioned in a letter to the *San Francisco Alta California* that J. Ross Browne, who had been nominated to replace Burlingame as minister to China, "has kindly invited me to take a lucrative position on his staff in case he goes to China, and I have accepted. . . . I shall follow him out there as soon as I am free."[7] If Twain had gone to work for the U.S. minister to China, he would have been in a position analogous to that of Hank Morgan in *A Connecticut Yankee*, attempting to both participate in a country's modernization and profit from that process.

Efforts to modernize China and to represent Chinese immigrants as adaptable to U.S. civil society belied representations of an unchanging and ahistorical "Orient." This chapter presents two interrelated contexts for reading *A Connecticut Yankee*: popular historical romances and China's efforts to access modern technology and institutions. Along with his antagonism toward the racist and romantic conventions of popular adventure novels, Twain's own involvements with China's "Self-Strengthening" inform his satirical account of the Connecticut Yankee's failed scheme to modernize and democratize medieval England. Tracing Twain's personal connections with proponents of Chinese reform, this chapter compares three efforts to counteract the logic of imperial romance: *A Connecticut Yankee*, which travesties the notion that the nineteenth century and its technologies are any more civilized than the sixth; the Chinese Educational Mission established by Yung Wing, which attempted to train Chinese boys in Western technology and ideas between 1872 and 1881; and Wong Chin Foo's writings, which provocatively present China as a technological, political, and ethical model for the United States. Whereas Yung's project demonstrates Twain's firsthand support of an enterprise designed to bring Western technologies and ideas to China, Wong shared Twain's interest in experimenting with a range of forms and personae to shift public sentiment about race and empire. In addition to suggesting that the Chinese Educational Mission influenced Twain's novel, the comparative readings in this chapter demonstrate how *A Connecticut Yankee* collaborated with Yung and Wong's writings in critiquing Western interventions in China. I do not intend to reduce the novel to an allegory of Chinese modernization or to suggest that Twain's medieval setting is interchangeable with an idealized Orient; instead, I hope to demonstrate that Twain's long-standing interest in China's relations with the United States provides significant points of reference for *A Connecticut Yankee*'s critical representations of colonial governance and education.

I. A Connecticut Yankee and Imperial Romance

In *No Place of Grace: Antimodernism and the Transformation of American Culture, 1880–1920*, the historian T. J. Jackson Lears documents how proponents of "antimodernism" sought outlets for anxieties about industrial "overcivilization" and fears about "urban culture as a source of both bodily and spiritual enervation."[8] In response to the closing of the U.S. "frontier" and the rise of industrial capitalism, antimodernism projected notions of force, passion, spirituality, and martial prowess onto medieval and "Oriental" cultures.[9] Romantic adventure novels of the 1880s and 1890s, in turn, projected this fantasized physicality back onto American heroes, who spontaneously rise to challenges posed in foreign and medieval fields. These fantasies—which Amy Kaplan describes as "romance[s] of empire"[10]—imagined exotic and premodern societies as ideal settings for the regeneration of U.S. manhood. Kaplan argues that popular romances of the 1890s—such as Richard Harding Davis's *Soldiers of Fortune* (1897), Charles Major's *When Knighthood Was in Flower* (1898), and F. Marion Crawford's *Via Crucis* (1899)— aligned ideas about gender and race with U.S. imperialist ideology. "The nostalgia for a lost wholeness in the distant past expressed in the swashbuckling romances of the 1890s," writes Kaplan, "created fanciful realms on which to project contemporary desires for unlimited global expansion."[11] These romances—which feature masculine American (or proto-American) heroes rescuing kingdoms and romancing exoticized women in historical and/or foreign settings—provided an imaginative domain for remasculinizing white American men whose physical force and racial superiority were at risk of being vitiated by overcivilization. Referencing Twain's supposition that "there must be two Americas"— one democratic, the other imperialist—Kaplan claims that, "through the medium of the white male body, [imperial romances] work to close the gap between Twain's two Americas, to merge the narratives of liberation and domination, to narrate the new empire as consistent with the history of the republic, to map overseas colonies as contiguous to continental expansion."[12]

While the rage for historical romances and imperialist adventure novels swelled with the availability of cheaper periodicals in the 1890s, the groundwork for this genre's success was laid in the 1880s.[13] Lew Wallace's historical novel *Ben-Hur* (1880), which sold more copies than Harriet Beecher Stowe's *Uncle Tom's Cabin*, presented early Christian history as an allegory for U.S. exceptionalism: as Kaplan explains, "The birth of Christianity that frames the historical romance figures the birth of America as a new empire, one that fuses the universalism of

Rome with the chosenness of the Jews into a new global power and the promise of a future beyond history."[14] America in the 1880s also saw the revival of interest in Sir Walter Scott by critics who saw in his corpus "the emblem of a larger, fuller life";[15] the increasingly popular series of Frank Reade dime novels, in which "the hero invents a fantastic, technologically enhanced form of transportation and uses it to travel to some remote destination where he has a series of adventures";[16] and the rage for medieval narratives by Sir Thomas Malory and Alfred, Lord Tennyson, as well as H. Rider Haggard's bestselling imperial romances.[17]

Whereas imperial romances idealize medieval and Oriental cultures, *A Connecticut Yankee* offers a bracing critique of popular beliefs about imperialism, modernity, and "civilization." Just as his travelogues highlight the ubiquitous mediation of foreign sites by popular guidebooks and the tourist industry, Twain's historical novels refuse to definitively demarcate the past from the present. As John Carlos Rowe writes, "Twain's historical romances, as I think such works as *Huckleberry Finn*, *Pudd'nhead Wilson*, *A Connecticut Yankee* and *The Prince and the Pauper* deserve to be called, employ historical distance to suggest how little the contemporary reader's society has progressed from the serfdom of either medieval England or antebellum America."[18] *A Connecticut Yankee* questions teleological models of history by noting troublesome continuities between past and present: aristocrats are like capitalist robber barons, peasants are like southern freedmen, and the nineteenth-century protagonist ends up committing its most lawless, violent acts. Hank Morgan, the novel's utilitarian narrator, offers a satirical counterpoint to the popular romantic heroes of the 1880s. In an allegory of colonial administration and development,[19] Morgan introduces modern technologies of transportation, communication, education, hygiene, governance, and war to medieval England. However, these reforms give rise to increasingly strident forms of resistance, to which Morgan responds with increasingly violent measures that culminate in the novel's explosive finale. The contradictory nature of Morgan's design is eloquently expressed by his mixed metaphors of enlightenment: he figures modernity as both a benign mechanical lever ready to "flood the midnight world with light at any moment" and a "serene volcano . . . giving no sign of the rising hell in its bowels" (*CY*, 51). If historical romances fantasize that medieval valor could be reenacted in foreign battlefields of the present, *A Connecticut Yankee* dispels this fantasy's assumptions about the past and the present. First, it undermines the romanticization of the past by juxtaposing medieval romances like Malory's *Morte d'Arthur* (1485) with historical analysis gleaned from works—such as William Lecky's *History of European Morals from Augustus to Charlemagne* (1869) and *History of England in the Eighteenth Century* (1878–1890)—that exposed how chivalric ideals masked the oppressive regimes of the Catholic Church and feudal state. Second, the novel emphasizes that modern warfare is diametrically opposed to chivalry by dramatizing Morgan's cold and mechanical massacring of innumerable knights. In addition to redefining masculinity around technical prowess and efficiency, Twain frequently hints at Morgan's queer sexual proclivities: as Elizabeth Freeman has noted, Twain's Yankee not only avoids his wife and child but also eagerly seeks out his page Clarence, who "was pretty enough to frame" in his "blue silk," "dainty laces," and "plumed pink satin cap" (*CY*, 15).[20] Twain's novel exposes the violence and hypocrisy underlying the ideals of physical force, chivalric masculinity, and historical progress that were central to late nineteenth-century antimodern discourses and historical romances.

Although *A Connecticut Yankee*'s references to imperialism are often circuitous, they are also more ubiquitous and compelling than its references to antebellum slavery and Gilded Age capitalism. The novel invokes imperialist scenarios by alluding to the use of eclipse predictions and Gatling guns against "savage" populations (*CY*, 64). More important, imperialist ideas inform Morgan's entire project of modernizing the sixth century through technological, political, and behavioral transformations. From his conviction that this goal of progress justifies his violent and deceptive methods to his attempts to refashion England's knights (whom he calls "white Indians") into disciplined subjects, Morgan embodies both an outlook and a set of strategies characteristic of imperial regimes (*CY*, 19). Critics including Amy Kaplan, Stephen Sumida, Susan Harris, and John Carlos Rowe have associated these aspects of *A Connecticut Yankee* with historical contexts such as European colonialism, Western incursions on Hawai'i, and U.S. policies of Indian Removal and assimilation.[21] Sumida argues that the novel expands upon themes that Twain had explored in an earlier, unfinished novel about Hawai'ian characters experiencing the effects of Christianity, missionary education, and leprosy.[22] Pointing out the importance of education in Hank Morgan's scheme of "transform[ing] the British populace from monarchical subjects to republican consumer-citizens," Harris compares the plot of *A Connecticut Yankee* to the U.S. colonial administration in the Philippines, which attempted to assimilate young Filipinos through "free universal public schools, instruction in English, and the training of native teachers."[23] Rowe links Twain's novel to a different site of transpacific colonialism, suggesting that Morgan's duel with five hundred knights echoes the celebrated death of the British colonial officer Charles George Gordon: although he died while fighting Madhists in Khartoum, "The legend of Chinese Gordon as imperialist hero begins with his appointment in 1863 as military commander of the forces organized by the United States and Great Britain to quell the Taiping Rebellion . . . and to prop up the tottering Manchu dynasty in China."[24] Gordon's nickname was a reference to his leadership of China's "Ever Victorious Army"—an army of several thousand Chinese soldiers led by British officers—against much larger forces. The spectacular success of Western military discipline and weaponry in suppressing the Taiping Rebellion was one of the motivating factors behind China's "Self-Strengthening" movement, which I discuss in the following section.

A Connecticut Yankee famously concludes with a brutal massacre that exposes the impracticable and zealous nature of Morgan's scheme to transform Arthurian England. Trapped in Merlin's cave by a wall of massacred knights and "made sick by the poisonous air bred by those dead thousands" (*CY*, 256), Morgan and his army of modernized boys are reduced to conditions of unconsciousness, captivity, and slow death. Ironically, the Yankee who sets out to civilize "white Indians" ends up confined to a cave like Injun Joe (*CY*, 19). The most spectacular moment in the war between Morgan's "Republic" and tens of thousands of knights occurs when thousands of "dynamite torpedoes" explode beneath a forty-foot sand belt swarming with knights: "Great Scott! Why, the whole front of that host shot into the sky with a thunder-crash, and became a whirling tempest of rags and fragments; and along the ground lay a thick wall of smoke that hid what was left of the multitude from our sight" (*CY*, 249). Morgan's lurid fascination with the devastation inflicted by his mines is enabled by his blindness to the suffering of the knights, symbolized here by the wall of smoke that "hid what was left"—either the remains of the knights or those who remain alive—from sight. This lack of sympathy correlates, in part, with the impossibility of counting the dead: "As to destruction of life, it was amazing. Moreover, it was beyond estimate. Of course we could not *count* the dead, because they did not exist as individuals, but merely as homogeneous protoplasm, with alloys of iron and buttons" (*CY*, 249). An excised passage from Twain's manuscript draft of *A Connecticut Yankee* extends Morgan's commentary on the problem of counting the dead (a problem whose colonial implications I explore at length in Chapter 5):

> Several methods were tried, with a view to getting at the solid contents of the mass: by triangulation, very good approximate measurements were secured; then, by taking the mean distance of the sun from the nearest fixed star, & computing the difference between the meridian of London & the number of people engaged in the fight—however, never mind those details, they wouldn't inform anybody but scientists. It is sufficient to say that after they got the mass measured, they weighed the earth by the ordinary processes known to astronomers, then they subtracted the estimated weight of this mess or mass of protoplasm from the sum of the earth's weight. After that the rest was easy. By determining the proportions of a cubic foot of this slush—so much horse, so much man, so much dry-goods, so much iron—& then adding up all of the man by itself & charging up the rest to profit & loss & debtor & sundries, it was demonstrated that we had killed 1,069,362 pounds.[25]

If Morgan's problem with knights is that their feudal system discourages individualism, his solution to this problem literally dissolves them into a mass that "did not exist as individuals." This deindividualizing mode of quantification forecloses sympathy and thus minimizes any moral unease Morgan might feel about slaughtering knights: "So I felt quite safe in believing that the utmost force that could for the future be brought against us would be but some trifle over 4,000,000 pounds of meat, that is, knights."[26] The pivotal role of dynamite[27] in Morgan's pyrrhic victory over the knights also resonates with nineteenth-century reactions to the new explosive substance: from 1869 to 1873, California's white miners organized a series of strikes that combined demands for the prohibition of dynamite (which they perceived as a threat to their labor power and health) with demands for the prohibition of Chinese laborers (who were frequently skilled in handling dynamite from their experience working on the Central Pacific Railroad).[28]

Although *A Connecticut Yankee* does not explicitly mention U.S. relations with Asia, its critique of forced modernization and colonial governance may have influenced later writings about China and the Philippines. For example, Alexander Saxton has suggested that the conclusion of Ignatius Donnelly's speculative narrative, *Caesar's Column: A Story of the Twentieth Century* (1890)—in which the protagonist and a group of Anglo Americans barricade themselves against an oligarchy whose power is founded upon an "Orientalized proletariat"[29]—echoes the siege that concludes *A Connecticut Yankee*.[30] Vachel Lindsay's "The Golden-Faced People: A Story of the Chinese Conquest of America" (1914), published in W. E. B. Du Bois's *Crisis* magazine, appropriates Twain's mechanism for time travel, in which the factory superintendent Hank Morgan is struck on the head with a crowbar during an altercation with a worker.[31] After he is struck by a broomstick during an altercation with a Chinese laundryman, Lindsay's narrator dreams he has been transported into the thirtieth century. In this dystopian future, he learns how China had conquered and enslaved white Americans, then granted them formal equality before the law. While being pursued by a Chinese mob for asserting his social equality, the narrator awakens to learn that the laundryman who hit him—along with a Japanese, a Greek, and a black man, have been hanged by a white mob on Lincoln's birthday. Lindsay's story deploys anxieties about China's modernity to critique Jim Crow practices in the United States; like Twain's novel, it uses an apparently remote temporal setting to satirize contemporary legal and social practices.

Twain also returned to themes he first explored in *Yankee* in his later writings about the U.S.-Philippine War. For example, he echoes Morgan's cynical designation of an explosive massacre as "The Battle of the Sand Belt" when describing a U.S. colonial massacre of Moros in the Philippines: "The battle began—*it is officially called by that name*— our forces firing down into the crater with their artillery and their deadly small arms of precision; the savages furiously returning the fire, probably with brickbats."³² Throughout his anti-imperialist writings, Twain deploys premodern notions of honor and chivalry to highlight U.S. atrocities in the Philippines and China: for example, "A Defence of General Funston" (1902) debunks accounts of Funston's heroic capture of Filipino president Emilio Aguinaldo by pointing out that Funston found it expedient "to persuade or bribe a courier to betray his trust; to remove the badges of his honorable rank and disguise himself; to lie, to practise treachery, to forge . . . to accept of courteous welcome, and assassinate the welcomers while their hands are still warm from the friendly handshake."³³ Elsewhere, Twain undermines the claim that missionaries would help modernize non-Western populations by describing Christian missionaries in China in medieval and romantic terms—the missionary, he writes, is "made up of faith, zeal, courage, sentiment, emotion, enthusiasm; and so he is a mixture of poet, devotee and knight-errant."³⁴ To further explore *A Connecticut Yankee*'s transpacific connections, the following section considers a suggestive analogue (and one possible source) for Twain's satire of Hank Morgan's efforts to reform Arthurian England: the Chinese Educational Mission organized by Yung Wing, which provided Twain with numerous opportunities to learn about Chinese modernization and its pitfalls.

II. Transpacific "Self-Strengthening" and the Chinese Educational Mission

Between 1872 and 1881, the Chinese government sent 120 boys to New England to study English, along with Western science, technology, and military tactics. The Chinese Educational Mission (CEM) was largely the project of Yung Wing, a naturalized U.S. citizen, the first Chinese graduate of Yale, and later the author of *My Life in China and America* (1909). The CEM placed students with host families scattered throughout the region and periodically brought the students to its headquarters in Hartford, Connecticut, to instruct them in Chinese. It also supported the boys when they later attended schools and universities, including Hartford High School, Holyoke High School, Phillips Exeter, Rensselaer Polytechnic Institute, Harvard, and Yale. As Joseph Hopkins Twichell observed in an address to Yale law students, "A visitor to the City of Hartford, at the present time, will be likely to meet on the streets groups of Chinese boys, in their native dress, though somewhat modified, and speaking their native tongue, yet seeming, withal, to be very much at home. He will also occasionally meet Chinese men who, by their bearing, will impress them as being gentlemen of their race."[35] In the decade before passage of the Chinese Exclusion Act, New Englanders—and especially Hartford residents like Twain—witnessed the emergence and demise of an ambitious project of cultural exchange in which Chinese boys were trained in a way that undercut popular stereotypes about Chinese "coolies." Mission students lived with middle-class families, spoke fluent English, adapted Western dress, and excelled in Latin composition, German, mathematics, and hunting, as well as two activities enjoyed by the knights of Twain's Round Table: bicycling and baseball (Figure 4.1).[36]

The Chinese Educational Mission was an important component of China's reformist "Self-Strengthening" movement, which aimed to appropriate Western technologies in order to better defend against foreign encroachments. In response to China's defeats in the Opium Wars (1839–1842, 1856–1860) and the effectiveness of Western tactics and armaments in suppressing the Taiping Rebellion (1850–1864), reformists such as Prince Gong and Li Hongzhang established arsenals of modern weaponry, technical schools, the Fuzhou Navy Yard, and a new Office of Foreign Affairs (Zongli Yamen). Whereas imperialist discourses generally aligned technological proficiency and self-reliance with Western heroes, "Self-Strengthening" attempted to transfer Western technologies on China's own terms, without relying on foreign officers and interventions. As Twain put it in his assessment of Article 8 of the Burlingame Treaty:[37] "They want railways and telegraphs, but they fear to put these engines of power into the hands of strangers without a guaranty that they will not be used for their own oppression, possibly their destruction."[38] In "The Chinese Must Stay" (*North American Review*, 1889), Yan Phou Lee—a prominent graduate of the CEM and Yale University and author of *When I was a Boy in China* (1887)—supports his argument against Chinese Exclusion with a triumphalist assessment of Chinese modernization: "In the last fifteen years the Chinese Government has educated upwards of two hundred students in Europe and America, has built arsenals and navy-yards, established schools and colleges on Western models, disciplined an army that

Figure 4.1: The "Orientals," baseball club of the Chinese Education Mission boys, taken in front of the Chinese Educational Mission Headquarters, Collins Street, Hartford, Connecticut. Thomas La Fargue Collection, Washington State University.

whipped the Russians, created a navy that would put the American navy to shame, put up thousands of miles of telegraph wires; and it is now busily opening up mines, building railroads, and availing itself of American capital and experience to put up telephones and establish a national bank. The Chinese are not ashamed to own that they appreciate the Americans."[39]

After helping to negotiate a purchase of military materials from the United States, Yung promoted a plan to send Chinese boys to the United States to study the scientific foundations of Western technological advances and, ideally, to attend the public military and naval academies that the Burlingame Treaty ostensibly made accessible to Chinese students.[40] Despite its government funding, the CEM had many detractors among the Qing dynasty's more conservative Manchu leaders. While Manchus were well represented among bureaucrats and the students of translators' colleges, the 120 students recruited by the CEM were all Han Chinese.[41] Furthermore, none of the CEM students were ever admitted to the U.S. Military Academy or Naval Academy, and officials worried that the boys' education would come at the cost of Chinese language skills, cultural identity, and ethical compass. In his history of the CEM, Edward Rhoads details the factors that contributed to the recall of the students in 1881, which included reports that students were neglecting their Chinese studies, converting to Christianity, and (in two cases) cutting their queues.[42] The anti-Chinese movement in the United States—which led to the 1880 Angell Treaty's agreement that the United States could "regulate, limit, or suspend" the immigration of Chinese laborers—also contributed to the recall: "As Yung Wing summed up the situation in mid-December 1880 for his friend Joseph Twichell, 'Woo's [Wu Zideng's] representations of the students together with the new treaty concerning Chinese immigration & the howl of the Pacific coast against Chinese all contributed to disgust Li [Hongzhang] & he has finally to my utter sorrow decided to give up the scheme.'"[43]

Twain was connected to the CEM by both geographical proximity and Hartford's social networks. The CEM's administrative buildings, where students would periodically gather for weeks to study Chinese intensively, were all located in the Asylum Hill neighborhood of Hartford, less than a mile north of Twain's Nook Farm home. Twain was acquainted with Yung Wing through his neighbor, pastor, and close friend Twichell, who wrote of the CEM that "I don't think I was ever more excited in my sympathies and admirations by anything of the kind in my life."[44] Yung and the Chinese students sometimes circulated through Twain's familial and social circles. While in Hartford, writes Anne Hamilton, the CEM students "were the toast of the town—and danced with Mark Twain's daughters at Hartford soirees."[45] One of

Twain's daughters was a classmate of the CEM student Yung Shang Him,[46] and Yung Wing was married to Marie Louise Kellogg, the daughter of Twain's family doctor.[47]

Twain supported the CEM on several occasions. Twichell's biographer, Steve Courtney, reports that "the Clemenses held at least one neighborhood reception for Yung Wing in their new Farmington Avenue mansion."[48] When Twichell and Yung started a subscription drive to support Rong Kui's Yale education after Rong had been officially dismissed by the CEM for having his queue cut off, Twain made an annual contribution of $25.[49] When Chinese officials were deciding whether to recall the CEM in late 1880, Twain helped Twichell secure a meeting with former President Ulysses S. Grant.[50] After speaking with Twain and Twichell, Grant decided to write a personal letter to Li Hongzhang requesting continuance of the CEM. Li's summary of Grant's letter indicates the extent to which technology transfer motivated the program: "The boys are making good progress and it may be expected that they will learn building railroads, opening mines, constructing fortifications, and manufacturing machines. It would be a great pity if they were to be recalled."[51] Twain also signed a statement addressed to China's Office of Foreign Affairs by "instructors, guardians, and friends of the students who were sent to this country under the care of the Chinese Educational Commission," which vouched for the morals and progress of the students and protested the dissolution of the CEM.[52] Despite these efforts "to stay the work of retrogression,"[53] the CEM was dissolved in 1881. However, many of its students—whom Yung praised as "the vanguard of the pioneers of modern education in China"[54]—would be influential in developing China's railroads, mines, telegraph lines, and navy and would also play prominent roles in China's foreign diplomacy and in the Revolution of 1911.[55] Twain continued supporting Yung's efforts to modernize China after the closure of the CEM: a few years later, Twain and Yung visited Grant to persuade the former president to support a project to build military railroads in China. According to Twain, Grant told the visitors that "he now felt . . . sure that such a system would be a great salvation for [China] and also the beginning of the country's liberation from the Tartar rule and thraldom."[56]

Did Twain's familiarity with Yung and the CEM shift his views about the Chinese, which were largely formed from his earlier impressions of working-class Chinese migrants on the West Coast?[57] Did the reformist, modernizing aims and the discontinuation of the CEM influence the plot of *A Connecticut Yankee*, in which technology transfer and the training of a small group of boys play central roles? Like the CEM's supporters, Twain's Yankee believed that education and industrial training would form the "nuclei of future vast factories, the iron and steel missionaries of my future civilization. In these were gathered together the brightest young minds I could find, and I kept agents out raking the country for more, all the time. I was training a crowd of ignorant folk into experts—experts in every sort of handiwork and scientific calling" (*CY*, 50). In their efforts to modernize England, Morgan and his followers accomplish many of the CEM's goals, building mines, railroads, factories, armories, and technical schools. The CEM's reasons for seeking out younger boys are also echoed in Clarence's explanation of his decision to select only boys to defend the Republic against the Church and knights: "Because all the others were born in an atmosphere of superstition and reared in it. It is in their blood and bones. . . . With boys it was different. Such as have been under our training from seven to ten years have had no acquaintance with the Church's terrors, and it was among these that I found my fifty-two" (*CY*, 242).

As with the CEM, Morgan's modernization scheme gives rise to anxieties about whether industrial education can be isolated from cultural assimilation. Would new technologies improve the lives of a nation's subjects, or would they just make available more brutal and efficient forms of warfare and domination? Would a nineteenth-century Western education empower medieval and Chinese students, or would it make them subservient to different forms of power—such as the genocidal schemes of the Yankee "Boss" or the rhetoric of Christian conversion? While the CEM's brief career provided Twain with an opportunity to question the efficacy and ethnocentric limitations of technological "training," Wong Chin Foo's writings provide a different kind of analogue to Twain's novel about anachronistic modernization. Wong spent most of his life in the United States mobilizing print culture, the lecture platform, and courtrooms to strengthen the position of the American Chinese and, at times, of anti-Manchu reformers in China. As I show in the following section, his historical novel *Wu Chih Tien* deploys scenarios of Chinese modernization to critique the imperialist preoccupations of popular historical romances.

III. Wu Chih Tien and Chinese Modernization

Unlike Yung Wing, the platform lecturer, magazine writer, entrepreneur, newspaper editor, and political organizer Wong Chin Foo was not personally acquainted with Twain. Yet their lectures and magazine writings circulated among similar audiences, and Twain encountered Wong's writing on at least one occasion. As the illustrator Daniel Carter Beard recalls, his numerous collaborations with Twain began when the latter read an unnamed "Chinese Story":

> Mr Fred Hall, Mark Twain's partner in the publishing business, came to my studio in the old Judge Building and told me that Mark Twain wanted to meet the man who had made the illustrations for a Chinese story in the *Cosmopolitan* and he wanted that man to illustrate his new book, *A Connecticut Yankee in King Arthur's Court*. The manuscript was sent to me to read. I read it through three times with great enjoyment.[58]

The Chinese story in question was *Wu Chih Tien*, a serialized novel purportedly "translated from the original" by Wong and the first novel published by a "Chinese American." (In fact, Wong coined the term "Chinese-American," and was one of the first Chinese immigrants to be naturalized in the United States).[59] Beard's illustrations for *Wu Chih Tien*—whose plot features a prince leading a revolt against a usurping empress—may have appealed to Twain on numerous levels: they present historical scenarios from roughly 140 b.c.e. to 120 b.c.e.; they depict period costumes, depraved aristocrats, epic journeys, expert horsemanship, and magical events with versatility and grace; and they elegantly supplement a plot that pits a national populace against a brutal and corrupt regime. Twain's interest in *Wu Chih Tien* did not stop at Beard's illustrations: a passage from his notebooks dismisses a travelogue published in the February 1889 issue of *Cosmopolitan* by contrasting it with Wong's novel: "Pity to put that flatulence between the same leaves with that charming Chinese story."[60]

Given Twain's interest in both the "charming Chinese story" and its illustrator, it seems likely that he continued to peruse chapters from the novel as they appeared in subsequent months. While Twain was editing and revising the typescript of *A Connecticut Yankee*, he may have read

"Now break the right, and the center will not fight."

This is what Wu Chih Tien said, when she saw the standards of her horsemen waving to the left.

At once a hundred thousand men, a force greater than that of all General Mah's army, and made up of men chosen for their strength and skill, advanced against the right, where, firm as the rocks beneath their feet, Ta Teen and his fifteen thousand heavy archers awaited the onset.

Thick and fast the iron bolts flew, and the first lines of Wu Chih Tien went down like grass before the hailstorm, but still on pushed the others, till at length the bolts of Ta Teen's men were exhausted, and only their swords were left. Surrounded and outnumbered, the men on the right would have fallen back, had it not been for the example of Ta Teen.

Towering above friend and foe, he seized the fallen standard of the prince from the grasp of a dead man, and, shouting for the others to follow his example, his mighty sword whistled and crashed to the right and left, and the skulls and armor of men were severed as a knife might sever a spider's thread.

Wherever he went, the

THE EXPLOSION.
(See the close of Chapter XXII.)

Figure 4.2: "The Explosion." Daniel Beard, illustrator, *Wu Chih Tien, the Celestial Empress. Cosmopolitan* 7, no. 1 (May 1889): 67. Courtesy of the University of Michigan Library.

the May 1889 installment of *Wu Chih Tien*, which describes a stratagem that incorporates both the technology of gunpowder and the military tactics of Sun Tzu's *Art of War*. "In the pass, through which ran the main road to the camp, [General Mah] ordered deep pits to be dug, and these were filled with powder that was to be exploded by fuses if the foe succeeded in entering the defile."[61] A few pages later, the explosion kills thousands of the corrupt empress's soldiers:

> At length they gained the pass, and poured in till the foremost men could see the white tent of the prince, with his banner above it.
> Then they cheered till the echoes trembled; and, as if this had been the signal, the rocks from the tops of the pass came thundering down, and the powder-pits at the bottom were fired, and twenty thousand men were hurled into the sky.[62]

The toppled rocks and explosion lead to a momentary victory, as enemy soldiers retreat from a pass suddenly filled with "blood and the limbs of torn men."[63] Whether he read this passage or not, Twain likely noticed Beard's rendering of this scene in one of *Wu Chih Tien*'s largest and most striking illustrations (Figure 4.2). This image may have been instrumental in establishing Beard as a prominent illustrator of Twain's writings: Beard was offered the contract for illustrating *A Connecticut Yankee* in June, just a few weeks after his illustration of "The Explosion" appeared in the May 1889 issue of *Cosmopolitan*.[64] Thematically, this scene from *Wu Chih Tien* resonates with the explosions that pervade *A Connecticut Yankee*, for which Beard provided similar illustrations titled "Another Miracle" and "After the Explosion" (Figures 4.3 and 4.4). However, the affinities between *A Connecticut Yankee* and *Wu Chih Tien* extend far beyond their showcasing of brutally effective explosives. Both novels anachronistically project modern practices into the past to counteract conventional opinions about the progressive nature of history and the temporally backward status of non-Western civilizations.[65] While it shares many concerns with *A Connecticut Yankee*, however, *Wu Chih Tien* also revises imperialist representations of white masculinity in a distinctive way—by presenting a democratic and masculine *Chinese* protagonist who embodies his nation's struggles for reform and modernization.

ANOTHER MIRACLE.

Figure 4.3: Daniel Beard, illustrator, "Another Miracle," *A Connecticut Yankee in King Arthur's Court* by Mark Twain (New York: Charles L. Webster & Co., 1889), 356. Courtesy of the Mark Twain Project, Bancroft Library, University of California, Berkeley.

Wong's own experiences in China and the United States help contextualize *Wu Chih Tien's* critical stance toward the ethnocentric correlation of masculinity, progress, and liberalism with whiteness. Like Twain, Wong made a name for himself by creating and manipulating controversy in the periodical press. Wong's prolific publications—mostly in the form of nonfiction essays and sketches—appeared in many periodicals that Twain published in around the turn of the century, including the *Cosmopolitan, Independent, Youth's Companion, Harper's, North American Review, Atlantic,* and *Chautauquan*. Wong sometimes supplemented his income by lecturing on Chinese history, culture, and religion, and his lectures were organized by prestigious

about him, except that his plumes swished about a little in the night wind. We rose up and looked in through the bars of his visor, but couldn't make out whether we knew him or not—features too dim and shadowed. We heard muffled sounds approaching, and we sank down to the ground where we were. We made out another knight vaguely; he was coming very stealthily, and feeling his way. He was near enough, now, for us to see him put out a hand, find an upper wire, then bend and step under it and over the lower one. Now he arrived at the first knight—and started slightly when he discovered him. He stood a moment—no doubt wondering why the other one didn't move on; then he said, in a low voice, "Why dreamest thou here, good Sir Mar—" then he laid his hand on the corpse's shoulder—and just uttered a little soft moan and sunk down dead.

AFTER THE EXPLOSION.

Figure 4.4: Daniel Beard, illustrator, "After the Explosion," *A Connecticut Yankee in King Arthur's Court* by Mark Twain (New York: Charles L. Webster & Co., 1889), 562. Courtesy of the Mark Twain Project, Bancroft Library, University of California, Berkeley.

managers—the abolitionists James C. Redpath and James B. Pond—whose clients included Mark Twain, Susan B. Anthony, Frederick Douglass, and Booker T. Washington.[66] Throughout his public career, Wong's careful self-fashioning as an exiled Chinese nationalist makes it difficult to distinguish between his public persona and biographical facts. In 1873, he told the *New York Times* that he had been sponsored by "an American lady philanthropist" to attend "a Pennsylvania college"[67] where he graduated with honors and then observed American forms of civil society ("social and political clubs, benevolent societies, trade unions, &c.") before returning to China.[68] While the biographies he provided to newspapers are sometimes inconsistent, vague, or unsupported by documentary evidence,[69] they generally reiterate the following incidents reported in the *Shaker Manifesto* in 1879:

> Though only 26, he has visited this country twice, has been an officer of the imperial government at Shanghai, and a rebel against the present Tartar emperor. For this last a price was set on his head, and he was hunted for months, never getting into such serious danger as when he put himself into the hands of English missionaries, who, finding out who he was, decided to give him up to the emperor. He remonstrated against their betrayal of him to torture and final execution by cutting him into 18 pieces; but they promised to obtain him the favor of simply having his head cut off, and thereupon locked him in a room, and told him to put his trust in Jesus. Disregarding this very practical advice, he broke out and got to the coast, where an irreligious seaman gave him passage to Japan. Thence he came to San Francisco on a steamer which carried in the steerage 200 Chinese young women of the lower class, imported for infamous purposes; and on arriving he went into the courts and secured their freedom and return to their country.[70]

Wong came of age during a turbulent period in China's history, when Western missionaries and traders were encroaching on the cultural and political hegemony of the Qing dynasty's Manchu (or Tartar) rulers. While presenting a satirical indictment of Christian missionaries (which in many ways parallels Twain's critiques of missionary hypocrisy in "To the Person Sitting in Darkness" [1901]), Wong fashions himself as an exilic hero: a nationalist rebel with "a price ... on his head" who manages to appeal to U.S. laws to liberate 200 Chinese slave women "on arriving." In "Wong Chin Foo's Periodical Writing and Chinese Exclusion," I have documented Wong's attempts to sway public opinion in favor of the Chinese by mobilizing cosmopolitan, parodic, satirical, and protest discourses in a variety of periodicals and newspapers.[71] These strategies ranged from a yellowface poem to publicly challenging anti-Chinese demagogue Denis Kearney to a duel, from touring as a "Buddhist missionary" lecturer to founding the first Chinese newspaper in the United States, the *Chinese-American*.

Although Wong presented *Wu Chih Tien, the Celestial Empress: A Chinese Historical Novel* as a "translation" of a Chinese narrative, I have not been able to identify a plausible source text.[72] Whether he translated the novel or composed it himself, Wong is responsible for both its language and its intervention in conceptions of history, race, and masculinity propagated by U.S. historical romances. Loosely based on the controversial regime of the Empress Wu Zetian from a.d. 655 to a.d. 705, the novel begins with the concubine Wu Chih Tien usurping the throne, forcing the emperor's newborn son into exile, and subjecting the populace to brutal taxes intended to fund her extravagant lifestyle. The narrative focus then shifts from the empress to the prince, Li Tan, who grows into a tall, beautiful, talented, eloquent, and sympathetic young man. Hounded by the empress's soldiers, Li Tan exchanges clothing with a swineherd to escape. He is then pursued by Tartars intending to sell him into slavery, but he escapes slavery—at least nominally—by indenturing himself to the cruel merchant Wu Deah. Just as the adoption of a swineherd's clothes and the threat of being duplicitously sold into slavery echo recurring motifs in Twain's novels, Wu Deah's offer to Li Tan resonates with Twain's interest in the blurry boundaries between "free," forced, and indentured labor: "If you will pledge yourself to work for me for five years, I will give you fine raiment, plenty of food, and a nice bed where my slaves sleep; and when your time is up I will give you a new suit of clothes and five taels; and then you will be a very rich man—for a swineherd."[73] Immediately after Li Tan saves himself from slavery by accepting this offer, Wu Deah has him brutally whipped for failing to kowtow properly.

At Wu Deah's palace, the novel changes modes again as a romantic relationship develops between the prince and Wu Deah's poor niece, Sho Kai. After the two pledge their love, Li Tan leaves to rejoin the rebel army. Sho Kai is tricked into believing Li Tan has died and marries another suitor in despair; Li Tan nearly marries another woman when he learns of Sho Kai's apparent infidelity. Once these romantic complications are resolved, Li Tan and Sho Kai are finally married, and the novel comes to a swift conclusion: the final battle for China's capital is narrated in two short pages. The novel's conclusion shifts from scenarios of punishment (including a graphic illustration of the empress's half-naked body ablaze) to an account of the new emperor's happy and fruitful marriage. Li Tan's love match with Sho Kai (which succeeds despite the fact that each believes the other is of lower rank and despite others' attempts to arrange marriages that would interfere with their relationship) signals a shift away from polygamy and arranged marriage towards a model of contractual marriage that, as Nancy Armstrong has shown, plays an essential role in Western liberalism's conception of freedom.[74] In a period when U.S. law presumed that Chinese women seeking to enter the country were prostitutes and when missionaries and other writers focused disproportionate attention on misogynistic Chinese practices such as footbinding, prostitution, polygamy, and infanticide, Wong presents an exemplary monogamous marriage that crosses class lines: "although [the emperor] might have had many wives besides Sho Kai, he was too happy to want another."[75] The arc of the novel thus moves from the polygamous situation from which the empress rose to power to a monogamous, self-contracted, and prolific marriage.

Drawing on the conventions of historical romance, *Wu Chih Tien* represents heroic and liberally minded Chinese men in an era characterized by Chinese Exclusion and racist stereotypes ranging from the "Heathen Chinee" and "Yellow Peril" to Twain's own effeminizing notion (in *Roughing It*) of "The Gentle, Inoffensive Chinese." By taking as its protagonist the handsome, robust, intelligent, and sympathetic prince, *Wu Chih Tien* resists the equation of whiteness with imperial manhood that, according to Kaplan, would underwrite historical novels of the 1890s.[76] However, Wong is only able to appropriate the genre of the historical romance by reproducing its misogynist logic, contrasting his idealized male hero with both the passive Sho Kai—who is ultimately rescued—and the demonized usurping empress—who is ultimately burned alive. Wong's later writings would continue to invert—but not criticize—the notion of imperial masculinity: for example, in a commentary on the Sino-Japanese War (1894–1895) he praised China for embodying "the virility of Oriental civilization" and predicted that its "older, manlier, grander civilization will triumph over the woman-ruled races and effeminate creeds of the West."[77]

In addition to invoking liberal models of freedom through both its critique of servitude and its marriage subplot, the novel's plot suggestively parallels Wong's own engagement with contemporary Chinese politics. Wong appears to have told the *Buffalo Daily Courier* that, while in China, he formed a secret society "to gain control over the government and change the whole internal system of the empire. He says the society rapidly extended and gained strength among the higher classes. The American and European residents were let into the secret and promised hearty cooperation."[78] When this plan for a coup d'état was discovered by authorities, Wong claimed that he fled and "for two months he wandered about, often being compelled to flee to the mountains and for days subsist upon herbs."[79] Wong's self-fashioning as a frustrated revolutionary hiding in the mountains and "a Chinese rebel chief ... now an exile for the part he took in the rebellion to overthrow the present Tartar dynasty," align him with the novel's exiled, revolutionary protagonist.

Likewise, Wong's choice of subject suggests parallels between the usurping empress and the contemporary regime of the Manchu Empress Dowager Cixi in China. Cixi, who like Wu Chih Tien maneuvered herself from the position of a low-ranking concubine to the most powerful woman in China, opposed foreign influence and Self-Strengthening reforms. Supported by other conservative Manchu officials, she engaged in a power struggle against the reformist Prince Gong, who she believed had become too favorable to foreigners (Gong was a prominent member of the Office of Foreign Affairs that supported the Chinese Educational Mission until 1881). In 1884, Cixi consolidated her power by forcing the prince to retire to private life. Exiled (like Gong) for promoting pro-Han and modernizing reforms in China, Wong framed his story of the revolutionary removal of Wu Chih Tien as an allegory—and an argument—for the overthrow of the Qing (Manchu or Tartar) dynasty in China (an overthrow that eventually occurred in the 1911 Xinhai Revolution).[80] As Western nations were competing for commercial, religious, and political influence in China, Wong's novel endorsed self-rule and reforms designed to strengthen the nation against foreign encroachments, as well as to protect the rights of Chinese living abroad. Generating support for a political revolution in China, of course, counteracts racist thinking by suggesting that the Chinese are capable of self-rule—even if that self-rule must be allegorized through the installation of a rightful emperor whose interests are aligned with the nation's. Unlike many historical romances set in foreign countries, national liberation in *Wu Chih Tien* does not call for the intervention of a heroic American man. By imagining Li Tan as an enlightened despot capable of ruling China objectively and responsibly, Wong reaffirms an earlier *Harper's* article on "Political Honors in China" (1883), in which he argued that China's system of rule is grounded in democratic systems of meritocracy and substantive (as well as merely formal) justice.[81]

Wu Chih Tien suggests that China can adapt modern technologies of war and governance without the help of colonial rulers—indeed, the novel suggests that China had *already* been ruled by an enlightened, monogamous, and liberal emperor over a century before the birth of Christ. As Wong put it in his controversial essay "Why Am I a Heathen?" "We [Chinese] decline to admit all the advantages of your boasted civilization; or that the white race is the only civilized one. Its civilization is borrowed, adapted, and shaped from our older form."[82] *Wu Chih Tien*'s depictions of the buried gunpowder strategem and an egalitarian Chinese emperor—published months before the satirical anachronisms dramatized in *A Connecticut Yankee*—unsettle Eurocentric notions of technological and political progress. Through its strategic use of anachronism, Wong's novel implicitly argues that, far from being "unassimilable" (as anti-Chinese agitators had long believed and as numerous Chinese exclusion acts presumed) to Western liberal practices, the Chinese had in fact invented many of those practices.

Wong's argument about China's prior invention of civilized practices highlights the ways in which *Wu Chih Tien*, rather than being merely anachronistic, unravels Western discourses about Chinese anachronism. By arguing that egalitarian institutions (such as cross-class marriage alliances and government positions distributed through an examination system) and technological innovations had already existed for centuries in China, Wong's novel refutes Orientalist claims such as Rounsevelle Wildman's assertion that "A story like Mark Twain's delightful 'A Yankee in King Arthur's Court' would be impossible from a Chinese standpoint. If Confucius had returned to China a thousand years after his death, he would have found everything substantially as he left it."[83] Wong's novel emphasizes modern aspects of seventh-century

China in order to refute representations of China as—to borrow Anne McClintock's term—an "anachronistic space," or an atavistic nation remote from historical "progress."[84] Reading *A Connecticut Yankee* with *Wu Chih Tien* situates China as a concrete reference point (though by no means the only one) for the anti-imperialist allegory of Twain's novel and shows that Twain was not alone in strategically deploying literary anachronism to combat the imperialist tendency to represent real and potential colonies as temporally backward. While *A Connecticut Yankee* has already been linked to multiple imperialist contexts ranging from the trans-Mississippi frontier and Hawai'i to Africa and India,[85] Wong's "Chinese Historical Novel" introduces a non-Western, nonwhite nation that, in the second century b.c., was (by Hank Morgan's standards) already more politically and technologically "advanced" than sixth-century England. Explosives, gunpowder, and meritocracy were not exclusively Western inventions: they could have been transported into sixth-century England from sixth-century China, rather than transferred from nineteenth-century Connecticut.

Years after Wong returned to China in 1896, his position as the Redpath Agency's lecturer on Chinese topics was filled by Ng Poon Chew, a Christian minister, advocate for Chinese immigrants' rights, and editor of the first daily Chinese newspaper in the United States. Because he deployed a blend of humor and incisive critique on the lecture platform (and possibly also on account of his moustache) Ng was widely promoted as "the Chinese Mark Twain" in Redpath agency advertisements and newspaper accounts: as one brochure explains, "It was his keen wit and his wholesome fun-making that gave him the title 'The Chinese Mark Twain.'"[86] Ng, who addressed topics such as anti-Chinese laws and the revolution that established a Chinese republic in 1911–1912, may have been influenced by the satirical style of Twain's lectures and political writings. Like Twain, he draws on biblical language to highlight the hypocrisy underlying racist U.S. policies: "It is easier for a rich, fat American millionaire, with his tainted dollars on his back, to climb to heaven through the fire escape than for a Chinese to come through the ports of the United States. (Laughter.)"[87] Like Wong and Yung, the "Chinese Mark Twain" would endorse Chinese modernization while mobilizing examples of modernized and assimilated Chinese subjects (including his own performances in fluent English) to refute racist discourses.

If Ng's reputation as "the Chinese Mark Twain" helped draw crowds to his lectures, it also obscured the "Chinese" side of Mark Twain's own career. In addition to his treatments of Chinese immigration explored in previous chapters, Twain meditated on China's role in the world's future in an unpublished and underexamined (it was marked "not valuable" by Twain's literary executor Alfred Bigelow Paine)[88] manuscript narrative entitled "Fable of the Yellow Terror" (1904–1905). Whereas *A Connecticut Yankee* and *Wu Chih Tien* offer oblique and allegorical references to late nineteenth-century China, "Fable" draws explicit connections between the themes of technology transfer, imperialism, and Chinese modernization.

IV. "The Fable of the Yellow Terror"

A cautionary parable about Western incursions on China's economy and sovereignty, "Fable" focuses on a nation of Butterflies that lived "A long, long time ago" in "a vast territory which was flowery and fragrant and beautiful."[89] Unsatisfied with their possessions, the Butterflies began to send missionaries—along with "trader-bugs"—among "all the pagan insects" ("YT," 369). The Butterfly was able to spread its civilization because he had mastered the "art of killing" in the form of a sting that—in a formulation reminiscent of Hank Morgan's title—"made him Boss" (370). Eventually, the scientific application of the sting enabled the Butterflies to spread the market for their honey even into the "vast empire of the Bees" (370). Although the peaceable Bees at first showed no interest in honey and never used their stings, the influence of the Butterflies eventually rubbed off: "One clever tribe of Bees even began to learn how to make honey itself" (371), and Bees "learned to be remarkable prompt and handy with their stings" (372).

Like Lindsay's "The Golden-Faced People," Twain's "Fable" revises the conventions of xenophobic Chinese invasion narratives. Along with Twain's other late-career experiments in the genre of counterfactual history,[90] this story of Bees and Butterflies leverages a possible future to put contemporary U.S. foreign interventions in perspective. Twain's "Fable" ends with a Grasshopper explaining to the Butterflies how they have brought the invasion of Bees upon themselves:

You have taught one tribe of Bees how to use its sting, it will teach its brother-tribe. The two together will be able to banish all the Butterflies some day, and keep them out; for they are uncountable in numbers and will be unconquerable when educated. . . . They will make as prime an article of honey as any Butterfly can turn out; they will make it cheaper than any Butterfly can make it; they are here on the spot, you are the other side of the world, transportation will cost them nothing—you can't compete. . . . If you do not subdue them now, before they get well trained and civilized, they may break over the frontiers some day and go land-grabbing in Europe, to do honor to your teaching. It may be that you will lose your stings and your honey-art by and by, from lack of practice, and be and remain merely elegant and ornamental. Maybe you ought to have let the Yellow Peril alone, as long as there wasn't any. ("YT," 372)

Ironically, the Butterflies' cross-cultural transfer of technology and economic desire produces the very "Yellow Peril" that they had feared.

While "Fable" expresses anxiety about the sheer size and potential influence of modernized Asian populations, Twain's anti-imperialist and anti-Christian attitudes depart from more conventional accounts of the "Yellow Peril." Jack London's June 1904 essay on the topic, for example, deploys a somewhat circular argument about the "integrity" of Western imperialism to differentiate it from future varieties of "yellow" imperialism:

Back of our own great race adventure, back of our robberies by sea and land, our lusts and violences and all the evil things we have done, there is a certain integrity, a sternness of conscience, a melancholy responsibility of life, a sympathy and comradeship and warm human feel, which is ours, indubitably ours, and which we cannot teach to the Oriental as we would teach logarithms or the trajectory of projectiles.[91]

Twain's fable, which concludes by holding the Butterflies accountable as the initial aggressors motivated by egotism and greed, has no such illusions about the motivations for imperial expansion. Twain's cultural relativism also prevents him from suggesting that Western "civilization" has any moral values to teach the Chinese: the Butterflies teach the Bees no moral lessons, only the practical matters of how to use their stingers, produce and consume honey, and conquer other populations. Moreover, the title of Twain's fable highlights the subjective nature of racial stereotypes by shifting from a phrase that focuses on an external quality, "yellow *peril*," to a phrase designating the perceiver's own subjective state: "yellow *terror*."

Twain's choice of insects—possibly motivated by London's own use of the bee to symbolize Japanese subjects' lack of independent thought[92]—also runs against the grain of anti-Chinese discourse by emphasizing the contingency of group behavior. By asserting that the ornamental Butterfly and the industrious, hive-minded Bee were once otherwise, Twain's fable appears to confirm the grasshopper's prediction that the Bees would in time render Butterflies powerless and unproductive. "Fable" challenges readers to imagine how contact with imperialism and aggressive traders might transform the Bees' values and behaviors. The challenge of imagining a bee without its sting or an aggressive, deadly, and honey-producing butterfly conveys the difficulty of thinking against the grain of naturalized racial frameworks. London's "Yellow Peril," by contrast, relies on ahistorical (and implicitly biological) models of racism to assign traits to the Chinese and "other peoples": "The Chinese is the perfect type of industry. For sheer work no worker in the world can compare with him. Work is the breath of his nostrils. It is his solution of existence. It is to him what wandering and fighting in far lands and spiritual adventure have been to other peoples. Liberty to him epitomizes itself in access to the means of toil."[93] As opposed to London's account—which assigns unthinking industry to the Chinese and an imperial spirit of adventure to other (implicitly Western) groups—Twain's "Fable" suggests that China is capable of both technological and social transformation even as it questions whether adapting Western values would constitute a step toward civilization or savagery.

In addition to allegorizing an anticolonial reversal, "Fable" indicates the possibility of coalitions uniting "brother-tribes" of Bees against colonial Butterflies. The coloration of bees—black and yellow—hints at lateral alliances among heterogeneous racialized and colonized groups. Chapter 5 extends this analysis of Twain's anti-imperialist allegories, focusing on how his later writings mobilize demographic data to draw connections between different imperial sites and to characterize diverse racial and imperialist projects as regimes of premature death.

5

Body Counts and Comparative Anti-imperialism

"To the Person Sitting in Darkness" (1901), Twain's most widely distributed anti-imperialist statement,[1] draws a striking range of connections between corrupt Tammany Hall politics in New York, missionaries' demands for brutal reparations in the wake of China's Boxer uprising, colonial massacres in South Africa and the Philippines, and the spectacle of antebellum slavery's "Chains Repaired."[2] This method of comparison characterizes many of Twain's critiques of empire—and particularly the works he penned while serving as vice president of the Anti-Imperialist League from 1901 to 1910. For example, he compares the beating of a native servant in India with the daily brutality he experienced fifty years earlier in the slaveholding South (*FE*, 351–352); his December 30, 1900, "Salutation Speech from the Nineteenth Century to the Twentieth" presents the figure of "christendom—returning bedraggled, besmirched and dishonored from pirate raids in Kiaochow, Manchuria, South Africa and the Philippines";[3] his unpublished manuscript, "The Stupendous Procession" (1901), describes a procession of Western nations accompanied by subject populations, each represented by a "*Mutilated Figure in Chains*";[4] and his unpublished review of Edwin Wildman's biography of Philippine president Emilio Aguinaldo draws a series of parallels between the nationalist leader's youth and that of "a negro in a Gulf State, where his race is despised, detested, and kept down with a master-hand."[5] Emphasizing circumpacific sites such as India, China, Hawai'i, Australia, and the Philippines, Twain's anti-imperialist writings situate U.S. imperialism in a broader comparative context.[6] "To the Person" argues that U.S. actions in the Philippines indulge in "the European game" of imperial domination and thus betray the exceptionalist notion of the United States as a liberated, liberating nation ("PS," 32).[7]

Twain's comments on the Philippines are closely tied to his thinking about China. U.S. soldiers from the Philippines were deployed in the international Boxer Relief Expedition in 1900–1901, and on several occasions Twain discusses the suppression of the Boxers in conjunction with the U.S.-Philippine War. Supporters of annexation also viewed the Philippines as a stepping-stone for further U.S. influence in China, as Senator Albert Beveridge explains in an oft-quoted speech: "The Philippines are ours forever.... And just beyond the Philippines are China's illimitable markets. We will not retreat from either. We will not repudiate our duty in the archipelago. We will not abandon our opportunity in the Orient."[8] Although it echoes Twain's own early claims that U.S. access to the Pacific represented "the true Northwest Passage [to] vast Oriental wealth,"[9] Beveridge's cynical articulation of "duty" in the Philippines with economic "opportunity in the Orient" leverages the promise of Chinese trade to legitimize colonial violence. While Twain's critiques of imperialism frequently dwell on the U.S.'s transpacific incursions, they also connect China and the Philippines to global atrocities committed by Western colonial powers.

What grounds Twain's comparisons between such diverse scenarios of imperialism and racism? Does the breadth of his analogies detract from their specificity, or does it highlight particular modes of thinking common to all his local examples? This chapter argues that Twain's writings highlight how racist and imperialist regimes count (and in many cases discount) the dead through memorials and statistics and that he responds to these enumerative strategies with abstract figures and allegorical narratives. Twain's shift from psychologically sophisticated novels to allegorical nonfiction—and from a regional, folk style to the abstract language of statistics—should be understood as an attempt to engage with discourses that demarcate and count differentiated populations. Through close readings of Twain's anti-imperialist texts, I consider how racialization—in both domestic and imperial contexts—functions at the level of populations, as well as how monuments and mortality statistics train audiences to value and devalue differentiated lives. Twain's writings about Chinese Boxers, Filipino nationalists, and other imperial subjects bring allegorical forms such as imaginary monuments, processions, and fables to bear on the politically and ethically consequential ways in which we count the living and the dead.

I. "Among the Swarming Populations of the Globe"

Whereas Twain's fiction explores the psychological impacts of racial inequality on individual characters such as Ah Sin, Injun Joe, Jim, and Tom Driscoll, his nonfiction and allegorical writings frequently interrogate how populations are formed, policed, moved around, exploited, and exterminated. While Twain was sanguine about the migration of Chinese "coolies" in his *Letters from Hawai'i* and indifferent to the "swarming populations of the globe" that merely demonstrate the need for biometric identification in *Pudd'nhead Wilson*, his sketches in the 1870s dwell on the inhumane conditions and unequal protections faced by Chinese immigrants. His later writings, beginning with *Following the Equator*, expand these commentaries on the treatment of racialized populations into a rigorous critique of racial inequality and imperial governance.

Michel Foucault's discussion of "biopower" and modern forms of racism in *"Society Must Be Defended"* has provided an influential framework for understanding how states mobilize "race" in order to optimize the life and health of the population. Arguing that there emerged in the late eighteenth century a new mode of power that takes hold over life ("the power to 'make' live and 'let' die," rather than the sovereign "right to take life or let live"),[10] Foucault defines modern racism as

> primarily a way of introducing a break into the domain of life that is under power's control: the break between what must live and what must die. The appearance within the biological continuum of the human race of races, the distinction among races, the hierarchy of races, the fact that certain races are described as good and that others, in contrast, are described as inferior: all this is a way of fragmenting the field of the biological that power controls. It is a way of separating out the groups that exist within a population. It is, in short, a way of establishing a biological-type caesura within a population that appears to be a biological domain. This will allow power to treat that population as a mixture of races, or to be more accurate, to treat the species, to subdivide the species it controls, into the subspecies known, precisely, as races. That is the first function of racism: to fragment, to create caesuras within the biological continuum addressed by biopower.[11]

The mass migrations of the eighteenth and nineteenth century—the Middle Passage, Indian Removal, waves of immigration driven by war and famine—involved plenty of killing, but they also called forth biopolitical techniques focusing on reproduction and health. Through such practices as antimiscegenation laws, Jim Crow, the reservation system and a range of hygienic restrictions imposed on Chinese immigrants and Filipino subjects, the U.S. state attempted to impose health norms on racialized groups and to segregate those groups from contact with whites. In San Francisco's Chinatown and the Philippines, public health officials produced fastidious maps, statistics, and regulations in an effort to manage diseases among supposedly unsanitary populations.[12] In both the United States and the Philippines, the census configured racial taxonomies and prescribed how bodies should be counted amid volatile and heterogeneous populations.[13]

Building on Foucault's work, the literary critics Nancy Armstrong and Leonard Tennenhouse argue that the management of circulating populations has long been a preoccupation of American literature. Although they focus on Barbary captivity and circumatlantic slavery in antebellum novels, Armstrong and Tennenhouse address issues that are crucial to understanding the circulation of laborers, armies, resources, and capital across the Pacific Ocean in the 1890s. In contrast with the individual heroines and fixed national boundaries characteristic of domestic novels, they argue,

> Barbary narratives address the problem of people who are defined, not so much by their nation of origin, or home, as by their encounters in a world produced by the circulation of goods and peoples. . . . Such narratives raise this order of question: What enables bodies and commodities to circulate around the Atlantic? What is the role of government in facilitating this circulation? At what point does government intervene to guarantee the circulation of people and goods?[14]

To the extent that the War of 1898, the U.S.-Philippine War, the annexation of Hawai'i, and the suppression of the Boxer uprising secured U.S. access to transpacific markets, the emergence of U.S. overseas imperialism raises similar questions about how government affects the circulation of populations and goods. Whereas authors like Royall Tyler,

Herman Melville, and Harriet Beecher Stowe explored the problem of population through sweeping novels, Twain's nonfiction and allegorical writings took on the language of demography more directly, attending to both populations on the move and those immobilized by U.S. laws. Frequently—as in the cases of colonialism, slavery, and the racializing enforcement of vagrancy laws—the immobilization of specific populations enhanced the social and physical mobility of others.

In another influential response to Foucault's theorization of "biopolitics," Achille Mbembe argues that a focus on how the state organizes and optimizes the life of populations does not sufficiently account for contemporary colonies, where the state has just as frequently exercised the sovereign right to kill. Colonial spaces were crucibles for what Mbembe describes as contemporary "necropolitical" regimes where "weapons are deployed in the interest of maximum destruction of persons and the creation of *death-worlds*, new and unique forms of social existence in which vast populations are subjected to conditions of life conferring upon them the status of *living dead*."[15] Mbembe's description of the colony as a space of death resonates with the geographer Ruth Wilson Gilmore's influential reframing of U.S. racism in terms of structural violence and uneven vulnerabilities to premature death: for both colonial subjects and racialized populations in the United States, "Racism ... is the state-sanctioned or extralegal production and exploitation of group-differentiated vulnerability to premature death."[16] The consignment of colonial and racialized populations to hazardous or fatal spaces raises questions explored throughout Twain's late writings: "What place is given to life, death, and the human body (in particular the wounded or slain body)? How are they inscribed in the order of power?"[17]

As Susan Gillman has shown, Twain's shift from fiction and travelogues about national race relations to scathing critiques of U.S. imperialism was profoundly influenced by his direct observations of life under British imperial rule.[18] *Following the Equator* (1897), Twain's account of his 1895 lecture tour through much of the British empire, dwells on several instances of involuntary or constrained migration. In the Pacific Islands, Twain criticizes the practice of "blackbirding," whereby British "vessels fitted up like old-time slavers" kidnapped tens of thousands of islanders to work as indentured laborers on Queensland sugar plantations. Using the discourses of morality and health to critique this practice of forced indenture, Twain notes that blackbirding "generally demoralizes and always impoverishes the Kanaka, deprives him of his citizenship," and "is fraught with danger to Australia and the islands on the score of health" (*FE*, 90). In South Africa, Twain excoriates Cecil Rhodes's Chartered Company for first displacing the black population and then hiring them under brutal conditions:

> The reduction of the population by Rhodesian methods to the desired limit is a return to the old-time slow-misery and lingering-death system of a discredited time and a crude "civilization." We humanely reduce an overplus of dogs by swift chloroform; the Boer humanely reduced an overplus of blacks by swift suffocation; the nameless but right-hearted Australian pioneer humanely reduced his overplus of aboriginal neighbors by a sweetened swift death concealed in a poisoned pudding. . . . You and I would rather suffer either of these deaths thirty times over in thirty successive days than linger out one of the Rhodesian twenty-year deaths, with its daily burden of insult, humiliation, and forced labor for a man whose entire race the victim hates. (*FE*, 691)

Although he disingenuously suggests that Americans only direct genocidal violence at "dogs," Twain's satirical comparisons present a scathing critique not only of the Rhodesian regime of forced labor and slow death but of the premature deaths imposed by all colonial regimes.

Elsewhere, Twain describes a more empowered migratory population when commenting on a group of migrants huddled on a ship bound for Mozambique: "Fifty Indians and Chinamen asleep in a big tent in the waist of the ship forward; they lie side by side with no space between; the former wrapped up, head and all, as in the Indian streets, the Chinamen uncovered; the lamp and things for opium smoking in the center" (*FE*, 636; see Figure 5.1). Twain's sharp eye for social satire and ethnographic detail—evident through much of *Following the Equator*—gives way, here, to a more impressionistic description. "Lie"—the only verb in these four clauses—emphasizes the passive, indistinguishable nature of these dormant bodies positioned "side by side with no space between." After noting some broad details and the customary "things for opium," Twain abruptly changes the topic. The brevity and vagueness of this description register the mixed group of Chinese and Indian migrants only as a mystery.

of the ship forward; they lie side by side with no space between; the former wrapped up, head and all, as in the Indian

INDIANS AND CHINAMEN.

streets, the Chinamen uncovered; the lamp and things for opium smoking in the center.

Figure 5.1: "Indians and Chinamen," *Following the Equator* (Hartford, Conn.: American Publishing Co., 1898), 636. Courtesy of the Mark Twain Project, Bancroft Library, University of California, Berkeley.

However, Twain's earlier comments on Mauritius—an island with "the largest variety of nationalities and complexions we have encountered yet"—provide a positive framework for this spectacle of migrant Asian laborers. While workers from India and China were frequently compelled to migrate by famines, wars, and displacements resulting from Western imperial incursions,[19] Twain witnessed the efficiency with which they adapted to new communities. For example, after noting the efficiency of Indian "coolies" of both sexes, he notes that "these thrifty coolies are said to be acquiring land a trifle at a time, and cultivating it; and may own the island by and by" (*FE*, 626). This passage revises the following excerpt from Twain's travel notebooks: "Passenger who has spent 2 yrs in Port Louis repeats what so many have said: that the island is gradually passing acre by acre into the hands of the Indians, Arabs, & Chinamen; that by & by it will be their property exclusively."[20] By adding terms like "thrifty" and "cultivating" and substituting the immigrants' activities ("acquiring" and "cultivating") for the passive phrase "is passing," Twain's revisions to "what so many have said" suggest that the immigrants have earned a claim to the place by mixing their labor with the land. By reducing the sweeping references to "Indians, Arabs, & Chinamen" to a more focused discussion of "Indian coolies," he shifts the account from a xenophobic perspective that views all nonwhite immigrants as invaders to an ethnographic one that considers the merits of each group. In another aside, Twain points out that, in the wake of the 1892 cyclone that devastated Port Louis, "It is said the Chinese fed the sufferers for days on free rice" (*FE*, 628). Whereas anti-immigrant discourses in the United States often represented Asiatics as unassimilable, Twain's favorable representations of Indian and Chinese migrants in Mauritius suggest that these groups make valuable contributions to a population composed of heterogeneous "nationalities and complexions."

II. Body Counts

Despite the impressionistic nature of Twain's description of the fifty Indian and Chinese migrants on board the *Arundel Castle*, he apparently took the trouble to count them. Similarly, he enumerates the population of Mauritius in 1851 (185,000) and in the present (375,000), claiming that the difference indicates the number and socioeconomic effects of Indian immigrants. In a striking analysis of seventeenth-century engagements with an emerging transatlantic discourse of population, the literary critic Molly Farrell has argued that counting bodies serves as an important colonial strategy: "Numbers ... offer the promise of drawing clear borders between peoples even as they mask the permeability of those boundaries."[21] During the nineteenth century, statisticians, epidemiologists, and eugenicists such as William Farr, Florence Nightingale, and Francis Galton became increasingly interested in birth and death statistics as tools for tracking and intervening in the health of populations.[22] The historian Drew Gilpin Faust observes that, "as the very term itself implies, statistics emerged in close alliance with notions of an expanding state, with the assessment of its resources, strength, and responsibilities."[23] Faust traces the rise of body counts in the United States to the years following the Civil War, when government officials, historians, and private citizens attempted to reckon the immense losses incurred on both sides: "Late-nineteenth-century Americans exhibited an unprecedented and growing interest in the numbers of dead, in the statistics of the conflict they had experienced."[24] But if counting serves the interests of population management, surveillance, and postwar mourning, it can also gauge the demographic impacts of migration, racial violence, colonialism, and specific techniques of governance. By critiquing conventional beliefs about who counts and by insistently counting colonial subjects (living and dead), Twain exposes how racism and empire work to distribute vulnerability, preventable deaths, and grief unevenly.

In *Frames of War: When Is Life Grievable?* the philosopher Judith Butler argues that states can only wage war in conjunction with a cultural "assault on the senses" that influences how people perceive specific lives and deaths:

> The assault can take various forms: rendering sensational losses that are borne by nations with whom identification is intensified through the individual icons of death, rendering insensate certain losses whose open mourning might challenge the rationale of war itself. . . . Waging war in some ways begins with the assault on the senses; the senses are the first target of war. Similarly, the implicit or explicit framing of a population as a war target is the initial action of destruction.[25]

Once rendered "ungrievable" by representational media such as photography, journalism, and fiction, lives can be devastated without guilt or mourning. In effect, Butler argues that representational media enact and reproduce the fragmentation and hierarchization of "races" described in Foucault's account of biopolitical racism. Using recent Israeli attacks on Palestinian civilians as an example, Butler argues that "to kill such a person, indeed, such a population, thus calls upon a racism that differentiates in advance who will count as a life, and who will not."[26]

Along with visual and narrative media, body counts play a crucial role in documenting or obfuscating losses. In addition to interrogating who counts, who is counted, and how the counting is done, Butler notes that numbers are always open to unexpected framings and interpretations:

> Numbers, especially the number of war dead, circulate not only as representations of war, but as part of the apparatus of war waging. Numbers are a way to frame the losses of war, but this does not mean that we know whether, when, or how numbers count. We may know how to count, or we may well rely on the reliability of certain humanitarian or humanitarian rights organizations to count well, but that is not the same as figuring out how and whether a life counts. Although numbers cannot tell us precisely whose lives count, and whose deaths count, we can note how numbers are framed and unframed to find out how norms that differentiate livable and grievable lives are at work in the context of war.[27]

Numbers require framing and interpretation: a high body count may be viewed as evidence of poor strategy, a nation's weakness, the enemy's ruthlessness, or God's disfavor. In the context of war, body counts are frequently withheld: in the U.S.-Philippine War, "statistics were deliberately not kept for Filipino casualties and losses";[28] in the current occupation of Iraq, the Iraq Body Count project—now drawing on classified war logs made available by WikiLeaks—tracks the number of documented violent civilian deaths since 2003 (107,953–117,954 at the time of this writing). News media carefully frame statistics, photographs, and testimonials of war losses on both sides so as to support the ideology of war making.[29]

Foucault notes that biopolitical racism may expose populations to death through diverse forms of discrimination and inequity: "When I say 'killing,' I obviously do not mean simply murder as such, but also every form of indirect murder: the fact of exposing someone to death, increasing the risk of death for some people, or, quite simply, political death, expulsion, rejection, and so on."[30] To the extent that counting renders some populations more vulnerable to legal and extralegal violence, it intersects with the status of "civil death" discussed in Chapter 2. Twain's sketches and novels critique the politics of counting in a range of situations that depend upon rendering a set of lives ungrievable. "Disgraceful Persecution of a Boy" satirizes the incommensurability between the narrator's sympathy for a boy who is disciplined for stoning Chinese men and his failure to register the suffering of Chinese men who are insufficiently protected from such assaults by the law. When Aunt Sally asks if anyone was hurt in a steamship accident in *Huckleberry Finn*, Huck's response—"No'm. killed a nigger"—dissimulates his interest in liberating Jim by rehearsing one of the central beliefs of the slaveholding South: that African American lives cannot be counted on the same terms as those of whites (*HF*, 230). As I discussed in Chapter 4, Twain's draft of *Connecticut Yankee* dwells on Hank Morgan's elaborate efforts to quantify the knights he massacred in the Battle of the Sand Belt: "Of course we could not *count* the dead, because they did not exist as individuals, but merely as homogeneous protoplasm."[31] *Pudd'nhead Wilson* and *Those Extraordinary Twins* satirize the ways of counting bodies that underlie legal fictions of race and individualism: in Roxy's case, "the one sixteenth of her which was black outvoted the other fifteen parts and made her a Negro" (*PW*, 9); in the case of the conjoined twins, the legal system goes from being unable to decide which twin is responsible for kicking Tom to deciding to hang Luigi even though his life is tied to Angelo's. In a recent essay, Thomas Peyser has noted that "Number 44, New Series 864,962," the title character of *No.44, The Mysterious Stranger*, invokes the panoply of statistics with which the period's "books, speeches, and periodicals had a way of practically reducing immigrants to numbers."[32] Whereas his fiction tends to examine how the politics of counting affects specific characters, Twain's later writings articulate broader anti-imperialist frameworks for interpreting body counts. In Twain's hands, statistics foreground not only how the scale of modern war and governance overshadows individual lives but how racialization and imperialism impose these deindividualizing forces on subject populations as well.

Following the Equator deploys death rates and population counts to refute imperialist beliefs that non-Western civilizations are unsanitary, undisciplined, and thus prone to disease and famine. For example, William Farr—who pioneered "the use of local life tables to compare the relative health of places"[33]—also connected health statistics to eugenicist and imperialist ideas about the racial inferiority of populations living in "unhealthy environments."[34] By contrast, Twain uses numbers to convey the deadly and unsustainable nature of colonialism and racialized labor. Commenting on the effects of blackbirding on Pacific Islanders forcibly "recruited" to work on plantations, he writes: "It is claimed that the traffic will depopulate its sources of supply within the next twenty or thirty years. Queensland is a very healthy place for white people—death-rate 12 in 1,000 of the population—but the Kanaka death-rate is away above that. The vital statistics for 1893 place it at 52; for 1894 (Mackay district), 68. . . . The death-rate among the new men has reached as high as 180 in the 1,000" (*FE*, 88). Whereas European commentators often expressed shock and disapproval at reports of infanticide among aborigines, Twain compares infanticide favorably to Western techniques of depopulation: "[The aborigine] diligently and deliberately kept population down by infanticide—largely; but mainly by certain other methods. He did not need to practice these artificialities any more after the white man came. The white man knew ways of keeping down population which were worth several of his. The white man knew ways of reducing a native population 80 per cent. in 20 years." Twain then cites statistics (along with anecdotes attesting to the cold-blooded killing of indigenous Australians by whites) showing a reduction of Gippsland aborigines from 1,000 to 200 and a reduction of the Geelong tribe from 173 to just one person over forty years (*FE*, 209).

"The United States of Lyncherdom" (1901), which Twain suppressed in order to avoid offending southerners, juxtaposes conversion rates in China with lynching statistics to support the argument that missionaries in China would be more appropriate and more effective in the U.S. South. Noting the increasing number of lynchings between 1899 and 1901, Twain explains that lynching does not reduce the incidence of "the usual crime" (i.e., the alleged rape of white women) so much as it inspires imitators to commit more lynchings.[35] After citing a telegram that graphically describes a lynching, Twain asks readers to

> picture the scene in their minds, and soberly ponder it; then multiply it by 115, add 88; place the 203 in a row, allowing 600 feet of space for each human torch, so that there be viewing room around it for 5,000 Christian American men, women, and children, youths and maidens[;] the eye can then take in the whole line of twenty-four miles of

blood-and-flesh bonfires unbroken. . . . There are more than a million persons present; the light from the fires flushes into vague outline against the night the spires of five thousand churches. O kind missionary, O compassionate missionary, leave China! Come home and convert these Christians![36]

As I show below, this passage anticipates similar mathematical thought experiments in "To the Person Sitting in Darkness" and *King Leopold's Soliloquy*. Here, Twain uses methodical calculations based on recorded numbers of lynchings to design a horrific imaginary tableau that contrasts with the relatively insignificant numbers of Christian converts in China. Drawing on actual missionary reports, Twain notes that there are 1,500 U.S. missionaries in China "converting two Chinamen apiece per annum against an uphill birth rate of 33,000 pagans per day."[37] Compared with the Sisyphean task of converting China's population at that rate, and given that "the Chinese are universally conceded to be excellent people, honest, honorable, industrious, trustworthy, kindhearted, and all that," Twain argues that these 1,500 missionaries should be shipped to the U.S. South to convert Christian lynchers. He thus exposes the hypocrisy of both evangelism and the civilizing project, showing how both missionary work and lynching function in the service of Chinese and African American racialization.

While most of Twain's writings on the U.S.-Philippine War "closely paralleled arguments that can be found in other anti-imperialist writings of the time," Twain's commentaries are distinguished by their obsession with counting dead and wounded bodies.[38] Whereas other anti-imperialist writers published casualty figures to provide concrete evidence that U.S. soldiers were killing wounded enemies and to appeal to the American public's fascination with war statistics,[39] Twain uses literary techniques such as repetition, irony, and (as I show below) ekphrastic descriptions of imaginary monuments to defamiliarize body counts. In numerous responses to the war (many of which he deemed too controversial to publish in his lifetime), Twain mobilizes casualty statistics to frame battles not as strategic victories but as war atrocities. Despite the uncertainty of casualty figures on the Philippine side,[40] he draws on unofficial estimates published by the Anti-Imperialist League[41] to indicate both the discrepancy between

U.S. and Philippine casualty figures and the discrepancy in the care with which those figures are counted. In his unpublished 1901–1902 review of Edwin Wildman's *Aguinaldo: A Narrative of Filipino Ambitions* (1901), Twain compares the four thousand Americans recorded dead with Filipino losses: "It is impossible to estimate [the Filipino] loss on the field, but one officer has estimated it at *one-sixth of the population*, which would be *over a million.*"[42] After calculating that about thirty thousand American men were on the field at any given time, Twain pauses to consider the implications:

> *Thirty thousand killed a million.* They must have killed all; a population of six million can by no possibility furnish more than one million fighting men. *Thirty thousand killed a million.* In eighteen months. It is 100 percent of the opposing force. And all killed dead in the field. It is 85 percent above any figure ever reached before in any age, even with flood and famine and massacre to help. *Thirty thousand killed a million.* It seems a pity that the historian let that get out; it is really a most embarrassing circumstance.[43]

In an unpublished response to a January 11, 1902, *New York Evening Post* graph depicting war losses between May 1900 and July 1901, Twain provided a more fine-grained (if somewhat inaccurate)[44] statistical analysis: "Consider what it means. The Filipinos killed 250 and wounded double as many—and that is the customary proportion in Civilized warfare—2 wounded to 1 killed. We killed 4,000, and wounded 200—the proportion customary to massacre."[45] The numbers reflect not only the more destructive weapons used by Americans but also an apparent refusal to spare Filipino prisoners or tend their wounded.

Twain provided a more extensive discussion of the relation between body counts and war crimes in his autobiography, which includes several pages of meditations on the Moro Massacre in the Philippines written between March 12 and March 14, 1906. After describing the incident—in which U.S. forces killed nine hundred Moros (indigenous Muslims who continued resisting U.S. rule until 1913), including women and children, camped in a crater bowl—Twain draws attention to how official reports exaggerate the heroism and wounds of American troops while obscuring Moro deaths:

The official report quite properly extolled and magnified the "heroism" and "gallantry" of our troops; lamented the loss of the fifteen who perished, and elaborated the wounds of thirty-two of our men who suffered injury, and even minutely and faithfully described the nature of the wounds, in the interest of future historians of the United States. It mentioned that a private had one of his elbows scraped by a missile, and the private's name was mentioned. Another private had the end of his nose scraped by a missile. His name was also mentioned—by cable, at one dollar and fifty cents a word.

Next day's news confirmed the previous day's report and named our fifteen killed and thirty-two wounded *again*, and once more described the wounds and gilded them with the right adjectives.[46]

Twain's satire of news reports resonates with Butler's analysis of the media "assault on the senses" that sensationalizes the nation's own war casualties while "rendering insensate certain losses whose open mourning might challenge the rationale of war itself."[47] Like President Theodore Roosevelt, who at first called the incident a "brilliant feat of arms . . . [which] upheld the honor of the American flag" (quoted in "CMM," 173), these official reports legitimate the massacre—and lay the groundwork for future massacres—by quietly rendering the dead Moro men, women, and children ungrievable. Even when newspapers began reporting that women and children were among the dead, General Leonard Wood (who Twain ironically reminds us was also a doctor) represents both wounded and civilian Moros as unworthy of sympathy: "He says there was 'no wanton destruction of women and children in the fight, though many of them were killed by force of necessity because the Moros used them as shields'[48] [and that] 'many of the Moros feigned death and butchered the American hospital men who were relieving the wounded'" ("CMM," 176). The accusation of feigning death suggests that the Moros are beyond the scope of grief: their corpses should be feared, not mourned.

In the case of the Moro massacre, Twain suggests that the glaring truth implicit in the statistics cannot possibly be ameliorated by patriotic platitudes. By simply juxtaposing an early count of Moro losses with a celebratory explanation, Twain exposes how the War of Philippine Independence conflated Christianity and U.S. "patriotism" with indiscriminate slaughter: "There, with six hundred engaged on each side, we lost fifteen men killed outright, and we had thirty-two wounded—counting that nose and that elbow. The enemy numbered six hundred—including women and children—and we abolished them utterly, leaving not even a baby alive to cry for its dead mother. *This is incomparably the greatest victory that was ever achieved by the Christian soldiers of the United States*" ("CMM," 172; emphasis in original). Twain's use of "abolish" as a term for murder eloquently evokes the contradiction between the U.S.'s discourse of liberation (which frequently invoked the rhetoric of abolitionism) and its brutal conquest of the Philippines. After five days pass without editorial commentary on the massacre in newspapers, Twain reframes the persistent silence about the Moro dead as a sign of "ominous paralysis" in the discursive apparatus of war making: "I hope that this silence will continue. It is about as eloquent and as damaging and effective as the most indignant words could be, I think. When a man is sleeping in a noise, his sleep goes placidly on; but if the noise stops, the stillness wakes him.... A five-day silence following a world-astonishing event has not happened on this planet since the daily newspaper was invented" ("CMM," 175). This may help explain why Twain never published his remarks about the massacre during his lifetime: the numbers and the silence spoke for themselves.

Twain's later works of speculative fiction largely forsake individual protagonists in favor of examining population dynamics allegorically represented in relations between microbes, bacilli, bees, butterflies, and souls in heaven.[49] *Extract from Captain Stormfield's Visit to Heaven* (1907–1908)[50] defamiliarizes population counts and body counts by presenting a demographic thought experiment in which heaven is inhabited by world populations from the entire span of human history. When Stormfield is surprised to see so few white angels in heaven, his friend Sandy explains that, whereas "America was occupied a billion years and more, by Injuns, and Aztecs, and that sort of folks, before a white man ever set foot in it," only about "fifty million whites have died in America from the beginning up to to-day."[51] This is why Heaven's America "is populated with a scattering of a few hundred thousand billions of red angels, with now and then a curiously complected *diseased* [i.e., white] one." And "the California district is a thousand times worse.

It swarms with a mean kind of leather-headed mud-colored angels—and your nearest white neighbor is likely to be a million miles away."[52] Under these conditions of immortality—where techniques of depopulation and genocide cannot be used to gain land and power—whites are a racialized and pathologized minority. And even the "transcendent, 'essential' racial category" of whiteness turns out to be a recent invention, as whites from different eras turn out to be "just simply foreigners" to Sandy.[53] As Stephanie LeMenager notes, "Twain uses the diachronic dimension of his Heaven to divorce national territories from ideological fictions that posited a monoracial future against multiracial, conflictual pasts."[54] Among Heaven's multiracial masses, the greatest heroes turn out to be publicly executed criminals such as Captain Kidd and the celebrated murderer Charles Peace: "Flocks came from all the departments. I saw Esquimaux there, and Tartars, Negroes, Chinamen—people from everywhere. You see a mixture like that in the Grand Choir, the first day you land here, but you hardly ever see it again."[55] Convicted criminals who die at the hands of the state turn out to be celebrities in Heaven, and only they bring together a mixed, multiracial crowd of millions in an otherwise largely self-segregated Heaven. By using the scale of deep time[56] to place notions of whiteness, nationalism, and criminality in perspective, Twain's demography of Heaven undermines the national and racial categories that conventionally determine which lives count most. The following section focuses on more direct critiques of the connection between nationalism and violence in Twain's treatments of public monuments.

III. Monumental Violence

In 1879, an architect writing for the *Atlantic Monthly* observed that the American public was "blazing lately with ardor, not yet spent, to cover the land with monuments, and set up statues to all their perishable celebrities."[57] In the wake of the Civil War, as Americans became obsessed with counting battlefield casualties, monuments functioned as sites of public mourning and national identification. The Civil War memorial at Arlington National Cemetery is among the earliest examples of the tombs of unknown soldiers that Benedict Anderson identifies as "arresting emblems of the modern culture of nationalism." "Void as these tombs are of identifiable mortal remains or immortal souls," writes Anderson, "they are nonetheless saturated with ghostly *national imaginings*" insofar as they weave the contingency of individual lives into the larger continuity of an imagined community.[58] In addition to producing patriotic feelings, monuments to U.S. wars and war heroes play an essential role in framing historical deployments of violence and in spectacularizing some lives at the expense of others: they unevenly distribute access to public mourning and identification.

Augustus Saint-Gaudens's monument to Colonel Robert Gould Shaw and the 54th Regiment (1884–1897), erected across the street from the State House on Boston Common, exemplifies how monuments distribute visibility and mourning. Inscriptions on the monument include Shaw's name, rank, and birth date, along with some verses by James Russell Lowell describing his heroic death; the names of sixty-two of the approximately 116 African American soldiers killed in the charge on Fort Wagner were not added to the monument until 1982. The bronze relief depicts Shaw riding in procession with several foot soldiers, whose faces were based not on the actual infantrymen but on live African American models. An inscription next to Shaw reads "omnia relinqvit / servare rempvblicam": "He relinquished everything to serve the Republic." The use of *he* instead of *they* singles out Shaw's sacrifice as exemplary and his death as much more deserving of public grief than the deaths of the anonymous black soldiers who died alongside him. Although a longer inscription includes some lines praising the courage and devotion of "the black rank and file," the monument clearly accords more grief and honor to Shaw than to the foot soldiers whose losses it does not enumerate and whose own faces it does not depict.[59]

As the historians James Loewen and Oscar Campomanes have shown, monuments to the War of 1898 go to great lengths to erase the subsequent war waged by the United States to suppress Philippine nationalist resistance (1899–1902).[60] Beginning in 1904, veterans erected over fifty monuments throughout the United States commemorating the "Spanish-American War, 1898–1902," and many of these feature a statue of a lone "Hiker." Both the dates and the name of the war are misleading, however: instead of referring to the "Spanish-American War," which was fought over the course of three months in 1898, "'the hiker' and 'hiking' were terms used by U.S. soldiers in the

Philippine-American War to describe themselves and their campaigns to root out Filipino Guerrillas from their mountain strongholds."[61] Although these monuments frequently include inscriptions designating colonial arenas—"Porto Rico," "Cuba," "The Philippines," and "China" (alluding to the 1901 campaign against the Boxers)—they never acknowledge the imperialist motives for the U.S.-Philippine War or the staggering and uncountable losses incurred by Filipino revolutionaries and civilians. Monuments to "The Hiker" single out the rugged U.S. soldier while obfuscating both the counterrevolutionary war of conquest in which he fought and the hundreds of thousands of Filipinos killed by U.S. soldiers, malnutrition, and disease during the war. Building on critical assessments of war monuments, Campomanes argues for an analysis of how a much broader range of cultural media contribute to public perceptions of war casualties: "I endeavor to expand the notion of the war monument, as Loewen and [Benedict] Anderson have used it, into a *complex* of representational genres and texts that would include contemporary U.S. mass communication and visual culture products."[62]

Twain counteracted the political violence enacted by this multimedia complex of war monuments by attending to populations "sitting in darkness" whose lives and deaths are denied public visibility. "The Treaty with China" dwells on the likelihood that peasants would resist the construction of railroads in the Chinese countryside because the land is filled with "graves . . . as precious as their own blood to the Chinese, for they worship their dead as ancestors. The first railroad that plows its pitiless way through these myriads of sacred hillocks would carry dismay and distress into countless households."[63] Although he empathizes with the distress that the Chinese would feel at the destruction of their ancestors' graves, Twain's 1868 article insists that "The railroads must be built. . . . They will tear heartstrings out by the roots, but they lead to the sources of unimaginable wealth, and they must be built."[64] In *The Innocents Abroad* and other travel writings, Twain poked fun at the trouble it took to visit Western monuments; his account of "Injun Joe's Cup" at the conclusion of *Tom Sawyer* dramatized how markers of Native American deaths become tourist attractions that evoke, at best, only an abstract grief that naturalizes genocidal violence (*TS*, 253), and in *A Connecticut Yankee* he envisions an alternative monument commemorating King Arthur's actions during a disease epidemic: a statue of the king not in the act of "killing a giant or a dragon" but "in commoner's garb [and] bearing [a child killed by smallpox] in his arms that a peasant mother might look her last upon her child and be comforted" (*CY*, 164–165).

In *Following the Equator*, Twain offers an extensive analysis of two war monuments at Wanganui, New Zealand. He objects to the depiction of Maoris in a memorial "in honor of white men 'who fell in defence of law and order against fanaticism and barbarism'" (*FE*, 321). Comparing indigenous resistance to "Thermopylae, or where [the Swiss national hero] Winkelried died, or upon Bunker Hill monument," Twain argues that those who fought against the colonizers should also be honored as patriots: "It was no shame to fight them. They fought for their homes, they fought for their country; they bravely fought and bravely fell" (322). While including some acknowledgment of the Maoris' heroism and war losses would improve the first monument, Twain claims that

> the other monument cannot be rectified. Except with dynamite. It is a mistake all through, and a strangely thoughtless one. It is a monument erected by white men to Maoris who fell fighting with the whites and *against their own people*, in the Maori war. "Sacred to the memory of the brave men who fell on the 14th of May, 1864," etc. On one side are the names of about twenty Maoris. It is not a fancy of mine; the monument exists. I saw it. It is an object-lesson to the rising generation. It invites to treachery, disloyalty, unpatriotism. Its lesson, in frank terms is, "Desert your flag, slay your people, burn their homes, shame your nationality—we honor such." (Ibid.)

Twain's critique focuses on how these monuments attempt to rewrite history by persuading the "rising generation" that only those who fight on the side of the colonizers are "brave" and worthy of mourning. In addition to commemorating events, monuments provide scripts for public memory and national belonging: as Twain notes, the second monument implicitly defines "nationality" as allegiance to the colonial government, not to neighbors and chiefs. Within the context of the New Zealand Land Wars (1845–1872), these monuments also lay claim to the landscape itself, obscuring prior histories of Maori settlement and land use.[65] Twain's fantasy of rectifying the latter monument "with dynamite" inverts the pattern established in *Connecticut Yankee*, in which Hank Morgan uses explosives to bring light and modernity to the "white Indians" of Arthurian England: here, Twain wants to detonate the legacy of land wars conducted in the name of modernizing the Maoris (*CY*, 19).

Whereas monuments generally aestheticize violence by reducing complex historical events to heroic figures and actions, "To the Person Sitting in Darkness" imagines a monument that would graphically depict the costs of the unjust reparations demanded by the American Board of Foreign Missions following the suppression of the Boxer uprising. Twain objects to the exorbitant fine (which was initially reported as thirteen times the indemnity but turned out to be one-and-a-third times the indemnity)[66] because it would expose "women and children" to "inevitable starvation and lingering death" and because "the blood-money so acquired [would] be *'used for the propagation of the Gospel'* ("PS," 27; emphasis in original). Twain's emphasis on the "inevitable starvation and lingering death" that result from exorbitant reparations shifts the perspective from the immediate deaths resulting from uprisings and battles—which are frequently commemorated in monuments and body counts—to the lingering and underdocumented "slow violence"[67] caused by environmental and infrastructural damage that continues long after battles have been fought. He later compares the United States' demands to Germany's "overcharge" for the killing of several missionaries in an earlier incident—a demand for devastating reparations (including a costly monument to the murdered missionaries) that, according to Twain, "*produced the Chinese revolt*, the indignant uprising of China's traduced patriots, the Boxers" ("PS," 30; emphasis in original). Twain suggests erecting a monument to honor Reverend William Scott Ament, who justified the United States' exorbitant demands by citing European Catholics' demand for 750,000 strings of cash and 680 heads (one for each Catholic killed):

> Designs must allegorically set forth the Thirteen Reduplications for the Indemnity, and the Object for which they were exacted; as Ornaments, the designs must exhibit 680 Heads, so disposed as to give a pleasing and pretty effect; for the Catholics have done nicely, and are entitled to notice in the monument. Mottoes may be suggested, if any shall be discovered that will satisfactorily cover the ground. ("PS," 26-27)

Twain's satire lays bare the cultural work of war monuments: to render violence into ornament that "give[s] a pleasing and pretty effect." But, insofar as it incorporates the sufferings and losses of the Chinese, his proposed monument is designed to fail: for no memorial could successfully beautify 680 severed heads and a thirteen-fold indemnity or elicit from such statistics the sense of religious or national identity characteristic of such structures.

By associating Ament's demands with the German Catholics' demand for 680 heads, Twain's projected monument situates American missionaries in the context of comparative colonialism. This comparative approach to political critique is characteristic of Twain's later allegorical writings. In "The Stupendous Procession," the "680 Chinese heads" appear again with the helmeted figure of "germania"; "france" bears "Chinese 'heads' and loot" alongside the mutilated figure of "Tonquin"; "russia"'s floats bear the corpses of "Massacred Manchurian peasants"; and the United States is accompanied by a *"Mutilated Figure in Chains*, labeled 'Filipino Independence,' and an allegorical Figure of the Administration caressing it with one hand, and stabbing it in the back with the other."[68] Along with monuments and parades, Twain appropriated nationalist genres such as the war prayer, the disembarkation speech, the "Battle Hymn of the Republic" (for which he wrote an alternate set of scathing, anti-imperialist lyrics), and the flag to criticize how patriotic discourse discounts the lives of enemies and colonial subjects. For the Philippine Province, Twain proposes, "we can have just our usual flag, with the white stripes painted black and the stars replaced by the skull and cross-bones" ("PS," 39).

In *King Leopold's Soliloquy: A Defense of His Congo Rule* (1905),[69] Twain developed earlier critiques and appropriations of imperial monuments into his most extravagant proposal for a monument to imperial violence. Railing against critics who accuse him of reducing the Congo population from twenty-five million (or from a projected figure of 30 million that would account for natural increase) to fifteen million in twenty years, Leopold describes one proposed monument to the atrocities of his regime—a monument entirely organized by body counts:

> Another madman wants to construct a memorial for the perpetuation of my name, out of my 15 000 000 skulls and skeletons, and is full of

"A memorial for the perpetuation of my name."— *Page 27.*

Figure 5.2: "A Memorial for the Perpetuation of My Name," *King Leopold's Soliloquy*. Courtesy of the Mark Twain Project, Bancroft Library, University of California, Berkeley.

vindictive enthusiasm over his strange project. He has it all ciphered out and drawn to scale. Out of the skulls he will build a combined monument and mausoleum to me which shall exactly duplicate the Great Pyramid of Cheops, whose base covers thirteen acres, and whose apex is 451 feet above ground. He desires to stuff me and stand me up in the sky on that apex, robed and crowned, with my "pirate flag" in one hand and a butcher-knife and pendant handcuffs in the other. He will build the pyramid in the center of a depopulated tract, a brooding solitude covered with weeds and the mouldering ruins of burned villages, where the spirits of the starved and murdered dead will voice their laments forever in the whispers of the wandering winds. Radiating from the pyramid, like the spokes of a wheel, there are to be forty grand avenues of approach, each thirty-five miles long, and each fenced on both sides by skulless skeletons standing a yard and a half apart and festooned together in line by short chains stretching from wrist to wrist and attached to tried and true old handcuffs stamped with my private trade-mark, a crucifix and butcher-knife crossed, with motto, "By this sign we prosper"; each osseous fence to consist of 200 000 skeletons on a side, which is 400 000 to each avenue.[70] (Figure 5.2)

The numbers in this passage build on death statistics scattered throughout *King Leopold's Soliloquy* (Twain highlighted and annotated many of the death counts in his personal copy of the published book, held at the Mark Twain Papers),[71] as well as Twain's own handwritten calculations of distance on the verso side of one of his manuscript pages (Figure 5.3). Twain's vision marshals the sublimity of a vast edifice (the Great Pyramid was, for thousands of years, the tallest manmade structure in the world) to convey the scale of Leopold's atrocities. Whereas the Great Pyramid of Cheops was intended to commemorate the pharaoh by preserving his body out of sight, this proposed monument for Leopold would put corpses—both his own and those of his estimated fifteen million victims—on display. The "skulless skeletons" joined by chains and handcuffs represent the war casualties generally obscured by monuments. Are these human remains, whose skulls have been removed to form the pyramid itself, part of the monument, or are they just accessories—mere fences, "avenues of approach," or the laments of the dead "in the whispers of the wandering winds"? Echoing the festering wall of massacred knights that entraps Hank Morgan and his fifty-two followers at the end of *Connecticut Yankee*, these "osseous fences" make it impossible to approach the sublime monument without confronting figures of death and bondage.

After describing this pyramid of skulls in the midst of "ruins of burned villages" and "a depopulated tract," Twain appends a strange analogy to his already overwrought allegory. The proposal abruptly superimposes the monument—a replica of an Egyptian pyramid erected in honor of a Belgian king of the Congo—onto the geography of the United States:

> It is remarked with satisfaction that it aggregates three or four thousand miles (single-ranked) of skeletons—15 000 000 all told—and would stretch across America from New York to San Francisco. It is remarked further, in the hopeful tone of a railroad company forecasting showy extensions of its mileage, that my output is 500 000 corpses a year when my plant is running full time, and that therefore if I am spared ten years longer there will be fresh skulls enough to add 175 feet to the pyramid, making it by a long way the loftiest architectural construction on the earth, and fresh skeletons enough to continue the transcontinental file (on piles) a thousand miles into the Pacific.[72]

While this image of fifteen million skeletons stretching from New York to San Francisco into the Pacific may be an analogy designed to illustrate the vast number of corpses for which Leopold is responsible, Twain's shift from the subjunctive ("*would* stretch") to the indicative ("there *will* be . . . fresh skeletons enough to continue"), as well as his retention of the analogy after it has been superseded (i.e., the size of America no longer seems pertinent when the skeletons stretch a thousand miles beyond it) suggest stronger connections between America and Leopold's reign. Imaginatively locating the line of skeletons in the United States obliquely registers that (as Twain points out elsewhere in the soliloquy) the United States was the first to recognize Leopold II's "International Association for the Exploration and Civilization of Central Africa" as an independent state and that U.S. capitalists had invested considerable sums in the Congo. Leopold's rant about the monument ends with the paranoid thought that Andrew Carnegie might fund its

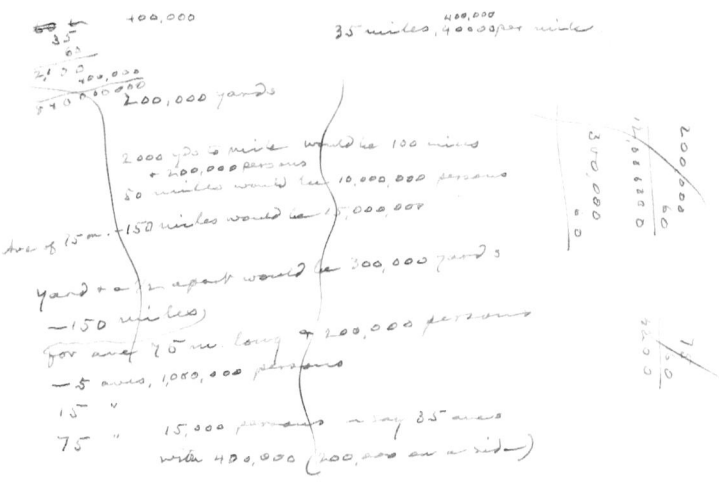

Figure 5.3: Twain's calculations for the monument to King Leopold, "King Leopold's Soliloquy," MS, p. 32 verso, Mark Twain Papers, CU-MarkWritingsFile 1905.09.00 (1905). Courtesy of the Mark Twain Project, Bancroft Library, University of California, Berkeley.

construction—but it remains unclear whether Carnegie would do this in the interest of discrediting Leopold, or as a way of acknowledging affinities between U.S. capitalism and Leopold's more direct approach to exploiting racialized labor. The transcontinental file of skeletons also invokes numerous parallels between atrocities in the Congo and U.S. practices of racial exploitation: the shackled skeletons recall slavery and disproportionately black chain gangs, the "depopulated tract" where the monument would be built invokes the violent wars and displacements that accompanied westward expansion, the "transcontinental" file forecast by a "railroad company" resonates with the employment of Chinese workers (particularly for more dangerous jobs) in the construction of the transcontinental railroad, and the extension of the file of human skeletons into the Pacific invokes the U.S.-Philippine War and Boxer "relief" expedition as well as the twentieth-century geographies of violence for which these would pave the way throughout the Pacific. Although they span diverse historical, legal, and discursive contexts of racialization, Twain's analogies between Leopold's atrocities and the histories of slavery, railroad labor, and transpacific imperialism are grounded in death rates: all these scenarios are sustained by racialized populations rendered vulnerable to premature death.

Twain's body counts—and the statistically informed monuments he develops from them—return us to the title of his great protest essay, "To the Person Sitting in Darkness," and to the title of this book. Twain derives the figure of the person sitting in darkness from Matthew 4:16, which presents Christ's preachings as a fulfillment of Isaiah's prophecy: "The people which sat in darkness saw great light; and to them which sat in the region and shadow of death light is sprung up."[73] If—as Twain's comparative colonial demographic data suggest—imperialism requires premature deaths and population reduction, then America's civilizing project does not shed a "great light" so much as it propagates a "region and shadow of death" across the colonized world. Like Hank Morgan's figuration of modernity's light as a "serene volcano" with "rising hell in its bowels" (*CY*, 51), Western efforts to civilize Filipinos, Chinese, Africans, and other groups invert Isaiah's prophecy by exposing nonwhite populations to darkness, captivity, civil death, and physical death. Twain deploys statistics to measure the depopulating effects of American and European incursions upon "the person sitting in darkness"—and he imagines extravagant allegorical monuments to visually represent those losses.

Twain's May 1901 poem "My Last Thought," whose comparative and historical implications have recently been illuminated by Susan Harris,[74] points toward one further way of understanding Twain's figure of the person sitting in darkness. Twain placed the poem in his copy of *An Eagle Flight* (1900)—an English-language version of José Rizal's great Filipino nationalist novel, *Noli Me Tangere* (1886). The poem's title echoes Rizal's farewell poem, "Mi Ultimo Adiós" (translated as "My Last Thought"), written on the eve of his execution by the Spanish colonial government in 1896 and included in the book's introduction. Rizal's poem apostrophizes the Philippines as the "Pearl of the Orient seas!" and proclaims the joy with which he gives his life for his country alongside other martyred patriots. Serving as a kind of literary monument to its author, "My Last Thought" proclaims that Rizal will become one with the nation: "I shall be air in thy streets, and I shall be space in thy meadows. / I shall be vibrant speech in thine ears, shall be fragrance and color, / Light and shout, and loved song forever repeating my message."[75] Twain's own rendering of "My Last Thought"—which on at least one occasion he read aloud along with Rizal's poem[76]—provides a stark counterpoint to Rizal's. Twain's speaker is a U.S. president who, in his dying moments, regrets his decision to wage a war of conquest that betrayed his nation's principles, produced starving widows and orphans, and crowned his head with "this poor tin glory . . . of World-Power, Conqueror of helpless tribes, / Extinguisher of struggling liberties!"[77] Like many of Twain's responses to the U.S.-Philippine War, the poem includes an allegorical vision: the American flag, but with a "Skull & Bones" in place of the stars, red bars "soaked with guiltless blood," and the "White Bars [turned] Black."[78] Where Rizal's poem memorializes its author and foresees him transfigured into the nation's "fragrance and color, / *Light* and shout, and loved song,"[79] Twain's speaker looks forward to being forgotten: "The night of Death is come: / Its shadows deepen—let me sleep. . . . / Sleep & forget, sleep and be forgotten."[80] Like Twain's early sketch "John Chinaman in New York," "My Last Thought" presents a dual portrait, juxtaposing a U.S. president with a Filipino hero in order to invite comparisons across national and racial boundaries. The poetic diptych formed by Twain and Rizal's poems counteracts ideological notions of Asiatic inarticulacy (evident, for example, in Twain's early poem, "The Mysterious Chinaman"[81]) by staging a disgraced American president and a prominent American author mimicking (and falling short of) the eloquence of a Filipino martyr. The speaker of Rizal's poem is more articulate and principled—more "civilized," by U.S. standards—than Twain's speaker, who ultimately regrets that he has betrayed his nation's trust. Whereas Rizal envisions himself transmuted into "Light," Twain's poem concludes with the American president sitting in darkness, longing for oblivion. As Harris puts it in her discussion of "To the Person Sitting in Darkness," "Suddenly the phrase 'people who sit in darkness' points not to the pagan world but to Americans themselves, people who, like Twain, believe that the United States is somehow different from other nations. To sit in darkness is to refuse to recognize that America's actions have destroyed its ideals."[82] Like his imaginary monuments to unmourned deaths, this pair of poems inverts imperial historiography by memorializing the conditions of colonized subjects and anti-imperialist heroes while withholding honor (and even a name) from the dying president.

Conclusion

Post-racial Twain?

In 2011, Alan Gribben's NewSouth edition of *Tom Sawyer* and *Huckleberry Finn* sparked widespread debates about censorship, racially offensive language, and the ways in which we read and teach literature by replacing the terms "nigger," "Injun," and "half-breed" with "slave," "Indian," and "half-blood" throughout Twain's novels. Whereas Gribben believes that the expurgated edition makes the books more palatable to a broader audience and more appropriate for schoolchildren, critics have noted that the redacted racial slurs convey important literary effects and historical context, for example by stressing how difficult it is for Huck to overcome racial antipathies he has absorbed from his family, friends, and teachers. In his commentary on the edition, the anthropologist John L. Jackson, Jr., warns that "de-niggerizing *Huckleberry Finn* . . . might just give us all an inflated sense of protection from the most dishonorable aspects of our nation's history." Linking the NewSouth edition's historical obfuscations to contemporary efforts to forget historically sedimented racial inequalities, Jackson adds: "Is this what we mean by post-racial?"[1]

However, the NewSouth edition doesn't fully purge U.S. history of racism—it only does away with the racial slurs. While the epithets in question were deeply entangled with social, psychological, and legal aspects of racism, Twain's incisive stagings of structural racism retain much of their force even after Gribben's substitutions. The NewSouth edition's post-racial substitutions remind us that there are two interconnected critiques of racism in Twain's works: a critique of racial prejudice that loses its force when pejorative terms are excised, and a critique of racially uneven vulnerabilities that has much less to do with racial slurs. To the extent that the restricted movement, prolonged captivity, and vulnerability of "slave" Jim and "Indian" Joe remain intelligible after the language of racial antipathy has been removed, the NewSouth edition of *Tom Sawyer* and *Huckleberry Finn* allegorizes how racial legislation and customs function even in the absence of prejudicial intent. In a recent monograph on *Illegal Migrations and the Huckleberry Finn Problem*, the immigration scholar John Park sees in *Huckleberry Finn*, not a problem unique to black/white relations in the antebellum or post-Reconstruction South, but a moral and legal dilemma pertaining to the structural violence imposed upon contemporary "illegal" migrants.[2] The argument of *Sitting in Darkness* has been that Twain's accounts of structural racism frequently hinge upon such implicit or explicit cross-racial comparisons—not least because racialization in his era functioned through shifting processes of comparison and differentiation. Although Twain's comparative vision of race relations was limited in many respects (for example, in his occasional deployment of minstrelsy, yellowface, settler colonial hostility toward Native Americans, and the rhetoric of American exceptionalism), his writings consistently interrogate how structural inequalities reproduce racial hierarchies—how uneven access to testimony, mobility in public space, biometric surveillance, literary representations of civilizational capacity, monuments, and public mourning imposed a range of vulnerabilities on different racialized groups. In addition to offering some of his era's most complex literary accounts of anti-Chinese discrimination, Twain's career-long archive of writings about U.S. relations with Asia provides important points of comparison with his more familiar critiques of antiblack racism and European colonialism.

Of course, Twain was not the only postbellum author who tracked processes of comparative racialization across geographical regions and scales, linking the antebellum South with the multiracial spaces of the U.S. West and the imperial contexts of the "American Pacific." Nor was he alone in his commitment to dramatizing how the legal apparatuses and cultural imaginary of his era consigned racialized populations to various forms of representational and civil "darkness." Literary scholars have shown, for example, that racialized access to mobility and public space play pivotal roles in narratives by Bret Harte, Helen Hunt Jackson, John Rollin Ridge, George Washington Cable, and Charles Chesnutt; similarly, W. E. B. Du Bois's engagements with Asia, Sui Sin Far's

"The Alaska Widow," Winifred Eaton's *A Japanese Blossom*, and Jack London's diverse narratives of racial difference explore a range of transpacific and cross-racial affiliations and distinctions.[3]

However, Twain is distinguished by the depth and consistency with which his experiments with literary form engage with specific cross-racial comparisons. His works highlight and compare instances of racialized access and vulnerability through narrative interruptions and apparently inexplicable scenes—for example, the temporary appearance of Plunkett in *Ah Sin*, the captivity chapters of *Huck Finn*, the formerly conjoined texts of *Pudd'nhead* and *Twins*, the concluding massacre of *A Connecticut Yankee*, ekphrastic descriptions of numerically oriented monuments in "To the Person Sitting in Darkness" and *King Leopold's Soliloquy*. By deploying literary form to dramatize the legal and material mechanisms of comparative racialization, Twain serves as an important precursor for twentieth and twenty-first century authors working to represent and expose more recent incarnations of structural racism. Insofar as his formal experiments call for readings grounded in historical accounts of comparative racialization, Twain also challenges literary scholars to develop modes of reading adequate to the historical complexities of both his era and our own. Since it requires attention to the uneven access and vulnerability imposed upon different groups, a reading method that focuses on comparative racialization is also well adapted to interrogating contemporary forms of "post-racial" racism. Twain's writings about Asia and transpacific migration do not just prefigure contemporary concerns such as immigration reform, overseas imperialism, and China's rapid economic growth—they also illuminate issues of structural inequality that extend through the eras of Jim Crow, Civil Rights, and multiculturalism into the present and future predicaments of a nation that is at once racially stratified and immersed in "post-racial" rhetoric.

Notes

BIBLIOGRAPHIC ABBREVIATIONS USED IN NOTES AND TEXT

AS Mark Twain and Bret Harte, Ah Sin, in *The Chinese Other, 1850–1925: An Anthology of Plays*, ed. Dave Williams (Lanham, Md.: University Press of America, 1997).

"CMM" Mark Twain, "Comments on the Moro Massacre," in *Mark Twain's Weapons of Satire*, ed. Jim Zwick (Syracuse, N.Y.: Syracuse University Press, 1992).

CY Mark Twain, *A Connecticut Yankee in King Arthur's Court*, ed. Allison Ensor (New York: Norton, 1982).

"DP" Mark Twain, "Disgraceful Persecution of a Boy," in *The Complete Essays of Mark Twain*, ed. Charles Neider (Cambridge, Mass.: Da Capo Press, 1991).

ET Mark Twain, *Those Extraordinary Twins*, in *Pudd'nhead Wilson and Those Extraordinary Twins*, ed. Sidney E. Berger (New York: Norton, 2005).

FE Mark Twain, *Following the Equator* (Hartford, Conn.: American Publishing Co., 1898).

"GF" Mark Twain, "Goldsmith's Friend Abroad Again," in *Collected Tales, Sketches, Speeches, and Essays, 1852–1890*, ed. Louis Budd (New York: Library of America, 1992).

HF Mark Twain, *Adventures of Huckleberry Finn*, ed. Thomas Cooley (New York: Norton, 1999).

"PS" Mark Twain, "To the Person Sitting in Darkness," in *Mark Twain's Weapons of Satire: Anti-imperialist Writings on the Philippine-American War*, ed. Jim Zwick (Syracuse, N.Y.: Syracuse University Press, 1992).

PW Mark Twain, "Pudd'nhead Wilson" and "Those Extraordinary Twins," ed. Sidney Berger (New York: Norton, 2005).

TS Mark Twain, *The Adventures of Tom Sawyer*, ed. Shelley Fisher Fishkin (New York: Oxford University Press, 1996).

"TVT" Bret Harte, "Three Vagabonds of Trinidad," in *The Luck of Roaring Camp and Other Writings*, ed. Gary Scharnhorst (New York: Penguin, 2001).

"YT" Mark Twain, "The Fable of the Yellow Terror," in *The Devil's Race-Track: Mark Twain's Great Dark Writings*, ed. John S. Tuckey (Berkeley: University of California Press, 1980).

INTRODUCTION

1. Mark Twain, *Mark Twain's Adventures of Tom Sawyer* and *Huckleberry Finn*, ed. Alan Gribben (Montgomery, Ala.: NewSouth, 2011).
2. For a striking selection of international authors' responses to Twain, see Shelley Fisher Fishkin, ed., *The Mark Twain Anthology: Great Writers on His Life and Work* (New York: Library of America, 2010).
3. See Toni Morrison, *Playing in the Dark: Whiteness and the Literary Imagination* (Cambridge, Mass.: Harvard University Press, 1992), 54–57, on blackness in *Huck Finn*; Susan Gillman and Forrest Glen Robinson, eds., *Mark Twain's Pudd'nhead Wilson: Race, Conflict, and Culture* (Durham, N.C.: Duke University Press, 1990), on race in *Pudd'nhead Wilson*; and John Carlos Rowe, *Literary Culture and U.S. Imperialism: From the Revolution to World War II* (New York: Oxford University Press, 2000), and Amy Kaplan, *The Anarchy of Empire in the Making of U.S. Culture* (Cambridge, Mass.: Harvard University Press, 2002), on empire in Twain's work.
4. Morrison, *Playing in the Dark*, 54.
5. See Joseph Coulombe, *Mark Twain and the American West* (Columbia: University of Missouri Press, 2003); and Roy Morris, Jr., *Lighting Out for the Territory: How Samuel Clemens Headed West and Became Mark Twain* (New York: Simon & Schuster, 2010).
6. Lawrence De Graaf and Quintard Taylor, "Introduction: African Americans in California History, California in African American History," in *Seeking El Dorado: African Americans in California*, ed. Lawrence De Graaf, Kevin Mulroy, and Quintard Taylor (Los Angeles: Autry Museum of Western Heritage, 2001), 10.
7. *The Statutes of California Passed at the First Session of the Legislature* (San José: J. Winchester, State Printer, 1850), 230.
8. *People v. Hall*, 4 Cal. 339 (1854).
9. Joshua Paddison, *American Heathens: Religion, Race, and Reconstruction in California* (Berkeley: University of California Press, 2012), 6.
10. Forrest Robinson, "Mark Twain, 1835–1910: A Brief Biography," in *A Historical Guide to Mark Twain*, edited by Shelley Fisher Fishkin (Oxford: Oxford University Press, 2002), 38.
11. Shelley Fisher Fishkin, "Mark Twain and Race," in Fishkin, ed., *Historical Guide*, 135.
12. Martin Zehr, "Mark Twain, 'The Treaty with China,' and the Chinese Connection," *Journal of Transnational American Studies* 2, no. 1 (2010): 8, http://escholarship.org/uc/item/5t02n321.
13. See Ruth Wilson Gilmore, *Golden Gulag: Prisons, Surplus, Crisis, and Opposition in Globalizing California* (Berkeley: University of California Press, 2007), 28.
14. Lao emphasizes Twain's support of "the Chinese people's fierce struggle against imperialist aggression" and singles out his 1868 article "The Treaty with China,"

which was only recently rediscovered and reprinted by Martin Zehr in 2010. See Lao She, "Mark Twain: Exposer of the 'Dollar Empire,'" in Fishkin, ed., *The Mark Twain Anthology*, 284.
15. Margaret Duckett, *Mark Twain and Bret Harte* (Norman: University of Oklahoma Press, 1964), 57.
16. Zehr, "Mark Twain," 7.
17. Fishkin, "Mark Twain and Race," 136.
18. Colleen Lye, "The Afro-Asian Analogy," *PMLA* 123, no. 5 (October 2008): 1734.
19. Alexander Saxton, *The Indispensable Enemy: Labor and the Anti-Chinese Movement in California* (Berkeley: University of California Press, 1971), quoted in Lye, "The Afro-Asian Analogy," 1734.
20. *People v. Hall*.
21. On nineteenth-century uses of the term "coolie" in the United States, see Moon-ho Jung, "Coolie," in *Keywords for American Cultural Studies*, ed. Bruce Burgett and Glenn Hendler (New York: NYU Press, 2007), 64: "Represented as a coerced and submissive labor force by anti- and proslavery forces alike, 'coolies' came to embody slavery in the age of emancipation."
22. Morrison, *Playing in the Dark*, 6.
23. Lisa Lowe, "The Intimacies of Four Continents," in *Haunted by Empire: Geographies of Intimacy in North American History*, ed. Ann Laura Stoler (Durham, N.C.: Duke University Press, 2006), 195.
24. Moon-Ho Jung, *Coolies and Cane: Race, Labor, and Sugar in the Age of Emancipation* (Baltimore: Johns Hopkins University Press, 2006), 9.
25. Colleen Lye, *America's Asia: Racial Form and American Literature, 1893–1945* (Princeton, N.J.: Princeton University Press, 2004), 11.
26. Jung, *Coolies and Cane*, 76.
27. Lowe, "The Intimacies of Four Continents," 195.
28. Julia H. Lee, *Interracial Encounters: Reciprocal Representations in African and Asian American Literatures, 1896–1937* (New York: NYU Press, 2011), 2.
29. Helen Heran Jun, *Race for Citizenship: Black Orientalism and Asian Uplift from Pre-Emancipation to Neoliberal America* (New York: NYU Press, 2011), 15–31.
30. See Heike Raphael-Hernandez and Shannon Steen, eds., *AfroAsian Encounters: Culture, History, Politics* (New York: NYU Press, 2006).
31. For a broader view of culturally oriented work in the field of comparative racialization, see Shu-Mei Shih, ed., "Comparative Racialization," special issue of *PMLA* 123, no. 5 (October 2008); and Grace Kyungwon Hong and Roderick A. Ferguson, eds., *Strange Affinities: The Gender and Sexual Politics of Comparative Racialization* (Durham, N.C.: Duke University Press, 2011).
32. Mark Twain, "Sandwich Islands Lecture," in *Mark Twain Speaking*, ed. Paul Fatout (Iowa City: University of Iowa Press, 1976), 4–14.
33. Twain's optimistic tone concerning Hawai'i's sugar plantations can be explained by the *Sacramento Union*'s "clearly defined goals to promote California's economic interest in the growing sugar industry and to market the islands as

accessible to American travel and business and equally available to popular knowledge and fantasy" (Kaplan, *The Anarchy of Empire*, 61).

34. Mark Twain, *Mark Twain's Letters from Hawaii*, ed. A. Grove Day (Honolulu: University of Hawaii Press, 1975), 271–272. See also William Speer, *The Oldest and the Newest Empire* (Hartford: S.S. Scranton & Co., 1870), 667: "The chief dependence of these products and exports is based upon Chinese labor.... In the Sandwich Islands is illustrated a course of things which will be repeated successively in time all over the numerous island groups and upon the shores and in the interior of America and elsewhere in the world."
35. Twain, *Mark Twain's Letters from Hawaii*, 273.
36. Ibid., 274.
37. Ibid.
38. William G. Robbins, *Colony and Empire: The Capitalist Transformation of the American West* (Lawrence: University Press of Kansas, 1994), 3.
39. Gray Brechin, *Imperial San Francisco: Urban Power, Earthly Ruin* (Berkeley: University of California Press, 2006), 16.
40. Twain, *Mark Twain's Letters from Hawaii*, 274.
41. Saxton, *The Indispensable Enemy*, 7.
42. On Twain's frequently disparaging representations of Native Americans, see Helen Harris, "Mark Twain's Response to the Native American," *American Literature* 46, no. 4 (January 1975): 495–505; and James McNutt, "Mark Twain and the American Indian: Earthly Realism and Heavenly Idealism," *American Indian Quarterly* 4, no. 3 (August 1978): 223–242.
43. Writing about the early twentieth century, Julia Lee explains: "My justification for looking at this particular relationship as it played out through African American and Asian American works is rooted in the extent and depth to which the two groups were paired with or pitted against each other *in this period*" (*Interracial Encounters*, 13).
44. Jung, *Coolies and Cane*, 7.
45. See Jean Pfaelzer, *Driven Out: The Forgotten War against Chinese Americans* (Berkeley: University of California Press, 2007), xi.
46. Richard A. Walker, "California's Golden Road to Riches: Natural Resources and Regional Capitalism, 1848–1940," *Annals of the Association of American Geographers* 91, no. 1 (March 2001): 180. See also Robbins, *Colony and Empire*.
47. Mark Twain, *The Works of Mark Twain: Early Tales and Sketches*, vol. 2: 1864–1865, ed. Edgar Marquess Branch, Robert H. Hirst, and Harriet Elinor Smith (Berkeley: University of California Press, 1981), 62.
48. Ibid., 62.
49. Ibid., 64–65.
50. Ibid., 64.
51. Albert Bigelow Paine, *Mark Twain, a Biography: The Personal and Literary Life of Samuel Langhorne Clemens* (New York: Harper, 1912), 255–256.
52. "California's Dull," poem attributed to Mark Twain, in *On the Poetry of Mark Twain: With Selections from His Verse*, ed. Arthur Lincoln Scott (Urbana:

University of Illinois Press, 1966), 69. First published in the *Buffalo Express*, this poem is included in a section of the newspaper that Twain enclosed in an August 19, 1869, letter to Olivia L. Langdon (reprinted as "Letter to Olivia L. Langdon, Appendix B" in *Mark Twain's Letters*, ed. Victor Fischer and Michael Frank [Berkeley: University of California Press, 1992], 3:469).

53. *Daily Morning Call* (July 12, August 30, 1864).
54. For an extensive analysis of this text, see Cynthia Wu, "The Siamese Twins in Late-Nineteenth-Century Narratives of Conflict and Reconciliation," *American Literature* 80, no. 1 (2008): 29–55.
55. Mark Twain, *The Autobiography of Mark Twain*, ed. Charles Neider (New York: Harper Perennial, 1990), 157.
56. Morris, *Lighting Out for the Territory*, 157.
57. Burlingame's successor, J. Ross Browne, invited Twain to China in 1868 to "take a lucrative position on his staff," and Twain claimed that he planned to accept the offer. Ou suggests that Browne's opposition to Burlingame's policies may have dissuaded Twain from taking the position in China. Hsin-yun Ou, "Mark Twain, Anson Burlingame, Joseph Hopkins Twichell, and the Chinese," *Ariel: A Review of International English Literature* 42, no. 2 (2012): 50.
58. Mark Twain, "The Treaty with China: Its Provisions Explained," *Journal of Transnational American Studies* 2, no.1 (2010): 10, http://escholarship.org/uc/item/2r87m2o3.
59. "Although many offenders of importance go unpunished, they infallibly snaffle every Chinese chicken-thief that attempts to drive his trade, and are duly glorified by name in the papers for it?" (Mark Twain, "What Have the Police Been Doing?" *San Francisco Golden Era* 14 (January 21, 1866): 5).
60. Twain, "The Treaty with China," 4.
61. Ibid., 6.
62. Mark Twain, "John Chinaman in New York," in *The Complete Humorous Sketches and Tales of Mark Twain*, ed. Charles Neider (Cambridge, Mass.: Da Capo Press, 1996), 134, 135. This story may allude to a series of caricatures published the previous year as "John Chinaman in San Francisco," *Harper's Weekly* 13 (1869): 439.
63. Twain, "John Chinaman in New York," 135.
64. For an extended reading of the ambivalence of ethnic caricature in this sketch, see Henry B. Wonham, *Playing the Races: Ethnic Caricature and American Literary Realism* (New York: Oxford University Press, 2004), 78–81.
65. Mark Twain, *Roughing It,* ed. Harriet Elinor Smith and Edgar Marquess Branch (Berkeley: University of California Press, 1993), 369.
66. Lye, "The Afro-Asian Analogy," 56.
67. Mark Twain, *Following the Equator* (Hartford, Conn.: American Publishing Co., 1898). Further references will be cited parenthetically in the text as *FE*.
68. The passage from *Roughing It* ("if the government sells a gang of Coolies to a foreigner for a five-year term . . . ") is a revision of a passage from "The Treaty

with China," which focuses on "coolies" outside the United States: "Even the contracts which consign the wretched Coolies to slavery at $5 a month salary and two suits of clothes a year stipulate that if he dies in Cuba, the Sandwich Islands, or any other foreign land, his body must be sent home" (Twain, *Roughing It*, 372, and "The Treaty with China," 6).

69. Mark Twain, "Concerning the Jews," in *The Complete Essays of Mark Twain*, ed. Charles Neider (Cambridge, Mass.: Da Capo Press, 1991), 242.
70. Mark Twain, "The Fable of the Yellow Terror," in *The Devil's Race-Track: Mark Twain's Great Dark Writings*, ed. John S. Tuckey (Berkeley: University of California Press, 1980), 369–372.
71. Jim Zwick, introduction to *Mark Twain's Weapons of Satire: Anti-imperialist Writings on the Philippine-American War*, ed. Jim Zwick (Syracuse, N.Y.: Syracuse University Press, 1992), xvii.
72. Mark Twain, "To My Missionary Critics," in Neider, ed., *The Complete Essays of Mark Twain*, 296–311.
73. Mark Twain, "The United States of Lyncherdom," in Neider, ed., *The Complete Essays of Mark Twain*, 679.
74. Mark Twain, "Public Education Association. Address at a Meeting of the Berkeley Lyceum, New York, Nov. 23, 1900," in *Mark Twain's Speeches*, ed. William Dean Howells (New York: Harper & Bros., 1910), 145.
75. Mark Twain, "The Chronicle of Young Satan," in *The Mysterious Stranger Manuscripts*, ed. William Gibson (Berkeley: University of California Press, 2005), 136, 137.
76. Mark Twain, *The Adventures of Tom Sawyer*, ed. Shelley Fisher Fishkin (New York: Oxford University Press, 1996), *The Adventures of Huckleberry Finn*, ed. Thomas Cooley (New York: Norton, 1999), *A Connecticut Yankee in King Arthur's Court*, ed. Allison Ensor (New York: Norton, 1982), and *"Pudd'nhead Wilson" and "Those Extraordinary Twins,"* ed. Sidney Berger (New York: Norton, 2005).
77. Bret Harte, "Three Vagabonds of Trinidad," in *The Luck of Roaring Camp and Other Writings*, ed. Gary Scharnhorst (New York: Penguin, 2001), 155–167.
78. *Santa Clara County v. Southern Pacific R. Co.*, 118 U.S. 394 (1886).
79. Wong Chin Foo, *Wu Chih Tien, The Celestial Empress: A Chinese Historical Novel*, published in installments in *Cosmopolitan*: 6, no. 4 (February 1889): 327–334; 6, no. 5 (March 1889): 477–485; 6, no. 6 (April 1889): 564–572; 7, no. 1 (May 1889): 65–72; 7, no. 2 (June 1889): 128–132; 7, no. 3 (July 1889): 289–299; 7, no. 4 (August 1889): 361–368; 7, no. 5 (September 1889): 449–459.

CHAPTER 1. "A WITNESS MORE POWERFUL THAN HIMSELF"

1. Mark Twain and Bret Harte, *Ah Sin*, in *The Chinese Other, 1850–1925: An Anthology of Plays*, ed. Dave Williams (Lanham, Md.: University Press of America, 1997), 69. Further references to this edition will be cited parenthetically in the text as *AS*.
2. For example, a piece titled "chinese oaths" in the "General Intelligence" section of the Albany magazine the *Country Gentleman* claims that "the Chinese, when

brought into court as witnesses in California, are sworn in the manner peculiar to their country. An oath, written in Chinese characters upon tissue paper, is subscribed with their names, and burned to ashes. The purport of the oath is, that, if the witness does not tell the truth, he hopes that his soul may be burned and destroyed as is the paper which he holds in his hands. Notwithstanding the severity of this oath, the evidence of the Chinese taken in court is not generally of a very reliable character" ("chinese oaths," *Country Gentleman* 3, no. 1 [January 4, 1853]: 66).

3. William Speer, *An Answer to the Common Objections to Chinese Testimony; and an Earnest Appeal to the Legislature of California, for Their Protection by our Law* (San Francisco: Chinese Mission House, 1857), 13.
4. John R. Wunder, "Chinese in Trouble: Criminal Law and Race on the Trans-Mississippi West Frontier," *Western Historical Quarterly* 17, no. 1 (January 1986): 33.
5. Charles J. McClain, *In Search of Equality: The Chinese Struggle against Discrimination in Nineteenth-Century America* (Berkeley: University of California Press, 1994), 22–23.
6. *People v. Hall*, 4 Cal. 399 (1854).
7. Ibid.
8. John Durham Peters, *Courting the Abyss: Free Speech and the Liberal Tradition* (Chicago: University of Chicago Press, 2005), 254, 255.
9. Najia Aarim-Heriot, *Chinese Immigrants, African Americans, and Racial Anxiety in the United States, 1848–82* (Urbana: University of Illinois Press, 2003), 38.
10. *People v. Hall*.
11. Eric Hayot, *The Hypothetical Mandarin: Sympathy, Modernity, and Chinese Pain* (New York: Oxford University Press, 2009), 45.
12. On Chinese invasion narratives such as Pierton W. Dooner's *The Last Days of the Republic* (1880), Arthur Vinton's *Looking Further Backward* (1890), and Jack London's "The Unparalleled Invasion" (1910), see ibid., 135–171; and Edlie Wong, "In a Future Tense: Immigration Law, Counterfactual Histories, and Chinese Invasion Fiction," *American Literary History* (in press).
13. Initially a monthly tax of three dollars, the amount was increased to "four dollars in 1853 and six dollars in 1855, with a two dollar increase each year thereafter" (See Jean Pfaelzer, *Driven Out: The Forgotten War aAgainst Chinese Americans* [(Berkeley: University of California Press, 2007], 31). "Between 1852 and 1870, years in which one billion dollars' worth of *untaxed* gold was mined in California, Chinese miners paid a staggering fifty-eight million dollars to the state, ranging from one fourth to one half of California's revenue" (ibid., 31). Okihiro notes that "from 1855 to 1870 all authorities concede that the Chinese paid practically the whole of the tax." (Gary Y. Okihiro, *The Columbia Guide to Asian American History* [New York: Columbia University Press, 2001], 81).
14. Sucheng Chan, "A People of Exceptional Character: Ethnic Diversity, Nativism, and Racism in the California Gold Rush," in *Rooted in Barbarous Soil: People,*

Culture, and Community in Gold Rush California," ed. Kevin Starr and Richard J. Orsi (Berkeley: University of California Press, 2000), 76.

15. Speer, *An Answer to the Common Objections*, 14. Even Speer qualifies his endorsement of Chinese testimony, suggesting that the state restrict it to Asiatics who show "that they comprehend the responsibility of an oath" and their capability of memory and mind and that "their testimony shall not be received as conclusive evidence of the facts sworn to by them, except so far as the same may be confirmed by circumstantial evidence, or corroborated by the testimony of other witnesses" (ibid., 8).

16. William Speer, *An Humble Plea, Addressed to the Legislature of California, in Behalf of the Immigrants from the Empire of China to this State* (San Francisco: Office of the Oriental, 1856), 32. Twain enumerates several of these abuses by Foreign Miners' Tax collectors in "The Treaty with China: Its Provisions Explained" (*Journal of Transnational American Studies* 2, no.1 [2010]: 7, http://escholarship.org/uc/item/2r87m203), and *Roughing It* (ed. Harriet Elinor Smith and Edgar Marquess Branch [Berkeley: University of California Press, 1993], 370).

17. Aarim-Heriot, *Chinese Immigrants*, 45.

18. Speer, *An Humble Plea*, 36.

19. Ibid., 37.

20. Speer, *An Answer to the Common Objections*, 12.

21. Ibid., 15.

22. Lai Chun-chuen, *Remarks of the Chinese Merchants of San Francisco, upon Governor John Bigler's Message and some Common Objections,* trans. William Speer (San Francisco: Whitton, Towne, & Co., 1855), 5.

23. Pun Chi, "A Remonstrance from the Chinese in California to the Congress of the United States," trans. William Speer (1868), in *The Oldest and the Newest Empire: China and the United States* by William Speer (Cincinnati: National Publishing Co., 1870): 595.

24. Ibid., 600.

25. Frederick Douglass, "Our Composite Nationality: An Address Delivered in Boston, Massachusetts, on 7 December 1869," in *The Frederick Douglass Papers*, ser. 1: *Speeches, Debates, and Interviews*, vol. 4: *1864–1880,* ed. John Blassingame and John McKivigan (New Haven, Conn.: Yale University Press, 1991), 257.

26. Ibid., 258.

27. Ibid.

28. *People of the State of California v. Brady*, 40 Cal. 198 (1870). Italics added.

29. Attributed to Mark Twain: "In Bad Company," *San Francisco Daily Morning Call* (September 7, 1864): 3, "Discharged," *San Francisco Daily Morning Call* (September 10, 1864): 3, and "The Battered Chinaman Case," *San Francisco Daily Morning Call* (September 11, 1864): 3. These attributions are from Edgar Branch, *Clemens of the "Call": Mark Twain in San Francisco* (Berkeley: University of California Press, 1969); and Barbara Schmidt, "*San Francisco Daily Morning*

Call, 1863–1864," *Mark Twain Quotations, Newspaper Collections, and Related Resources,* www.twainquotes.com/callindex.html.
30. Attributed to Mark Twain, "Astonishing Freak of Nature," *San Francisco Daily Morning Call* (July 22, 1864): 3; attribution by Branch, *Clemens of the "Call."*
31. Attributed to Mark Twain, "Police Court," *San Francisco Daily Morning Call* (September 18, 1864): 3, attribution by Schmidt, "*San Francisco Daily Morning Call, 1863–1864.*"
32. Forrest Robinson, "Mark Twain, 1835–1910: A Brief Biography," in *A Historical Guide to Mark Twain,* edited by Shelley Fisher Fishkin (Oxford: Oxford University Press, 2002), 38.
33. Mark Twain, "Disgraceful Persecution of a Boy," in *The Complete Essays of Mark Twain,* ed. Charles Neider (Cambridge, Mass.: Da Capo Press, 1991), 9, 9n2. Further references will be cited parenthetically in the text as "DP."
34. *Scott v. Sandford,* 60 U.S. 407 (1856).
35. "To string *incongruities* and absurdities together in a wandering and sometimes purposeless way, and seem innocently unaware that they are absurdities, is the basis of the American art [of story-telling]" (Mark Twain, "How to Tell a Story," in *How to Tell a Story and Other Essays* [Hartford, Conn.: American Publishing Co., 1901], 11, emphasis added).
36. "Strangely enough, this third and best *Galaxy* satire attacking abuse of Chinese is the only one not republished in the authorized edition of MT's writings" (Margaret Duckett, *Mark Twain and Bret Harte* [Norman: University of Oklahoma Press, 1964], 55).
37. See my discussion of this incident in the Introduction.
38. Mark Twain, "Goldsmith's Friend Abroad Again," in *Collected Tales, Sketches, Speeches, and Essays, 1852–1890,* ed. Louis Budd (New York: Library of America, 1992), 459. Further references will be cited parenthetically in the text as "GF."
39. Twain, *Roughing It,* 369.
40. Duckett, *Twain and Harte,* 57.
41. *Autobiography of Mark Twain,* ed. Charles Neider (New York: Harper, 1990), 165. For an extended account of Harte's poem and his work as editor of *Overland Monthly,* see Tara Penry, "The Chinese in Bret Harte's *Overland*: A Context for Truthful James," *American Literary Realism* 43, no. 1 (Fall 2010): 74–82.
42. Axel Nissen, *Bret Harte: Prince and Pauper* (Jackson: University Press of Mississippi, 2000), 111.
43. Bret Harte, "The Iliad of Sandy Bar," in *The Luck of Roaring Camp and Other Writings,* ed. Gary Scharnhorst (New York: Penguin Books, 2001), 87.
44. Ibid.
45. Bret Harte, "Wan Lee, the Pagan," in Scharnhorst, ed., *The Luck of Roaring Camp and Other Writings,* 137.
46. Profits from the play were to be split three ways between Parsloe and the two authors.
47. See Eric Lott, *Love and Theft: Blackface Minstrelsy and the American Working Class* (New York: Oxford University Press, 1995), 30–35.

48. Ibid., 6.
49. Mark Twain, "Curtain Speech. Opening of *Ah Sin*, Fifth Avenue Theatre, New York, July 31, 1877," in *Mark Twain Speaking*, ed. Paul Fatout (Iowa City: University of Iowa Press, 1976), 103–105.
50. "Amusements. Fifth Avenue Theatre," *New York Times* (August 1, 1877), 5; and "'Ah Sin' at the Fifth Avenue Theatre," *New York Herald* (August 1, 1877).
51. Trinculo, "Causerie," *New York Spirit of the Times* (August 4, 1877).
52. "Amusements. Ah Sin," *New York Sun* (August 5, 1877).
53. Sean Metzger, "Charles Parsloe's Chinese Fetish: An Example of Yellowface Performance in Nineteenth-Century American Melodrama," *Theatre Journal* 56, no. 4 (December 2004): 643.
54. Dave Williams, *Misreading the Chinese Character: Images of the Chinese in Euroamerican Drama to 1925*, Asian Thought and Culture no. 40 (New York: Peter Lang, 2000), 113.
55. Trinculo, "Causerie."
56. Jerry Thomason, "*Ah Sin: The Heathen Chinee*," in *The Mark Twain Encyclopedia*, ed. J. R. LeMaster and James D. Wilson (New York: Routledge, 2011), 17.
57. Harold K. Bush, Jr., "'A Moralist in Disguise: Mark Twain and American Religion," in Fishkin, *Historical Guide*, 91n63.
58. James Moy, *Marginal Sights: Staging the Chinese in America* (Iowa City: University of Iowa Press, 1993), 31; Hsin-yun Ou, "Mark Twain, Anson Burlingame, Joseph Hopkins Twichell, and the Chinese," *Ariel: A Review of International English Literature* 42, no. 2 (2012): 60–61.
59. Brenda Murphy, *American Realism and American Drama, 1880–1940* (Cambridge: Cambridge University Press, 1987), 54.
60. "Amusements. Ah Sin," *New York Sun*.
61. See the discussion of *Huck Finn* in Chapter 2.
62. "His 'jabbering frantically in Chinese' provides a safety in unintelligibility and apparent stupidity that enables Ah Sin, mainly through subterfuge and trickery, to outwit his adversaries" (Randall Knoper, *Acting Naturally: Mark Twain in the Culture of Performance* [Berkeley: University of California Press, 1995], 47). A contemporary review suggests that Ah Sin's sly subterfuges appealed to some spectators: "As I watched it slowly unfold last evening, I asked, what is its object, and concluded that its crowning purpose was to display 'Ah Sin.' It was written for him—a new type of man in the American fabric, political and social—a creature at once shy and sly, reticent and talkative, cunning and amiable, weak, yet powerful, subtle as air, acute as quicksilver—a servant, a pariah, a thief, yet child of the oldest civilization on our earth—nothing short of absolute genius can depict him as he is, and he who can will outrank in special personalities Raymond or Joe Jefferson" (Mary Clemmer, "Ah Sin," *San Francisco Daily Evening Bulletin* [21 May 1877]).
63. Clemmer's review also praised Twain and Harte's courtroom farce: "The rude scenes of a far western trial, the fluctuations of the pendulous jury, the swaying

and surging of self-interest and passion, are crudely, yet powerfully, made manifest in this impromptu trial" (Clemmer, "Ah Sin").

64. See Metzger's claim that, unlike in other racial melodramas, "Ah Sin has no death scene that generates sympathy for his character; his actions, until the very end, seem motivated only by his greed and penchant for mischief" ("Parsloe's Chinese Fetish," 641).
65. Harry R. Williams, "Ah Sin. Chinese Song" (Detroit: Roe Stephens, 1877), 5, https://jscholarship.library.jhu.edu/handle/1774.2/9681?show=full.
66. Ibid.
67. "Amusements. Ah Sin"; and Clemmer, "Ah Sin."
68. Leslie Fiedler, "Come Back to the Raft Ag'in, Huck Honey!" in *Leslie Fiedler and American Culture*, ed. Steven G. Kellman and Irving Malin (Newark: University of Delaware Press, 1999): 29, 33.
69. I adapt this term from Nayan Shah, *Stranger Intimacy: Contesting Race, Sexuality and the Law in the North American West* (Berkeley: University of California Press, 2012). For another fictional treatment of intimacy between Chinese and white men, see Ambrose Bierce, "The Haunted Valley," *Overland Monthly* 7, no. 1 (1871): 88–95.
70. Metzger, "Parsloe's Chinese Fetish," 632.
71. *Ah Sin*'s poker scene significantly revises that of Harte's "Plain Language from Truthful James" by framing the Chinese character's dissimulation not as an avaricious act but as a benevolent effort to protect Plunkett from Broderick's cheating (cf. Bret Harte, "Plain Language from Truthful James," in Scharnhorst, ed., *The Luck of Roaring Camp*, 215–216).
72. According to historian Randall E. Rohe, in 1861, "Probably the peak of Chinese mining, 80 to 85 per cent of the Chinese population [of California] engaged in mining.... By 1870, Chinese accounted for over half of the total mining population and, according to one report, they accounted for three-fifths of the miners in 1873" (Randall E. Rohe, "After the Gold Rush: Chinese Mining in the Far West, 1850–1890," in *Chinese on the American Frontier*, ed. Arif Dirlik [Lanham: Rowman & Littlefield, 2001], 6).
73. On the ways in which the prohibition on testimony endangers whites, see Speer: "Cargoes of ships may be lost, trusts abused by dishonest officers or seamen, vessels detained in port, crimes committed at sea, and, with hundreds of eyewitnesses, none avail" (Speer, *An Answer to the Common Objections*, 13).
74. Plunkett's friendship with Ah Sin is contrasted with Broderick's attitudes about race and class: the play's villain, a disaffected working-class miner whose name suggests Welsh or Irish roots, clearly resents both the "gentleman capitalist" York and Ah Sin, whom he calls an "unsolvable political problem" (*AS*, 40, 46).
75. Charles J. McClain, *In Search of Equality: The Chinese Struggle against Discrimination in Nineteenth-Century America* (Berkeley: University of California Press, 1994), 42. Although *People v. Elyea*, 14 Cal. 144 (1859), undercut *People v. Hall*, 4 Cal. 399 (1854), by "determining that skin color was a fallible test of witness

competence," white Americans nevertheless turned to "economic and moral grounds" for barring Chinese from testimony and other rights (see Reynolds J. Scott-Childress, "Race, Nation, and the Rhetoric of Color: Locating Japan and China, 1870–1907," in *Race and the Production of Modern American Nationalism*, ed. Reynolds J. Scott-Childress [New York: Taylor & Francis, 1999], 7).

76. Act of 5 May 1892, Chap. 60, 27 Stat. 25 (Geary Amendment).
77. Chinese Consolidated Benevolent Association, *Memorial of the Six Chinese Companies. An Address to the Senate and House of Representatives of the United States. Testimony of California's Leading Citizens* (San Francisco: Alta Print, 1877), 2, 3.
78. Ibid., 11.
79. Russell, *Reading Embodied*, 36.
80. Ibid., 38.
81. Mark Twain, *Pudd'nhead Wilson and Those Extraordinary Twins*, ed. Berger, 120. Further references to this edition will be cited parenthetically in the text as *PW*.
82. Sarah E. Chinn, *Technology and the Logic of American Racism: A Cultural History of the Body as Evidence*, Critical Research in Material Culture (New York: Continuum, 2000), 42.
83. Alfred W. McCoy, *Policing America's Empire: The United States, the Philippines, and the Rise of the Surveillance State* (Madison: University of Wisconsin Press, 2009), 21.
84. Simon A. Cole, *Suspect Identities: A History of Fingerprinting and Criminal Identification* (Cambridge, Mass.: Harvard University Press, 2002), 124–125. I discuss the connections between fingerprint identification and Chinese Exclusion in Chapter 3.
85. See Christian Parenti, *The Soft Cage: Surveillance in America from Slavery to the War on Terror* (New York: Basic Books, 2003), 61–76.
86. Alphonse Bertillon developed a system of identification based on ten anthropometric measurements, as well as a standardized method of taking photographs from which such measurements could be derived.
87. McCoy, *Policing America's Empire*, 28.

CHAPTER 2. VAGRANCY AND COMPARATIVE RACIALIZATION

1. T. S. Eliot, "Introduction to *Adventures of Huckleberry Finn*," in *Adventures of Huckleberry Finn* by Mark Twain, ed. Thomas Cooley (New York: Norton, 1999), 354.
2. Ibid.
3. Sau-Ling Cynthia Wong, *Reading Asian American Literature: From Necessity to Extravagance* (Princeton, N.J.: Princeton University Press, 1993), 121.
4. See Gail M. Hollander, "'Subject to Control': Shifting Geographies of Race and Labour in US Sugar Agroindustry, 1930–1950," *Cultural Geographies* 13, no. 2 (April 2006): 266–292.
5. In tracking Twain's intertextual and historical references across a range of temporal, spatial, and racial contexts, I build on Fishkin's suggestion that

Huckleberry Finn reflects the late-Reconstruction context of convict-lease, when "thousands of free black men were picked up throughout the South on 'vagrancy' charges, or, if poor, on charges of 'intent to steal.'" See Shelley Fisher Fishkin, *Was Huck Black? Mark Twain and African-American Voices* (New York: Oxford University Press, 1993), 73. For other accounts of *Huckleberry Finn*'s engagement with the years in which it was composed and published, see Neil Schmitz, "Twain, *Huckleberry Finn*, and the Reconstruction," *American Studies* 12–13 (1971–1972): 59–67; Axel Nissen, "A Tramp at Home: *Huckleberry Finn*, Romantic Friendship, and the Homeless Man," *Nineteenth-Century Literature* 60 (June 2005): 57–86; Christine MacLeod, "Telling the Truth in a Tight Place: *Huckleberry Finn* and the Reconstruction Era," *Southern Quarterly* 34 (Fall 1995): 5–16; and Brook Thomas, *Civic Myths: A Law-and-Literature Approach to Citizenship* (Chapel Hill: University of North Carolina Press, 2007), 125–176.

6. Joan [Colin] Dayan, "Legal Slaves and Civil Bodies," *Nepantla: Views from South* 2, no. 1 (2001): 6.
7. See Castronovo's study of "necro citizenship" "at the edges of legal incorporation and political dispossession" (Russ Castronovo, *Necro Citizenship: Death, Eroticism, and the Public Sphere in the Nineteenth-Century United States* [Durham, N.C.: Duke University Press, 2001], 3) and Holland's discussion of the nation's intimate relationship with "the death of black subjects" (Sharon Holland, *Raising the Dead: Readings of Death and (Black) Subjectivity* [Durham, N.C.: Duke University Press, 2000], 13–40).
8. "By the time he wrote *Huckleberry Finn* . . . Twain had figured out how to use a narrator's naïve responses to the world around him to unmask the hypocrisy and pretensions of that world, a strategy with which he had begun to experiment in 1870 and 1871 in 'Goldsmith's Friend Abroad Again'" (Fishkin, *Was Huck Black?* 22). On Chinese reprintings of "Goldsmith's Friend" and other writings by Twain, see Liu Haiming, "Mark Twain in China," trans. Stephen Fleming, *Chinese Literature: Fiction Poetry Art* (Beijing: Foreign Language Press, Autumn 1987), 190.
9. Twain also invoked Goldsmith's title in his obituary to Anson Burlingame: "He had outgrown the narrow citizenship of a state and become a citizen of the world; and his charity was large enough and his great heart warm enough to feel for all its races and to labor for them" (Mark Twain, "A Tribute to Anson Burlingame," in *Mark Twain at the Buffalo Express: Articles and Sketches by America's Favorite Humorist*, ed. Joseph B. McCullough and Janice McIntire Strasburg [DeKalb: Northern Illinois University Press, 1999], 153).
10. "The myth of the Chinese coolie laborer allowed white American workers, both native-born and immigrant, to racialize a stratum of wage work equated with wage slavery while reserving for whites a semi-artisan status within the wage labor system" (Robert Lee, *Orientals: Asian Americans in Popular Culture* [Philadelphia: Temple University Press, 1999], 60–61).

11. See Twain's dissonant portrait of an Irish man dressed up as a Chinese man to advertise for a tea shop in "John Chinaman in New York," in *The Complete Humorous Sketches and Tales of Mark Twain*, ed. Charles Neider (Cambridge, Mass.: Da Capo Press, 1996), 134–135.
12. On the plundering of black graves and other racist practices by which bodies were acquired for medical experimentation, see Harriet Washington, *Medical Apartheid: The Dark History of Medical Experimentation on Black Americans from Colonial Times to the Present* (New York: Doubleday, 2006), 101–142. An outtake from *Huckleberry Finn* rediscovered in 1990 associates Jim with such practices of racially discriminatory grave robbing (or "resurrection"): in an anecdote replete with images of blackness, darkness, and the animated dead, Jim recalls an incident when a former master—a medical student—asked him to prepare a cadaver for dissection (see Mark Twain, *Adventures of Huckleberry Finn*, ed. Justin Kaplan [New York: Ballantine, 1996]: 53–55).
13. Mark Twain, *The Adventures of Tom Sawyer*, ed. Shelley Fisher Fishkin (New York: Oxford University Press, 1996), 89–90. Further references will be cited parenthetically in the text as *TS*.
14. Shirley Ann Wilson Moore, "'We Feel the Want of Protection': The Politics of Law and Race in California, 1848–1878," in *Taming the Elephant: Politics, Government, and Law in Pioneer California*, ed. John F. Burns and Richard J. Orsi (Berkeley: University of California Press, 2003), 105.
15. Ironically, the span of Joe's captivity echoes the two weeks that Tom felt himself a "prisoner" earlier in the novel while convalescing at home from the measles.
16. See Dayan's discussion of Supreme Court decisions concerning physical and psychological harm inflicted upon prison inmates: "No matter how much actual suffering is experienced by a prisoner, if the intent requirement is not met [i.e., if the damage was not intended in the prisoner's sentence as part of the punishment], then the effect on the prisoner is not a matter for judicial review" ("Legal Slaves," 26).
17. John C. Gerber, "Sources for Characters," in *The Adventures of Tom Sawyer: 135th Anniversary Edition* by Mark Twain, ed. Paul Baender (Berkeley: University of California Press, 2010), 271.
18. Mark Twain, "Horrible Affair," *Virginia City Territorial Enterprise* (April 16–18, 1863), reprinted in *Early Tales and Sketches*, vol. 1: *1851–1864*, ed. Edgar Branch and Robert Hirst (Berkeley: University of California Press, 1979), 246–247.
19. Twain, *Adventures of Huckleberry Finn*, ed. Cooley, 41. Further references to this edition will be cited parenthetically in the text as *HF*.
20. Commenting on Twain's borrowings from blackface minstrelsy, Lott writes, "Twain's sly construction of this scene so that Pap, covered with mud after a drunken night in the gutter, is actually blacker than the hated 'mulatter' free man suggests the underlying 'racial' equations between black and working-class white men that occasionally called forth in the minstrel show interracial recognitions and identifications no less than the imperative to disavow them"

(Eric Lott, *Love and Theft: Blackface Minstrelsy and the American Working Class* [New York: Oxford University Press, 1995], 35). Pap's characterization also echoes Twain's source for Injun Joe: "Interestingly, there was a real Injun Joe in Hannibal, but he was more loafer than villain. His worst habit was to get drunk" (Gerber, "Sources for Characters," 271).

21. On the growth of the American sheet-music industry in the mid-nineteenth century, see Richard Crawford, "Introduction," in *The Civil War Songbook: Complete Original Sheet Music for 37 Songs*, ed. Richard Crawford (New York: Dover, 1977), vi.
22. Dena Epstein, *Music Publishing in Chicago before 1871: The Firm of Root & Cady, 1858–1871* (Detroit: Information Coordinators, Inc., 1969), 48, 52. Epstein writes, "Of *Tramp*, the *Tribune* for January 14 declared it 'has been sung all the week at the Academy of Music and other places of amusement, and has at times won a *double encore*, the company being compelled by the audience to sing it three times'" (52). "Tramp" circulated far beyond the Union: Confederate soldiers composed alternate Confederate lyrics to Root's composition, and the Japanese army adapted the tune as a marching song in the 1890s. Twain notes the popularity of Civil War songs on several occasions (see *Autobiography of Mark Twain*, ed. Neider, 74, and *Mark Twain's Letters from Hawaii*, ed. A. Grove Day [Honolulu: University of Hawaii Press, 1975], 65).
23. George Root, "Tramp, Tramp, Tramp," in Crawford, ed., *The Civil War Songbook*, 46.
24. Ibid., 48.
25. See Tim Cresswell, *The Tramp in America* (London: Reaktion, 2001); and Nissen, "Tramp at Home."
26. See Mikhail Bakhtin, "Forms of Time and of the Chronotope in the Novel," in *The Dialogic Imagination: Four Essays*, ed. Michael Holquist, trans. Caryl Emerson and Michael Holquist [Austin: University of Texas Press, 1994], 85). While Bakhtin explores numerous concepts—such as the open road, fools and clowns, and the time of labor—that resonate with the geography of *Huckleberry Finn*, Twain's novel depicts racially differentiated experiences of space and time.
27. Cresswell discusses tramp acts established in numerous states during the 1870s and 1880s, which built upon existing vagrancy codes inherited from British common law (*Tramp in America*, 50–52). See also Todd DePastino, *Citizen Hobo: How a Century of Homelessness Shaped America* (Chicago: University of Chicago Press, 2003), 3–58.
28. Michael Denning, *Mechanic Accents: Dime Novels and Working-Class Culture in America* (London: Verso, 1987), 149.
29. Quoted in Cresswell, *Tramp in America*, 9.
30. Frank Bellew, *The Tramp: His Tricks, Tallies, and Tell-Tales, With All His Signs, Countersigns, Grips, Pass-Words, and Villainies Exposed* (New York: Dick & Fitzgerald, 1878), 20. For discussions of Bellew's narrative in light of working-class and conspiratorial representations of tramp culture, see DePastino, *Citizen*

Hobo, 42–47; and Kenneth Kusmer, *Down and Out, on the Road: The Homeless in American History* (New York: Oxford University Press, 2002), 49.
31. Bellew, *The Tramp*, 12.
32. Saidiya Hartman, *Scenes of Subjection: Terror, Slavery, and Self-Making in Nineteenth-Century America* (New York: Oxford University Press, 1997), 150.
33. Ibid., 146.
34. DePastino, *Citizen Hobo*, 14. By contrast, "new immigrants, the Chinese, and newly freed African Americans . . . were reputed to be the most generous in giving to the homeless. One vagabond related to John McCook that blacks in the South readily gave food to tramps of both races. . . . In Chinatown, too, one tramp explained, there was 'always a bite to eat for the asking—no Chinaman refuses to feed a hungry man'" (Kusmer, *Down and Out*, 87).
35. Quoted in Ronald Takaki, *A Different Mirror: A History of Multicultural America* (Boston: Back Bay Books, 2008), 165.
36. Missouri, e.g., had banned free blacks from settling in the state in the 1840s.
37. Michelle Alexander, *The New Jim Crow: Mass Incarceration in the Age of Colorblindness* (New York: New Press, 2010), 28.
38. Quoted in Theodore Wilson, *The Black Codes of the South* (University: University of Alabama Press, 1965), 68.
39. Ibid. Wilson provides an overview of black codes in the years immediately following Emancipation. Some of these laws stayed in the books during Radical Reconstruction; others were reinstituted during post-Reconstruction. On the "outright peonage" that often resulted from vagrancy convictions, see Matthew Mancini, *One Dies, Get Another: Convict Leasing in the American South, 1866–1928* (Columbia: University of South Carolina Press, 1996), 184.
40. Jung notes one instance in which a gang of Chinese workers filing a complaint against their employer in Louisiana were told that "this was no place for vagrants, and that unless they went to work somewhere they would be arrested" (quoted in Moon-Ho Jung, *Coolies and Cane: Race, Labor, and Sugar in the Age of Emancipation* [Baltimore: Johns Hopkins University Press, 2006], 188).
41. W. E. B. Du Bois, "Reconstruction and Its Benefits," in *W. E. B. Du Bois: A Reader*, ed. David Levering Lewis (New York: Henry Holt & Co., 1995), 177.
42. A. L. Beier, *Masterless Men: The Vagrancy Problem in England, 1560–1640* (London: Methuen, 1986), xxii.
43. Bryan Wagner, *Disturbing the Peace: Black Culture and the Police Power after Slavery* (Cambridge, Mass.: Harvard University Press, 2009), 37.
44. Alex Lichtenstein, *Twice the Work of Free Labor: The Political Economy of Convict Labor in the New South* (London: Verso, 1995), 2. On "southern enclosure," see William Harris, *Deep Souths: Delta, Piedmont, and Sea Island Society in the Age of Segregation* (Baltimore: Johns Hopkins University Press, 2001). Wacquant's sweeping account of "sociospatial devices" of racialization provides a trenchant discussion of the "conjoint *extraction of labour* and *social ostracization*" characteristic of all "peculiar institutions" from slavery and Jim Crow, to the urban

ghetto and the carceral state (Loïc Wacquant, "From Slavery to Mass Incarceration: Rethinking the 'Race Question' in the US," *New Left Review* 13 [January 2002]: 44). For comprehensive overviews of the "penal lease system" imposed on blacks during Reconstruction in different Southern states, see Blake McKelvey, "Penal Slavery and Southern Reconstruction," *Journal of Negro History* 20 (1935): 153–179; and Mancini, *One Dies*.
45. *Ruffin v. Commonwealth*, 62 Va. 790 (1871).
46. For a detailed account of convict labor in Missouri from 1875 to 1900, see Gary Kremer, "Politics, Punishment, and Profit: Convict Labor in the Missouri State Penitentiary, 1875–1900," *Gateway Heritage* 13 (Summer 1992): 28–41.
47. Alexander, *The New Jim Crow*, 32.
48. On the construction of freedom as "indebted servitude" in post-emancipation liberalism, see Hartman, *Scenes of Subjection*, 125–163.
49. Dayan, "Legal Slaves," 6. Dayan lists the Vagrancy Act of 1547—which prescribed the enslavement of anyone convicted of vagrancy to the one who denounced him—among the Western "experiments in unfreedom" that preceded the slave trade (9).
50. Ibid., 3, 5.
51. Although the novel's scenes of mob violence all involve white victims, Twain's scorn towards the "mob" may reflect his attitude toward the racist lynchings of the post-Reconstruction period.
52. See Fishkin: "What could be more apt than that unsatisfying, burlesque, artificial ending to capture the travesty made of freedom and equality in the post-Reconstruction era?" (Shelley Fisher Fishkin, "Race and the Politics of Memory: Mark Twain and Paul Laurence Dunbar," *Journal of American Studies* 40 [2006]: 297). Du Bois deploys these lines from Hamlet's soliloquy in discussing Alexander Crummell's early confrontation with Church racism (W. E. B. Du Bois, *The Souls of Black Folk: Essays and Sketches* [Cambridge, Mass.: A.C. McClurg, 1903], 224).
53. Henry Louis Gates, Jr., "Frederick Douglass and the Language of the Self," in his *Figures in Black: Words, Signs, and the "Racial" Self* (New York: Oxford University Press, 1987), 100–101. Gates is commenting on Frederick Douglass's claim that "to be shut up entirely to the past and present, is abhorrent to the human mind; it is to the soul—whose life and happiness is unceasing progress—what the prison is to the body; a blight and mildew, a hell of horror" (200). Hartman also notes that "the 'time' of slavery negates the common-sense intuition of time as continuity or progression, then and now coexist; we are coeval with the dead" (Saidiya Hartman, "The Time of Slavery," *South Atlantic Quarterly* 101 [Fall 2002]: 759).
54. Hartman, "Time of Slavery," 770.
55. Twain, *Mark Twain's Letters from Hawaii*, 75–76.
56. Mark Twain, *Roughing It*, ed. Harriet Elinor Smith and Edgar Marquess Branch (Berkeley: University of California Press, 1993), 415.

57. Mark Twain, *The Prince and the Pauper* (Berkeley: University of California Press, 1979), 285.
58. Mark Twain, "Three Thousand Years among the Microbes," in *Mark Twain's "Which Was the Dream?" and Other Symbolic Writings of the Later Years*, ed. John S. Tuckey (Berkeley and Los Angeles: University of California Press, 1968), 436. For an analysis of ethnicity in "Three Thousand Years," see Henry B. Wonham, *Playing the Races: Ethnic Caricature and American Literary Realism* (New York: Oxford University Press, 2004), 69–71.
59. On the novel's Southwestern setting, see Stephanie LeMenager, *Manifest and Other Destinies: Territorial Fictions of the Nineteenth-Century United States* (Lincoln: University of Nebraska Press, 2004), 201–206.
60. In his discussion of personal and literary relations between Twain and Harte, Krauth suggests that "'Three Vagabonds of Trinidad' may . . . be Harte's revisioning of Twain's *Adventures of Huckleberry Finn*" (Leland Krauth, *Mark Twain & Company: Six Literary Relations* [Athens: University of Georgia Press, 2003], 33).
61. Bret Harte, "Three Vagabonds of Trinidad," in *The Luck of Roaring Camp and Other Writings*, ed. Gary Scharnhorst (New York: Penguin, 2001), 158. Further references will be cited parenthetically in the text as "TVT."
62. Jean Pfaelzer, *Driven Out: The Forgotten War against Chinese Americans* (Berkeley: University of California Press, 2007), 59.
63. Ibid., 60.
64. For a bracing discussion of the inequalities within and between groups that are often masked by rhetorics of multicultural solidarity, see James Kyung-Jin Lee, *Urban Triage: Race and the Fictions of Multiculturalism* (Minneapolis: University of Minnesota Press, 2004), 64–99.
65. *People v. Hall*, 4 Cal. 399 (1854). See Chapter 1.
66. *The Constitution of the State of California* (San Francisco: Bancroft-Whitney Co., 1902), 341.
67. Najia Aarim-Heriot, *Chinese Immigrants, African Americans, and Racial Anxiety in the United States, 1848–82* (Urbana: University of Illinois Press, 2003), 8.
68. Pfaelzer, *Driven Out*, 159.
69. Ibid., 75.
70. Ibid., 291. In 1893, "The Chinese remained trapped in legal purgatory, somewhere between deportation and endangered residence, imprisoned in all eleven counties covered by Judge Ross's southern U.S. District Court" (ibid., 320–321).
71. See the Yurok Tribe, "The Yurok Tribe: Background Information," www.yuroktribe.org/culture/history/history.htm, accessed March 1, 2008.
72. Bret Harte, "Indiscriminate Massacre of Indians, Women and Children Butchered," *Northern Californian* 2 (February 29, 1860): 1. See also Gary Scharnhorst, *Bret Harte: Opening the American Literary West* (Norman: University of Oklahoma Press, 2000), 13–4.

73. John Carlos Rowe, "Highway Robbery: 'Indian Removal,' the Mexican-American War, and American Identity in *The Life and Adventures of Joaquin Murieta*," *novel* 31 (Spring 1998): 151–152.
74. Karl Marx, *Grundrisse: Foundations of the Critique of Political Economy*, trans. Martin Nicolaus (New York: Penguin, 1993), 524.
75. Bruce Braun, "'On the Raggedy Edge of Risk': Articulations of Race and Nature after Biology," in *Race, Nature, and the Politics of Difference*, ed. Donald Moore, Jake Kosek, and Anand Pandian (Durham, N.C.: Duke University Press, 2003), 198.
76. Hartman, *Scenes of Subjection*, 150.
77. Pfaelzer, *Driven Out*, 161–162.

CHAPTER 3. "COOLIES" AND CORPORATE PERSONHOOD

1. Mark Twain, *Those Extraordinary Twins*, in *Pudd'nhead Wilson and Those Extraordinary Twins*, ed. Sidney E. Berger (New York: Norton, 2005), 163–164. Further references to this edition will be cited parenthetically in the text as ET.
2. Brook Thomas, *American Literary Realism and the Failed Promise of Contract* (Berkeley: University of California Press, 1997), 231. Blyn notes that the judge's anxiety in this scene resonates with the dangers that anti-corporate groups associated with the fiction of "corporate personhood" established in the U.S. Supreme Court's decision in *Santa Clara County v. Southern Pacific Railroad*, 118 U.S. 394 (1886) (Robin Blyn, "The Subject of Incorporation: Personhood under Reconstruction in *Those Extraordinary Twins*," paper presented at the American Literature Association Conference, Boston, May 24–27, 2007).
3. Thomas, *American Literary Realism*, 239.
4. Alan Trachtenberg, *The Incorporation of America: Culture and Society in the Gilded Age* (New York: Hill & Wang, 1982).
5. Elizabeth Dillon, "Fear of Formalism: Kant, Twain, and Cultural Studies in American Literature," *Diacritics* 27, no. 4 (1998): 66.
6. Leslie Fiedler, "'As Free as Any Cretur . . .'" in *The Devil Gets His Due: The Uncollected Essays of Leslie Fiedler*, ed. Samuele Pardini (Berkeley, Calif.: Counterpoint Press, 2008), 77.
7. For opposed readings of the vestigial status of the formerly conjoined twins in *Pudd'nhead*, see Hershel Parker, *Flawed Texts and Verbal Icons: Literary Authority in American Fiction* (Evanston, Ill.: Northwestern University Press, 1984), 134; and Emily Russell, *Reading Embodied Citizenship: Disability, Narrative, and the Body Politic* (New Brunswick, N.J.: Rutgers University Press, 2011), 23–58. On Twain's composition and revision process, see Anne P. Wigger, "The Composition of Mark Twain's 'Pudd'nhead Wilson and Those Extraordinary Twins': Chronology and Development," *Modern Philology* 55, no. 2 (November 1957): 93–102; and Parker, *Flawed Texts*, 115–145.
8. "New Books," *Hartford Times* (February 18, 1895): 8.

9. "Mark Twain's New Book," *Cincinnati Commercial Gazette* (February 3, 1895): 23; "About 'Pudd'nhead Wilson,'" *Springfield Republican* (February 3, 1895); "Literary Chat," *Munsey's Magazine* 13, no. 3 (June 1895): 315; "Pudd'nhead Wilson," *Public Opinion* 18, no. 7 (February 14, 1895): 161.
10. *The Critic; an Illustrated Monthly Review of Literature, Art, and Life*, unsigned review, 26 (May 11, 1895): 338–339, reprinted in Twain, *Pudd'nhead Wilson and Those Extraordinary Twins*, ed. Berger, 244.
11. Van Wyck Brooks, *The Ordeal of Mark Twain* (New York: E. P. Dutton & Co., 1920), 193.
12. Fiedler, "'As Free as Any Cretur . . . ,'" 77.
13. Nancy Fredricks, "Twain's Indelible Twins," *Nineteenth-Century Literature* 43, no. 4 (March 1989): 485.
14. Russell, *Reading Embodied*, 23–58.
15. Dillon, "Fear of Formalism," 63.
16. Russell notes that "many critics read this parallel between the disabled and the racially mixed protagonists as the secret theme of *Those Extraordinary Twins*" (*Reading Embodied*, 33).
17. Thomas, *American Literary Realism*, 236.
18. Mark Twain, "Introduction Speech," quoted in Major J. B. Pond, *Eccentricities of Genius: Memories of Famous Men and Women of the Platform* (New York: G. W. Dillingham Co., 1900), 248. For a thoughtful account of Twain's engagements with the theme of twins, see Stephen Railton's "Twain and Twins," *Mark Twain in His Times*, http://etext.virginia.edu/railton/wilson/mttwins.html.
19. "Mark Twain and Twin Cheer New Year's Party," *New York Times* (January 1, 1907): 1.
20. See Mark Twain, *No.44, The Mysterious Stranger* (Berkeley: University of California Press, 1969), 88–89. For an analysis of the theme of immigration in *No.44*, see Thomas Peyser, "Mark Twain, Immigration, and the American Narrative," *ELH* 79, no. 4 (December 2012): 1013–1037.
21. Alice Domurat Dreger, *One of Us: Conjoined Twins and the Future of the Normal* (Cambridge, Mass.: Harvard University Press, 2004), 31–32.
22. Stuart Hall, "Race, Articulation, and Societies Structured in Dominance," in *Sociological Theories: Race and Colonialism* (Paris: UNESCO, 1980), 325. Dreger points out that an archaic meaning of "individuality" is "indivisibility" (*One of Us*, 155).
23. Mark Twain, "Personal Habits of the Siamese Twins," in Mark Twain, *Collected Tales, Sketches, Speeches, and Essays, 1852–1890*, ed. Louis Budd (New York: Library of America, 1992), 296–299.
24. J. N. Moreheid, *Lives, Adventures, Anecdotes, Amusements, and Domestic Habits of the Siamese Twins* (Raleigh, N.C.: E. E. Barclay, 1850).
25. Cynthia Wu, "The Siamese Twins in Late-Nineteenth-Century Narratives of Conflict and Reconciliation," *American Literature* 80, no. 1 (2008): 38.
26. Ibid.

27. The *Scientific American* article that probably provided most of Twain's information about the Tocci brothers, however, notes that "they are able to stand, but have not yet succeeded in walking, as each leg is governed by its own brain" ("The Tocci Twins," *Scientific American* 65, no. 24 [December 12, 1891]: 374).
28. Vincenza Scarpaci, "Walking the Color Line: Italian Immigrants in Rural Louisiana, 1880–1910," in *Are Italians White? How Race Is Made in America* (New York: Routledge, 2003), 62.
29. On Twain's engagement with anti-Italian sentiment in *Pudd'nhead* and *Twins*, see Joseph Cosco, *Imagining Italians: The Clash of Romance and Race in American Perceptions, 1880–1910* (Albany, N.Y.: SUNY Press, 2003), 143–170; and Eric J. Sundquist, *To Wake the Nations: Race in the Making of American Literature* (Cambridge, Mass.: Harvard University Press, 1992), 261–263.
30. Trachtenberg, *Incorporation*, 82.
31. Frank Norris, *The Octopus* (New York: Penguin, 1986), 651. For an analysis of Asiatic racial form in Norris's novel, see Colleen Lye, *America's Asia: Racial Form and American Literature, 1893–1945* (Princeton, N.J.: Princeton University Press, 2004), 72–86.
32. Trachtenberg, *Incorporation*, 84, 7.
33. Mark Twain, "Concerning the Jews," in *The Complete Essays of Mark Twain*, ed. Charles Neider (Cambridge, Mass.: Da Capo Press, 1991), 247.
34. Loren Glass, *Authors Inc.: Literary Celebrity in the Modern United States, 1880–1980* (New York: NYU Press, 2004), 74.
35. Russell, *Reading Embodied*, 52.
36. Whereas critics often analogize the twins' conjoined status with racial inequality, the ease and economy with which they are able to move through trains, theaters, hotels, sitting rooms, and restaurants indicates that their physical condition does not subject them to Jim Crow policing of social relations and public space.
37. On "time-discipline" as a crucial factor in industrialization, see E. P. Thompson, "Time, Work-Discipline, and Industrial Capitalism," *Past & Present* 38, no. 1 (1967): 56–97.
38. Trachtenberg, *Incorporation*, 112. On the rapid growth of cities, transportation networks, and markets in the New South, see Henry Woodfin Grady, *The New South* (New York: Robert Bonner's Sons, 1890).
39. John Carlos Rowe, "Fatal Speculations: Murder, Money, and Manners in *Pudd'nhead Wilson*," in *Mark Twain's Pudd'nhead Wilson: Race, Conflict, and Culture*, ed. Susan Gillman and Forrest Glen Robinson (Durham, N.C.: Duke University Press, 1990), 147.
40. Ibid.
41. Ibid., 148.
42. William S. Laufer, *Corporate Bodies and Guilty Minds: The Failure of Corporate Criminal Liability* (Chicago: University of Chicago Press, 2008), 9, 12.
43. Mark Twain, *A Connecticut Yankee in King Arthur's Court*, ed. Allison Ensor (New York: Norton, 1982), 68.

44. Trachtenberg, *Incorporation*, 84.
45. Ibid., 5.
46. Morton J. Horwitz, *The Transformation of American Law, 1870–1960: The Crisis of Legal Orthodoxy* (New York: Oxford University Press, 1992), 73.
47. In this case, the court reporter turned out to be the former railroad company president J. C. Bancroft Davis. See Ted Nace, *Gangs of America: The Rise of Corporate Power and the Disabling of Democracy* (San Francisco: Berrett-Koehler Publishers, 2005), 102–109.
48. *Santa Clara County v. Southern Pacific Railroad*, 118 U.S. 396. "By 1911, six hundred and seven 14th Amendment cases had reached the Supreme Court. Three hundred and twelve involved corporations. Only thirty, including the failed effort of Homer Plessy, involved rights of minority groups" (Thomas, *American Literary Realism*, 235).
49. Horwitz, *Transformation*, 72. See also Martin J. Sklar, *The Corporate Reconstruction of American Capitalism, 1890–1916: The Market, the Law, and Politics* (Cambridge: Cambridge University Press, 1988), 48–51.
50. Mark Twain, "Pudd'nhead Wilson," Literary and Historical Manuscripts MA 881-2, MS, 1893, 354, Morgan Library, New York, copy at Mark Twain Papers, Bancroft Library, University of California, Berkeley.
51. *A Few Particulars Concerning Chang-Eng, the United Siamese Brothers* (New York: John M. Elliott, 1838), 12–13.
52. Amy Wallace and Irving Wallace, *The Two* (New York: Simon & Schuster, 1978), 107.
53. Moreheid, *Lives*, 23.
54. Roger Daniels, "The Immigrant Experience in the Gilded Age," in *The Gilded Age: Perspectives on the Origins of Modern America*, ed. Charles William Calhoun (Lanham, Md.: Rowman & Littlefield, 2007), 76.
55. Ibid., 78–79.
56. Trachtenberg, *Incorporation*, 88.
57. See Cosco, *Imagining Italians*, 143–170.
58. Dillon, "Fear of Formalism," 66.
59. Alexander Saxton, *Rise and Fall of the White Republic: Politics and Mass Culture in Nineteenth-Century America* (New York: Verso, 2003), 354.
60. Jim Zwick, "Mark Twain and Imperialism," in *A Historical Guide to Mark Twain*, ed. Shelley Fisher Fishkin (Oxford: Oxford University Press, 2002), 235. Today, George is perhaps best known for inspiring the satirical board game "Monopoly"; on George's attitudes concerning Chinese immigration, see Alexander Saxton, *The Indispensable Enemy: Labor and the Anti-Chinese Movement in California* (Berkeley: University of California Press, 1971), 92–103.
61. Saxton, *Indispensable*, 101. Thomas notes that corporations "were often the allies of Chinese seeking legal protections" (*American Literary Realism*, 238).
62. Charles J. McClain, *In Search of Equality: The Chinese Struggle against Discrimination in Nineteenth-Century America* (Berkeley: University of California Press, 1994), 82.

63. Ibid., 83–84.
64. See Ronald Rudy Higgens-Evenson, *The Price of Progress: Public Services, Taxation, and the American Corporate State, 1877 to 1929* (Baltimore: Johns Hopkins University Press, 2003), 21.
65. "A Fresh Eruption of the Pacific Coast Vesuvius," *Wasp*, vol. 8 (January–June 1882); "Theres Millions In It," *Wasp*, vol. 21 (July–December 1888); "Uncle Sam's Farm in Danger," *Wasp*, vol. 2 (August 1877–July 1878); "The Coming Man: Allee Sammee 'Melican Man Monopoleeee," *Wasp*, vol. 6 (January–June 1881); "The Hydra-Headed Vampire-Contending Contentments," *Wasp*, vol. 4 (August 1879–July1880); "The Chinese: Many-Handed But Soulless," *Wasp*, vol. 15 (July–December 1885); "Immigration East and West," *Wasp*, vol. 7 (July–December 1881): cover.
66. G. Frederick Keller, "The Curse of California," *Wasp* 9, no. 316 (August 19, 1882): 520–521.
67. G. Frederick Keller, "The Ogre of Mussel Slough," *Wasp* 8 (March 12, 1882).
68. G. Frederick Keller, "What Shall We Do With Our Boys?" *Wasp* 8 (March 3, 1882): 136–137.
69. Lye, *America's Asia*, 57.
70. Ibid., 55. Twain's early sketch endorsing "Coolies for California"—which I discussed in the Introduction—also associated Chinese "coolies" with "great mining, manufacturing, and public improvement corporations" and a type of mind-numbing "drudgery" distinct from the labor of white men.
71. Eric Hayot, *The Hypothetical Mandarin: Sympathy, Modernity, and Chinese Pain* (New York: Oxford University Press, 2009), 148. See Chapter 1n89. As Edlie Wong has documented, Chinese invasion narratives migrated from popular literature to the legal imagination, shaping anti-Chinese immigration law in cases such as *Chae Chan Ping v. U.S.*, 130 U.S. 581 (1889) (Edlie Wong, "In a Future Tense: Immigration Law, Counterfactual Histories, and Chinese Invasion Fiction," *American Literary History*, in press).
72. Ignatius Donnelly, *Caesar's Column: A Story of the Twentieth Century* (Chicago: Schulte & Co., 1890). For an assessment of how Donnelly's novel "metaphorically Orientalizes the world of monopoly capitalism," see Lye, *America's Asia*, 63–71, quote on 68.
73. L. E. Payson, "Texas and Pacific Railroad Company," *Executive Documents of the Senate of the United States for the First Session of the Forty-Eighth Congress* (Washington, D. C.: Government Printing Office, 1884), 1, no. 27:30; emphasis added.
74. Henry Osborn Taylor, *A Treatise on the Law of Private Corporations Having Capital Stock* (1884; reprint, Philadelphia: Kay & Bro., 1898), 29n1; emphasis added.
75. Anne P. Wigger, "The Source of Fingerprint Material in Mark Twain's *Pudd'nhead Wilson and Those Extraordinary Twins*," *American Literature* 28, no. 4 (January 1957): 517–520. The title page of one manuscript version of *Pudd'nhead Wilson* includes an image labeled, in Twain's crossed-out writing, "Finger prints of Francis Galton, F.R.S., etc." and accompanied by Twain's instruction: "Not to

be inserted in the book. SLC" (Mark Twain, "Pudd'nhead Wilson," MS, Mark Twain Papers, box 40, MS1, Bancroft Library, University of California, Berkeley, [ca.1892]; supplemental title page from the Shaun Speer Collection, available through the Mark Twain Project, Bancroft Library, University of California, Berkeley). On the relations between fingerprinting, individualization, and racial characteristics in the work of Twain and Galton, see Simon A. Cole, "Twins, Twain, Galton, and Gilman: Fingerprinting, Individualization, Brotherhood, and Race in *Pudd'nhead Wilson*," *Configurations* 15, no. 3 (2007): 227–265; Sarah Chinn, *Technology and the Logic of American Racism: A Cultural History of the Body as Evidence* (New York: Continuum, 2000), 24–52; Ronald Thomas, *Detective Fiction and the Rise of Forensic Science* (Cambridge: Cambridge University Press, 1999), 240–256; and Shawn Salvant, "Mark Twain and the Nature of Twins," *Nineteenth Century Literature* 67, no. 3 (December 2012): 366–396.

76. Sir Francis Galton, *Finger Prints* (New York: Macmillan & Co., 1892), 152–153.
77. Chinn, *Technology and the Logic of American Racism*, 47.
78. "They convicted one Chinaman, but when they found out it was the wrong one, they let him go. . . . You see, these Chinamen are all alike, and they cannot identify each other. . . . They cannot tell each other apart. There is only one way to manage this thing with strict equity: hang the gentle Chinamen promiscuously, until justice is satisfied" (Mark Twain, "The China Trial," *Territorial Enterprise* [February 19, 1863], reprinted in Mark Twain, *Early Tales and Sketches*, vol. 1: *1851–1864*, ed. Edgar Branch and Robert Hirst [Berkeley: University of California Press, 1979], 402–403).
79. Galton, *Finger Prints*, 26–27.
80. Mae Ngai, *The Lucky Ones: One Family and the Extraordinary Invention of Chinese America* (New York: Houghton Mifflin Harcourt, 2010), 62.
81. "Thumbs Down! The Latest Plan for Outwitting the Chinese," *San Francisco Daily Report* 34, no. 67 (September 19, 1885): 8. In addition to Taber, the former Alameda County Sheriff Harry Morse and San Francisco Mint Superintendent Franklin Lawton also proposed using thumbprints for identifying Chinese immigrants (Cole, "Twins, Twain, Galton, and Gilman," 248).
82. "Thumbs Down!" 8.
83. Ibid. The article also reproduces and briefly comments on thirteen sets of thumb marks, including seven belonging to subjects with Chinese names. One caption reads: "The thumb marks of Mon Shing, a Chinese laundry man. His marks are more easily recognized than his face" (ibid.).
84. Paul Rabinow, "Galton's Regret: Of Types and Individuals," in *DNA on Trial: Genetic Identification and Criminal Justice*, ed. Paul R. Billings (Plainview, N.Y.: Cold Spring Harbor Laboratory Press, 1992), 5–18.
85. Galton, *Finger Prints*, 14.
86. Cole, "Twins, Twain, Galton, and Gilman," 232. U.S. exclusion codes settled on Bertillonage to distinguish between Chinese migrants, but "lack of funds made this provision largely moot before 1905. After the [1905 anti-American] boycott,

proper Bertillonage and fingerprinting were formally dropped until the Chinese Exclusion Act expired in 1943" (Christian Parenti, *The Soft Cage: Surveillance in America from Slavery to the War on Terror* [New York: Basic Books, 2003], 76).

87. Pfaelzer details Chinese efforts to resist the Geary Act and describes the refusal to carry photographic identification by several thousand Chinese immigrants as "perhaps the largest organized act of civil disobedience in the United States" (Jean Pfaelzer, *Driven Out: The Forgotten War against Chinese Americans* [Berkeley: University of California Press, 2007], 291–335, quote on 292).

88. Cole, "Twins, Twain, Galton, and Gilman," 247, 239. Commenting on the persistence of racially segregated identification files alongside individualizing technologies of identification, Cole speculates "that individualization is not, as one would assume at first blush, the antidote to nefarious classification systems based on race: not only can biological individualization easily coexist with crude, artificial, 'embodied' racial classification; it also seems that individualizing technologies are so fine-grained that they may, in fact, *demand* such schemes" (259).

89. "Thumbs Down!" 8. The brief article notes the prior use of fingerprints in China three times, possibly in order to legitimate the idea of fingerprinting Chinese residents in the United States.

90. Karl de Leeuw and Jan Bergstra, eds., *The History of Information Security: A Comprehensive Handbook* (Amsterdam: Elsevier, 2007), 253.

91. Chinn, *Technology and the Logic of American Racism*, 42. Galton notes that, while "European practitioners of palmistry and cheiromancy do not seem to have paid particular attention to the ridges with which we are concerned," Chinese, Japanese, and African American practitioners attend closely to fingerprints (*Finger Prints*, 26).

92. Mark Twain, letter to Fred J. Hall (July 30, 1893), in *Mark Twain's Letters*, ed. Alfred Bigelow Paine, 2 vols. (New York: Harper & Bros., 1917), 2:590.

93. Mark Twain, "Pudd'nhead Wilson," MS, 1893, 627–628, Literary and Historical Manuscripts MA 881-2, Morgan Library, copy at Mark Twain Papers, Bancroft Library, University of California, Berkeley, Box 40 1892.00.00-1893.00.00.

94. Henry W. Grady, "The South and Her Problems," in *The Complete Orations and Speeches of Henry W. Grady*, ed. Edwin Shurter (New York: Hinds, Noble, & Eldredge), 38.

95. Booker T. Washington, *Up From Slavery*, ed. W. Fitzhugh Brundage (Boston: Bedford/St. Martin's, 2003), 143. Commenting elsewhere on black students' need for practical and locally grounded education, Washington writes that, "while they could locate the Desert of Sahara or the capital of China on an artificial globe, I found out that the girls could not locate the proper places for the knives and forks on an actual dinner-table, or the places on which the bread and meat should be set" (ibid., 97).

96. *Plessy v. Ferguson*, 163 U.S. 537, 561 (1896). Commenting on Harlan's invocation of a hypothetical "Chinaman," Lwin writes, "'A race so different from our own'

unveils the mutual imbrications of segregation and exclusion and ultimately exposes the embedded narratives of Asian American and African American racial formation that exist alongside each other" (Sanda Mayzaw Lwin, "'A Race So Different from Our Own': Segregation, Exclusion, and the Myth of Mobility," in *AfroAsian Encounters: Culture, History, Politics*, ed. Heike Raphael-Hernandez and Shannon Steen [New York: NYU Press, 2006], 29). On parallels between *Pudd'nhead* and *Plessy v. Ferguson*, see Sundquist, *To Wake the Nations*, 225–270.

97. Lisa Lowe, "The Intimacies of Four Continents," in *Haunted by Empire: Geographies of Intimacy in North American History*, ed. Ann Laura Stoler (Durham, N.C.: Duke University Press, 2006), 195.

CHAPTER 4. A CONNECTICUT YANKEE IN THE COURT OF WU CHIH TIEN

1. Mark Twain, "To William Dean Howells, 20 November 1874," in *Mark Twain's Letters*, vol. 6: *1874–1875*, ed. Michael Frank and Harriet Elinor Smith (Berkeley: University of California Press, 2002), 290.
2. Twain, "Autobiographical Dictation," transcript #19, September 12, 1908, at Mark Twain Papers, Bancroft Library, University of California, Berkeley.
3. Mark Twain, *A Connecticut Yankee in King Arthur's Court*, ed. Allison Ensor (New York: Norton, 1982), 239. Further references to this edition will be abbreviated as *CY* in the text.
4. On Twain's friendship with Burlingame, see Hsin-yun Ou, "Mark Twain, Anson Burlingame, Joseph Hopkins Twichell, and the Chinese," *Ariel: A Review of International English Literature* 42, no. 2 (2012): 48–53.
5. Mark Twain, "The Treaty with China: Its Provisions Explained," *Journal of Transnational American Studies* 2, no.1 (2010): 12, http://escholarship.org/uc/item/2r87m203. Gordon Chang persuasively argues that such a vision of China's commercial importance for America's future motivated U.S. "business, political, and religious leaders" to oppose nativists' calls for immigration restrictions for decades before the 1882 Exclusion Act (see Gordon Chang, "China and the Pursuit of America's Destiny: Nineteenth-Century Imagining and Why Immigration Restriction Took So Long," *Journal of Asian American Studies* 15, no. 2 [June 2012]: 147).
6. Ou, "Twain, Burlingame, Twichell," 50.
7. Twain quoted in ibid., 50.
8. T. J. Jackson Lears, *No Place of Grace: Antimodernism and the Transformation of American Culture, 1880–1920* (Chicago: University of Chicago Press, 1994), 28.
9. Ibid., xi.
10. Amy Kaplan, *The Anarchy of Empire in the Making of U.S. Culture* (Cambridge, Mass.: Harvard University Press, 2002), 119.
11. Ibid., 94.
12. Ibid.
13. On the historical romances of the 1890s, see William Dean Howells, "The New Historical Romance," *North American Review* 171 (1900): 935–948; George

Dekker, *The American Historical Romance* (Cambridge: Cambridge University Press, 1990); Lears, *No Place of Grace*, 117–124; Amy Kaplan, "Romancing the Empire," in *The Anarchy of Empire in the Making of U. S. Culture*, 92–120; and Andrew Hebard, "Romantic Sovereignty: Popular Romances and the American Imperial State," *American Quarterly* 57, no. 3 (September 2005): 805–830.

14. Amy Kaplan, "Imperial Melancholy in America," *Raritan* 28, no. 3 (Winter 2009): 27.
15. Lears, *No Place of Grace*, 105.
16. Nathaniel Williams, "*Frank Reade, Jr. in Cuba*: Dime-Novel Technology, U.S. Imperialism, and the 'American Jules Verne,'" *American Literature* 83, no. 2 (June 2011): 279. Twain's *Tom Sawyer Abroad* (1894)—in which Tom and Huck use a hot-air balloon to rescue Jim from the top of the Egyptian Sphinx (an imperial reenactment of their "rescue" of Jim in *Huck Finn*)—draws on the technological and imperial themes popularized by Frank Reade novels.
17. Like Twain's Yankee, the English adventurers in *King Solomon's Mines* (1886) gain influence over the "natives" by successfully predicting an eclipse. (See H. Rider Haggard, *King Solomon's Mines* [reprint, New York: Oxford University Press, 2006]).
18. John Carlos Rowe, *At Emerson's Tomb: The Politics of Classic American Literature* (New York: Columbia University Press, 1997), 138.
19. For an illuminating reading of *Yankee* as an allegory of colonial administration—and particularly of its mixture of realist and romantic modes—see Andrew Hebard, *The Poetics of Sovereignty in American Literature, 1885–1910* (Cambridge: Cambridge University Press, 2012), 49–73.
20. Elizabeth Freeman, "The Political Sensuality of the Archive: A Roundtable," conference presentation, "C19: The Society of Nineteenth-Century Americanists" (Berkeley, Calif.: April 12, 2012).
21. Kaplan, *The Anarchy of Empire*, 51–91; Stephen Sumida, "Reevaluating Mark Twain's Novel of Hawaii," *American Literature* 61, no. 4 (December 1989): 586–609; Susan K. Harris, *God's Arbiters: America and the Philippines, 1898–1902* (New York: Oxford University Press, 2011), 85–103; John Carlos Rowe, *Literary Culture and U.S. Imperialism: From the Revolution to World War II* (New York: Oxford University Press, 2000), 121–141.
22. "I start with Bill Ragsdale at 12 years of age, & the heroine at 4, in the midst of the ancient idolatrous system, with its picturesque & amazing customs and superstitions, 3 months before the arrival of the missionaries & the erection of a shallow Christianity upon the ruins of the old paganism. Then these two will become educated Christians, & highly civilized. And then I will jump 15 years, & do Ragsdale's leper business" (Twain, January 1884 letter to Howells, quoted in Sumida, "Reevaluating," 590). Around this time, Twain also proposed to co-author a Sandwich Islands play with William Dean Howells.
23. Harris, *God's Arbiters*, 88, 90.
24. Rowe, *Literary Culture*, 128.

25. Mark Twain, "A Connecticut Yankee in King Arthur's Court," MS, 1885–1889, Henry W. and Albert A. Berg Collection of English and American Literature, Berg Coll. MSS Clemens (holograph ms, continuous text, paginated in two series), paginated second series, 368–369, New York Public Library, New York. Copy in the Mark Twain Papers, box 41, 1885.12.00-1889.00.00, Bancroft Library, University of California, Berkeley.
26. Ibid., 370.
27. For a reading of "the presence, nearly everywhere in the book, of blasting powder, dynamite, rockets, grenades, and high-explosive destruction," see Bruce Michelson, "Realism, Romance, and Dynamite: The Quarrel of *A Connecticut Yankee in King Arthur's Court*," *New England Quarterly* 64, no. 4 (December 1991): 628.
28. See Alexander Saxton, *The Indispensable Enemy: Labor and the Anti-Chinese Movement in California* (Berkeley: University of California Press, 1971), 58. Ironically, the striking miners eventually succeeded in barring the employment of Chinese miners, but "the price was total surrender on the issue that actually had touched off the conflict—dynamite—and this in turn guaranteed a narrowing of their job opportunity" (ibid.).
29. Ibid., 283–284.
30. Ignatius Donnelly, *Caesar's Column: A Story of the Twentieth Century* (Chicago: Schulte & Co., 1890). For a more detailed analysis of how *Caesar's Column* renders oligarchy and proletarianization through Asiatic racial form, see Colleen Lye, *America's Asia: Racial Form and American Literature, 1893–1945* (Princeton, N.J.: Princeton University Press, 2004), 64–71.
31. Nicholas Vachel Lindsay, "The Golden-Faced People: A Story of the Chinese Conquest of America," *Crisis* 9, no. 1 (November 1914): 36–42. For a thorough analysis of this story, see Edlie Wong, "In a Future Tense: Immigration Law, Counterfactual Histories, and Chinese Invasion Fiction," *American Literary History* (in press).
32. Mark Twain, "Comments on the Moro Massacre," in *Mark Twain's Weapons of Satire: Anti-imperialist Writings on the Philippine-American War*, ed. Jim Zwick (Syracuse, N.Y.: Syracuse University Press, 1992), 170.
33. Mark Twain, "A Defence of General Funston," in Zwick, ed., *Mark Twain's Weapons of Satire*, 126-7.
34. Mark Twain, "To My Missionary Critics," in *The Complete Essays of Mark Twain*, ed. Charles Neider (Cambridge, Mass.: Da Capo Press, 1991), 534.
35. Joseph H. Twichell, "An Address by the Rev. Joseph H. Twichell," April 10, 1878, in Yung Wing, *My Life in China and America* (New York: Henry Holt & Co., 1909), 247.
36. Edward Rhoads, *Stepping Forth into the World: The Chinese Educational Mission to the United States, 1872–81* (Hong Kong: Hong Kong University Press, 2011), 130, 144–148.

37. Article 8 agreed that the United States would "freely disclaim any intention or right to intervene in the domestic administration of China in regard to the construction of railroads, telegraphs, or other material improvements" but would also provide assistance and "suitable engineers" if China's emperor requested assistance in constructing such works (quoted in Twain, "The Treaty with China," 10).
38. Ibid., 11. While Twain acknowledges the validity of Chinese resistance to railroad construction—dwelling on likelihood that it would destroy gravesites throughout the countryside—his 1868 essay nevertheless proclaims that the railroad "must be built" because it "would unlock the riches of 400,000,000 of Chinese subjects to the world" ("The Treaty with China," 11).
39. Yan Phou Lee, "The Chinese Must Stay," *North American Review* 148 (1889): 479.
40. Rhoads, *Stepping Forth*, 9–10.
41. Ibid., 14.
42. Ibid., 149–168.
43. Ibid., 172.
44. Steve Courtney, *Joseph Hopkins Twichell: The Life and Times of Mark Twain's Closest Friend* (Athens: University of Georgia Press, 2008), 146. For an extended account of how Twichell's involvement with the CEM may have influenced Twain, see Hsin-yun Ou, "Mark Twain, Anson Burlingame, Joseph Hopkins Twichell, and the Chinese," *Ariel: A Review of International English Literature* 42, no. 2 (2012): 57–61. In an 1881 letter to Howells, Twain poked fun at Twichell's interest in Yung and his Chinese missionary associates: "And he [Twichell] has gone and raked up the MS autobiography (written in 1848,) of Mrs. Phebe Brown, (author of [the hymn] 'I Love to Steal a While Away,') who educated Yung Wing in her family when he was a little boy; and I came near not getting to bed at all, last night, on account of the lurid fascinations of it. Why in the nation it has never got into print, I can't understand" (Twain, Letter to William Dean Howells (December 16, 1881), in *Mark Twain's Letters*, ed. Alfred Bigelow Paine, 2 vols. [New York: Harper & Bros., 1917], 1:411–412).
45. Anne Hamilton, "From China to Hartford, a Historic Connection," *Hartford Courant* (June 14, 2009). Online article. http://articles.courant.com/2009-06-14/news/exlife0614.art_1_first-chinese-graduate-chinese-government-chinese-families.
46. Kung Qien and J. Hu, *Chinese Educational Commission Studies* (Hong Kong: Chinese Books, 2003), 79.
47. Hamilton, "From China."
48. Courtney, *Joseph Hopkins Twichell*, 147.
49. Rhoads, *Stepping Forth*, 163.
50. Thomas LaFargue, *China's First Hundred: Educational Mission Students in the United States, 1872–1881* (Pullman: Washington State University Press, 1987), 50.
51. Li quoted in Rhoads, *Stepping Forth*, 173.

52. Yung Wing, *My Life in China and America*, 211–215.
53. Ibid., 211.
54. Ibid., iv.
55. On the role of the returned students in modernizing China, see LaFargue, *China's First Hundred*; and Rhoads, *Stepping Forth*, 183–214.
56. Harriet Elinor Smith et al., eds., *Autobiography of Mark Twain* (Berkeley, Calif.: University of California Press, 2010), 1:72.
57. It seems worth noting here that Americanized, middle-class Chinese such as Yung Wing and numerous CEM students were less than a mile away when Twain and Harte composed *Ah Sin* at his home in Hartford in 1876.
58. Daniel C. Beard, *Hardly a Man Is Now Alive: The Autobiography of Dan Beard* (New York: Doubleday, 1939), 336.
59. Wong repeatedly attempted to establish newspapers titled *The Chinese American* in New York City and Chicago; he was naturalized in Michigan in 1874 (Hsuan L. Hsu, "Wong Chin Foo's Periodical Writing and Chinese Exclusion," *Genre: Forms of Discourse and Culture* 39, nos. 3–4 [Fall/Winter 2006]: 85, 86).
60. Mark Twain, *Notebooks and Journals*, vol. 3: *1883–1891*, ed. Frederick Anderson et al. (Berkeley: University of California Press, 1979), 457; see also 457–458n.
61. Wong Chin Foo, *Wu Chih Tien* (serial installment), *Cosmopolitan* 7, no. 1 (May 1889): 65.
62. Ibid., 68.
63. Ibid.
64. M. Thomas Inge, "About the Illustrations," in *A Connecticut Yankee in King Arthur's Court*, ed. M. Thomas Inge (New York: Oxford University Press, 1997), xx. When Beard later illustrated Ernest Howard Crosby's satire of the U.S.-Philippine War and the suppression of the Boxer uprising, *Captain Jinks, Hero* (1902), he included a reference to Twain: a barrel of beer and colonial tax bills labeled "For Him Who Sits in Darkness." Twain wrote to Beard about the Captain Jinks illustrations: "I cannot tell you how much I like the pictures. I think you have not made better nor bitterer ones, nor any that were redder with the bloody truth" (Mark Twain, "Letter to Daniel Beard [January 18, 1902]," in Zwick, ed., *Mark Twain's Weapons of Satire*, 109).
65. See Fabian's critique of "*a persistent and systematic tendency to place the referent(s) of anthropology in a Time other than the present of the producer of anthropological discourse*" (Johannes Fabian, *Time and the Other: How Anthropology Makes Its Object* [New York: Columbia University Press, 2002], 31; emphasis in original).
66. Scott Seligman, *The First Chinese American: The Remarkable Life of Wong Chin Foo* (Hong Kong: Hong Kong University Press, 2013), 63, 153.
67. An 1897 article identifies Wong as a "former student at Columbian University"—now George Washington University ("Cues Must Come Off," *The Washington* [December 20, 1897]: 4–5).
68. "Wong Chin Foo," *New York Times* (October 4, 1873): 4.

69. Bonner observes that "the story [Wong] told the *World* varied from the one that formed the basis of the *Times* editorial" (Arthur Bonner, *alas! What Brought Thee Hither? The Chinese in New York, 1800–1950* [Madison, N.J.: Fairleigh Dickinson University Press, 1997], 54).
70. "A Heathen Missionary," *Shaker Manifesto* 9, no. 11 (November 1879): 260.
71. Hsu, "Wong Chin Foo's Periodical Writing," 83–105; see also Seligman, *First Chinese American*.
72. Calling the text "anything but" a direct translation, Seligman suggests that "Wong rewrote stories he had heard in his childhood, taking liberties with them as he saw fit, and filling in gaps where his memory failed him" (*First Chinese American*, 165). In the early 1880s, several periodicals announced that Wong Chin Foo was going to translate "The Fan Yong: or the Royal Slave," a Chinese historical novel written by "Kong Ming" "twenty-two hundred years ago" ("The Bookshelf," *The Continent: An Illustrated Weekly Magazine* 3, no. 16 [April 18, 1883]: 510; "Literary Intelligence," *Trübner's American, European and Oriental Literary Record* 4 [1883]: 3). These announcements seem misleading, however, because Kong Ming was the style name of Zhuge Liang (a.d.181–234), a celebrated scholar and military tactician who is not known to have written such a novel because "The Royal Slave" may be an invention modeled on the subtitle of Aphra Behn's *Oroonoko* and because the earliest Chinese novels were not written until the fourteenth century.
73. Wong Chin Foo, *Wu Chih Tien* (serial installment), *Cosmopolitan* 7, no. 2 (June 1889): 130.
74. Nancy Armstrong, *Desire and Domestic Fiction: A Political History of the Novel* (New York: Oxford University Press, 1987).
75. Wong Chin Foo, *Wu Chih Tien* (serial installment), *Cosmopolitan* 7, no. 5 (September 1889): 459.
76. Kaplan, *The Anarchy of Empire*, 92–120.
77. Quoted in Seligman, *First Chinese American*, 252.
78. Quoted in ibid., 33.
79. Quoted in ibid., 35.
80. Wong contributed to the Xinhai Revolution by writing in support of nationalist leader Sun Yat-Sen and attempting to form a revolutionary junta, based in Chicago, that would instigate the overthrow of the Manchus (ibid., 254–260).
81. Alluding to the Fifteenth Amendment, Wong argued that China's system of assigning government positions based on competitive examinations differs from U.S. politics insofar as it makes "no distinctions . . . relative to nationality, color, or previous condition to servitude" (Wong Chin Foo, "Political Honors in China," *Harper's New Monthly Magazine* [July 1883]: 300). Competitive examinations for military posts—as system that China had instituted in the sixth century—are among the innovations that Hang Morgan introduces in *Connecticut Yankee*.

82. Wong Chin Foo, "Why Am I a Heathen?" *North American Review* 145, no. 369 (August 1887): 174.
83. Rounsevelle Wildman, *China's Open Door: A Sketch of Chinese Life and History* (Boston: Lothrop Publishing, 1900), 1–2.
84. Anne McClintock, *Imperial Leather: Race, Gender, and Sexuality in the Colonial Contest* (New York: Routledge, 1995).
85. See Kerry Driscoll, "'Man Factories' and the 'White Indians' of Camelot: Rereading the Native Subtext of *A Connecticut Yankee in King Arthur's Court*," *Mark Twain Annual* 2, no. 1 (September 2004): 7–23; Kaplan, *The Anarchy of Empire*, 51–91; Sumida, "Reevaluating"; Rowe, *Literary Culture*, 121–141.
86. "Ng Poon Chew: Chinese Statesman and Journalist" (Boston: Redpath Lyceum Bureau, [1910s]), 3. Ng appears to have drawn extensively on a political cartoons and newspaper coverage of issues relating to China and Chinese immigration in preparing his lectures: his papers include four scrapbooks filled with clippings on these topics from an eclectic range of newspapers (Ng Poon Chew Papers, Asian American Studies Archive, University of California, Berkeley, scrapbooks in box 2 and box 3).
87. "Ng Poon Chew Speaks for China," *National Civic Federation Review* 1–2 (January–February 1906), 16.
88. Mark Twain, "The Fable of the Yellow Terror," Mark Twain Papers, MS171, DV359a. typescript, 8 pp., Bancroft Library, University of California, Berkeley.
89. Mark Twain, "The Fable of the Yellow Terror," in *The Devil's Race-Track: Mark Twain's Great Dark Writings*, ed. John S. Tuckey (Berkeley: University of California Press, 1980), 369. Further references to this edition will be cited parenthetically in the text as "YT."
90. Mark Twain, "History 1,000 Years from Now: A Translation" (1901), "The Fall of the Great Republic," and "The Secret History of Eddypus, the World-Empire" (1901–1902; all in Zwick, ed., *Mark Twain's Weapons of Satire*) view the U.S.-Philippine War from the perspective of a distant future in which imperialist tyranny has undermined the United States' democratic principles. Inverting the Chinese invasion narrative, "The Secret History" describes a future in which enlightened civilization exists only in China—the only region to have successfully resisted the imperial encroachments of "The World-Empire of Holy Eddypus" (see Twain, "The Secret History of Eddypus, the World Empire," in Zwick, ed., *Mark Twain's Weapons of Satire*, 83).
91. Jack London, "The Yellow Peril," in *Jack London Reports: War Correspondence, Sports Articles, and Miscellaneous Writings*, ed. King Hendricks and Irving Shepard (New York: Doubleday, 1970): 348.
92. "He relates himself to the State as, amongst bees, the worker is related to the hive; himself nothing, the State everything; his reasons for existence the exaltation and glorification of the State" (ibid., 350).
93. Ibid.," 343.

CHAPTER 5. BODY COUNTS AND COMPARATIVE ANTI-IMPERIALISM

1. After the essay appeared in the *North American Review* in February 1901, it was widely excerpted and debated and reprinted as a pamphlet by the Anti-Imperialist League of New York.
2. Mark Twain, "To the Person Sitting in Darkness," in *Mark Twain's Weapons of Satire: Anti-imperialist Writings on the Philippine-American War*, ed. Jim Zwick (Syracuse, N.Y.: Syracuse University Press, 1992), 38. Further references to this edition will be cited parenthetically in the text as "PS."
3. Mark Twain, "Salutation Speech from the Nineteenth Century to the Twentieth," in Zwick, ed., *Mark Twain's Weapons of Satire*, 12–13.
4. Mark Twain, "The Stupendous Procession," in Zwick, ed., *Mark Twain's Weapons of Satire*, 44–45.
5. Mark Twain, "Aguinaldo," in Zwick, ed., *Mark Twain's Weapons of Satire*, 89.
6. This chapter focuses on the rhetorical and aesthetic uses of body counts and other statistics in Twain's later writings. For extensive accounts of Twain's anti-imperialist writings in their historical context, see Susan Harris, *God's Arbiters: Americans and the Philippines, 1898-1902* (New York: Oxford University Press, 2011); and Jim Zwick, ed., *Confronting Imperialism: Essays on Mark Twain and the Anti-Imperialist League* (West Conshohocken, Pa.: Infinity Publishing Co., 2007).
7. Kaplan notes, however, that Twain's argument depends on an exceptionalist view of U.S. history: "His powerful condemnation of imperialism works here in part by disavowing its centrality to U.S. identity, by representing imperialism as a foreign activity, an aberration from the national commitment to freeing the captive" (Amy Kaplan, *The Anarchy of Empire in the Making of U.S. Culture* [Cambridge, Mass.: Harvard University Press, 2002], 92).
8. Albert Beveridge, "Our Philippine Policy," in *The Philippines Reader: A History of Colonialism, Neocolonialism, Dictatorship, and Resistance*, ed. Daniel B. Schirmer and Stephen Rosskamm Shalom (Boston: South End Press, 1987), 23.
9. See the Introduction.
10. Michel Foucault, *"Society Must Be Defended": Lectures at the Collège de France, 1975—1976*, trans. David Macey (New York: Picador, 2003), 241.
11. Ibid., 254–255.
12. Nayan Shah, *Contagious Divides: Epidemics and Race in San Francisco's Chinatown* (Berkeley: University of California Press, 2001); Warwick Anderson, *Colonial Pathologies: American Tropical Medicine, Race, and Hygiene in the Philippines* (Durham, N.C.: Duke University Press, 2006).
13. "In the early period of U.S. rule, one of the most instructive documents of the colonial wish to establish total and continuous supervision for the sake of tutelage was the four-volume *Census of the Philippine Islands*, begun in 1903 and published in 1905" (Vicente Rafael, *White Love and Other Events in Filipino History* [Durham, N.C.: Duke University Press, 2000], 24). See also Martha Hodes, "Fractions and Fictions in the United States Census of 1890," in *Haunted by*

Empire: Geographies of Intimacy in North American History, ed. Ann Laura Stoler (Durham, N.C.: Duke University Press, 2006), 240–270.

14. Nancy Armstrong and Leonard Tennenhouse, "The Problem of Population and the Form of the American Novel," *American Literary History* 20, no. 4 (Winter 2008): 672.
15. Achille Mbembe, "Necropolitics," trans. Libby Meintjes, *Public Culture* 15, no. 1 (Winter 2003): 40.
16. See Ruth Wilson Gilmore, *Golden Gulag: Prisons, Surplus, Crisis, and Opposition in Globalizing California* (Berkeley: University of California Press, 2007), 28. For geographically oriented scholarship that engages with the concept of necropolitics, see the essays collected in Michael McIntyre and Heidi J. Nast, eds., "Bio(necro)polis: Marx, Surplus Populations, and the Spatial Dialectics of Reproduction and 'Race,'" special issue of *Antipode: A Radical Journal of Geography* 43, no. 5 (November 2011).
17. Mbembe, "Necropolitics," 12.
18. Susan Gillman, *Blood Talk: American Race Melodrama and the Culture of the Occult* (Chicago: University of Chicago Press, 2003), 133–147.
19. As Twain probably knew from his friendships with Burlingame and Twichell, the mass migration of Asian laborers to the United States, the Caribbean, Latin America, Africa, Australia, and elsewhere was in part motivated by European incursions in India and China, where the commercialization of agriculture, the Opium Wars, and the Taiping Rebellion dispossessed or expropriated millions.
20. Mark Twain, "Notebook #38," supplemental pages from the Henry W. and Albert A. Berg Collection, Berg Coll MSS Clemens, New York Public Library, New York, Typescript, May 4, 1896, p. 33, in the Mark Twain Papers, Bancroft Library, University of California, Berkeley. In Twain's notebook, this passage immediately follows the description of fifty Indians and Chinamen sleeping on the ship, quoted above.
21. Molly Farrell, "'Beyond My Skil': Mary Rowlandson's Counting," *Early American Literature* 47, no. 1 (2012): 60.
22. See John Eyler, *Victorian Social Medicine: The Ideas and Methods of William Farr* (Baltimore: Johns Hopkins University Press, 1979); Louise Penner, *Victorian Medicine and Social Reform: Florence Nightingale among the Novelists* (New York: Palgrave, 2010); and Gérard Jorland et al., eds., *Body Counts: Medical Quantification in Historical and Sociological Perspectives* (Montreal: McGill-Queens University Press, 2005). Twain was influenced by Sir Francis Galton's *Finger Prints* (New York: Macmillan & Co., 1892; see Chapter 3) and refers to Nightingale in "Woman—The Pride of Any Profession, and the Jewel of Ours" and *No. 44*, which features a cat named "Mary Florence Fortescue Baker G. Nightingale" (Mark Twain, "Woman—The Pride of Any Profession, and the Jewel of Ours," in *Mark Twain Speaking*, ed. Paul Fatout [Iowa City: University of Iowa Press, 1976], 22, and *No.44: The Mysterious Stranger* [Berkeley: University of California Press, 1969], 257).

23. Drew Gilpin Faust, "'Numbers on Top of Numbers': Counting the Civil War Dead," *Journal of Military History* 70, no. 4 (October 2006): 998. See also Vanessa Steinroetter, "'Reading the List': Casualty Lists and Civil War Poetry," *ESQ: A Journal of the American Renaissance* 59, no. 1 (2013): 48–78.
24. Faust, "Numbers on Top of Numbers," 996.
25. Judith Butler, *Frames of War: When Is Life Grievable?* (London: Verso, 2009), xvi.
26. Ibid., xxix–xxx.
27. Ibid., xx.
28. Oscar Campomanes, "Casualty Figures of the American Soldier and the Other: Post-1898 Allegories of Imperial Nation-Building as 'Love and War,'" in *Vestiges of War: The Philippine-American War and the Aftermath of an Imperial Dream, 1899–1999*, ed. Angel Velasco Shaw and Luis H. Francia (New York: NYU Press, 2002), 138.
29. In many ways, the U.S.-Philippine War inaugurated the media disinformation campaigns that have accompanied twentieth- and twenty-first-century U.S. foreign wars: as McCoy notes, "The war in Iraq has produced a succession of parallels with this Philippine past too numerous to dismiss as merely incidental or ironic" (Alfred McCoy, *Policing America's Empire: The United States, the Philippines, and the Rise of the Surveillance State* [Madison: University of Wisconsin Press, 2009], 3–4).
30. Foucault, *"Society Must Be Defended,"* 256.
31. Mark Twain, "A Connecticut Yankee in King Arthur's Court," MS, 1885–1889, Henry W. and Albert A. Berg Collection of English and American Literature, Berg Coll. MSS Clemens (holograph ms, continuous text, paginated in two series), paginated second series, 368, New York Public Library, New York. Copy in the Mark Twain Papers, box 41, 1885.12.00-1889.00.00, Bancroft Library, University of California, Berkeley.
32. Thomas Peyser, "Mark Twain, Immigration, and the American Narrative," *ELH* 79, no. 4 (Winter 2012): 1017.
33. Eyler, *Victorian Social Medicine*, 133.
34. Ibid., 158.
35. Mark Twain, "The United States of Lyncherdom," in *The Complete Essays of Mark Twain*, ed. Charles Neider (Cambridge, Mass.: Da Capo Press, 1991), 674.
36. Ibid., 678–679.
37. Ibid., 677–678.
38. Jim Zwick, "'Prodigally Endowed with Sympathy for the Cause': Mark Twain's Involvement with the Anti-Imperialist League," in Zwick, ed., *Confronting Imperialism*, 133.
39. See, e.g., the comparison and assessment of numbers of American and Filipino wounded and dead in Moorfield Storey and Julian Codman, *Secretary Root's Record: "Marked Severities" in Philippine Warfare* (Boston: Geo. H. Ellis Co., 1902), 21–27.
40. Noting that "statistics were deliberately not kept for Filipino casualties and losses," historian Oscar Campomanes cites "conventionalized figures of 16,000

casualties for the Filipino army, from an estimated 1898 strength of 20,000 to 30,000—which apparently is by itself a case of undercounting—and civilian or noncombatant deaths of 200,000 'from famine, pestilence, or the unfortunate happenstance of being too close to the fighting.' I have seen a more consensual figure of 250,000 Filipino deaths but those who cite it do not explain the basis for their common agreement. Indeed estimates have ranged from a low one hundred thousand to a high of one million, which at its worst would have meant the depopulation, by one-sixth, of the turn-of-the-century Philippines" (Campomanes, "Casualty Figures," 138).
41. See Zwick, "Prodigally Endowed," 122.
42. Twain, "Aguinaldo," 103.
43. Ibid.
44. According to Zwick, "[Twain's] notes say that the Filipinos suffered 200 wounded in 400 days, but his rounding of the figure should have brought it to 2,000. . . . He seems to have halved the 400 days instead of the 4,000 killed. . . . The missatement is made twice and may have been intentional" (Zwick's annotation in Twain, "Aguinaldo," 114n).
45. Mark Twain, "Notes on Patriotism," in Zwick, ed., *Mark Twain's Weapons of Satire*, 114.
46. Mark Twain, "Comments on the Moro Massacre," in Zwick, ed., *Mark Twain's Weapons of Satire*, 171. Further references will be cited parenthetically in the text as "CMM."
47. Butler, *Frames of War*, xvi.
48. See Butler's discussion of the accusation that Hamas "uses children to shield itself": "If the Palestinian children who are killed by mortar and phosphorous bombs are human shields, then they are not children at all, but rather bits of armament, military instruments and materiel, aiding and abetting an assault in Israel" (ibid., xxvi).
49. See Mark Twain, "The Fable of the Yellow Terror" (1904–1905), in *The Devil's Race-Track: Mark Twain's Great Dark Writings*, ed. John S. Tuckey (Berkeley: University of California Press, 1980), 369–372, and "Three Thousand Years among the Microbes" (1905), in *Mark Twain's "Which Was the Dream?" and Other Symbolic Writings of the Later Years*, ed. John S. Tuckey (Berkeley and Los Angeles: University of California Press, 1968), 433–473.
50. Although the story first appeared in *Harper's Magazine* (December 1907 and January 1908), Twain had begun working on it as early as 1868.
51. Mark Twain, *Extract from Captain Stormfield's Visit to Heaven* (New York: Harper & Bros., 1909), 103.
52. Ibid., 106.
53. Stephanie LeMenager, *Manifest and Other Destinies: Territorial Fictions of the Nineteenth-Century United States* (Lincoln: University of Nebraska Press, 2004), 217.

54. Ibid.
55. Twain, *Extract from Captain Stormfield's Visit to Heaven*, 77.
56. See Wai Chee Dimock, "Deep Time: American Literature and World History," *American Literary History* 13, no. 4 (Winter 2001): 755–775.
57. An Architect, "The Washington Monument, and Mr. Story's Design," *Atlantic Monthly* 43, no. 258 (April 1879): 524.
58. Benedict Anderson, *Imagined Communities: Reflections on the Origin and Spread of Nationalism* (London: Verso, 2006), 9.
59. For the inscriptions, see *The Monument to Robert Gould Shaw: Its Inception, Completion and Unveiling, 1865–1897* (Boston: Houghton, Mifflin, & Co., 1897), 15–16.
60. For an extended discussion of the historical inaccuracies perpetrated by these monuments, see James Loewen, *Lies across America: What Our Historic Sites Get Wrong* (New York: New Press, 1999), 122–130.
61. Ibid., 125.
62. Campomanes, "Casualty Figures," 145.
63. Mark Twain, "The Treaty with China: Its Provisions Explained." *Journal of Transnational American Studies*, 2, no.1 (2010): 1–12, http://escholarship.org/uc/item/2r87m203.11.
64. Ibid.
65. See Danny Keenan, *Wars without End: The Land Wars in Nineteenth Century New Zealand* (New York: Penguin, 2009).
66. In a response to attacks from missionaries and their supporters, Twain refused to retract his initial statement, explaining that expanding the indemnity by one-third was still "theft and extortion" (Mark Twain, "To My Missionary Critics," in Neider, ed., *The Complete Essays of Mark Twain*, 305).
67. See Rob Nixon, *Slow Violence and the Environmentalism of the Poor* (Cambridge, Mass.: Harvard University Press, 2011).
68. Twain, "The Stupendous Procession," 45–46.
69. As Heym notes, the title echoes two of Twain's earlier political pieces (and thus draws an implicit comparison between their topics): "'In *Defense* of General Funston' [a satire of the officer who used deception and betrayal to capture General Emilio Aguinaldo in the Philippines] and 'The Czar's *Soliloquy*' are merged to become 'King Leopold's *Soliloquy—A Defense* of his Congo Rule'" (Stefan Heym, "Introduction," in *King Leopold's Soliloquy*, by Mark Twain [New York: International Publishers, 1970], 18).
70. Twain, *King Leopold's Soliloquy* (New York: International Publishers, 1970), 54–55.
71. In Twain's copy, statistics have been marked on pp. 16, 21, 23, 24, 25, and 27; there are also marginalia in Twain's hand: "15M" next to "[they] make my total death-harvest 15,000,000" and "1/2 M per year" next to "my output is 500,000 corpses a year" (Mark Twain's copy of *King Leopold's Soliloquy*, pp. 25, 27, in

the Mark Twain Papers, Bancroft Library, University of California, Berkeley, uncatalogued).
72. Twain, *King Leopold's Soliloquy*, 55.
73. Matthew 4:16 (King James Version).
74. See Harris, *God's Arbiters*, 154–157.
75. José Rizal, "My Last Thought," in *An Eagle Flight* (New York: McClure, Phillips, & Co., 1901), xiii.
76. Harris, *God's Arbiters*, 226n3.
77. Mark Twain, "My Last Thought," in *On the Poetry of Mark Twain with Selections from His Verse*, ed. Arthur Lincoln Scott (Urbana: University of Illinois Press, 1966), 130.
78. Ibid.
79. Emphasis added.
80. Ibid., 131.
81. See the Introduction.
82. Harris, *God's Arbiters*, 54.

CONCLUSION
1. John L. Jackson, Jr., "Censoring Twain," *Chronicle of Higher Education* (January 5, 2011), http://chronicle.com/blogs/brainstorm/censoring-mark-twains-ghost/30789.
2. John S. W. Park, *Illegal Migrations and the Huckleberry Finn Problem* (Philadelphia: Temple University Press, 2013).
3. On Harte and comparative racialization, see Chapter 2. On Jackson's *Ramona*, see Bryan Wagner, "Helen Hunt Jackson's Errant Local Color," *Arizona Quarterly* 58, no. 4 (Winter 2002): 1–23. On Ridge's *Life and Adventures of Joaquin Murieta*, see John Carlos Rowe, "Highway Robbery: 'Indian Removal,' the Mexican-American War, and American Identity in *The Life and Adventures of Joaquin Murieta*," *NOVEL* 31 (Spring 1998): 149–173. On Cable's *Grandissimes*, see Byan Wagner, *Disturbing the Peace: Black Culture and the Police Power after Slavery* (Cambridge, Mass.: Harvard University Press, 2009), 79–103. On Chesnutt, see Julia H. Lee, *Interracial Encounters: Reciprocal Representations in African and Asian American Literatures, 1896–1937* (New York: NYU Press, 2011), 48–69. On Du Bois and Asia, see Bill Mullen and Cathryn Watson, eds., *W. E. B. Du Bois on Asia: Crossing the World Color Line* (Jackson: University Press of Mississippi, 2005). On "The Alaska Widow," see Mary Chapman, "Cross-Cultural Affinities between Native American and White Women in 'The Alaska Widow' by Edith Eaton (Sui Sin Far)," *Melus* 38, no. 1 (Spring 2013): 155–163. On Winnifred Eaton, see Gretchen Murphy, *Shadowing the White Man's Burden: U.S. Imperialism and the Problem of the Color Line* (New York: NYU Press, 2010),159–186. On Jack London's career-long engagements with race, see Jeanne Campbell Reesman, *Jack London's Racial Lives: A Critical Biography* (Athens: University of Georgia Press, 2009).

Works Cited

Aarim-Heriot, Najia. *Chinese Immigrants, African Americans, and Racial Anxiety in the United States, 1848–82*. Urbana: University of Illinois Press, 2003.
"About 'Pudd'nhead Wilson.'" *Springfield Republican* (February 3, 1895).
Act of 5 May 1892 (Geary Amendment). Chap. 60, 27 Stat. 25.
"'Ah Sin' at the Fifth Avenue Theatre." *New York Herald* (August 1, 1877).
Alexander, Michelle. *The New Jim Crow: Mass Incarceration in the Age of Colorblindness*. New York: New Press, 2010.
"Amusements. Ah Sin." *New York Sun* (August 5, 1877).
"Amusements. Fifth Avenue Theatre." *New York Times* (August 1, 1877): 5.
An Architect. "The Washington Monument, and Mr. Story's Design." *Atlantic Monthly* 43, no. 258 (April 1879): 524–527.
Anderson, Benedict. *Imagined Communities: Reflections on the Origin and Spread of Nationalism*. London: Verso, 2006.
Anderson, Warwick. *Colonial Pathologies: American Tropical Medicine, Race, and Hygiene in the Philippines*. Durham, N.C.: Duke University Press, 2006.
Armstrong, Nancy. *Desire and Domestic Fiction: A Political History of the Novel*. New York: Oxford University Press, 1987.
Armstrong, Nancy, and Leonard Tennenhouse. "The Problem of Population and the Form of the American Novel." *American Literary History* 20, no. 4 (Winter 2008): 667–685.
Bakhtin, Mikhail. "Forms of Time and of the Chronotope in the Novel." In *The Dialogic Imagination: Four Essays*, ed. Michael Holquist, trans. Caryl Emerson and Michael Holquist. Austin: University of Texas Press, 1994.
Beard, Daniel C. *Hardly a Man Is Now Alive: The Autobiography of Dan Beard*. New York: Doubleday, 1939.
Beier, A. L. *Masterless Men: The Vagrancy Problem in England, 1560–1640*. London: Methuen, 1986.
Bellew, Frank. *The Tramp: His Tricks, Tallies, and Tell-Tales, With All His Signs, Countersigns, Grips, Pass-Words, and Villainies Exposed*. New York: Dick & Fitzgerald, 1878.
Beveridge, Albert. "Our Philippine Policy." In *The Philippines Reader: A History of Colonialism, Neocolonialism, Dictatorship, and Resistance*, ed. Daniel B. Schirmer and Stephen Rosskamm Shalom, 23–26. Boston: South End Press, 1987.
Bierce, Ambrose. "The Haunted Valley." *Overland Monthly* 7, no. 1 (1871): 88–95.
Blyn, Robin. "The Subject of Incorporation: Personhood under Reconstruction in *Those Extraordinary Twins*." Paper presented at the American Literature Association Conference, Boston, May 24–27, 2007.

Bonner, Arthur. *ALAS! What Brought Thee Hither? The Chinese in New York, 1800–1950*. Madison, N.J.: Fairleigh Dickinson University Press, 1997.

"The Bookshelf." *The Continent: An Illustrated Weekly Magazine* 3, no. 16 (April 18, 1883): 510–11.

Branch, Edgar. *Clemens of the "Call": Mark Twain in San Francisco*. Berkeley: University of California Press, 1969.

Braun, Bruce. "'On the Raggedy Edge of Risk': Articulations of Race and Nature after Biology." In *Race, Nature, and the Politics of Difference*, ed. Donald Moore, Jake Kosek, and Anand Pandian, 175–203. Durham, N.C.: Duke University Press, 2003.

Brechin, Gray. *Imperial San Francisco: Urban Power, Earthly Ruin*. Berkeley: University of California Press, 2006.

Brooks, Van Wyck. *The Ordeal of Mark Twain*. New York: E. P. Dutton & Co., 1920.

Bush, Harold K., Jr. "'A Moralist in Disguise: Mark Twain and American Religion." In *A Historical Guide to Mark Twain*, ed. Shelley Fisher Fishkin, 55–94. New York: Oxford University Press, 2002.

Butler, Judith. *Frames of War: When Is Life Grievable?* London: Verso, 2009.

Campomanes, Oscar V. "Casualty Figures of the American Soldier and the Other: Post-1898 Allegories of Imperial Nation-Building as 'Love and War.'" In *Vestiges of War: The Philippine-American War and the Aftermath of an Imperial Dream, 1899–1999*, ed. Angel Velasco Shaw and Luis H. Francia, 134–162. New York: NYU Press, 2002.

Castronovo, Russ. *Necro Citizenship: Death, Eroticism, and the Public Sphere in the Nineteenth-Century United States*. Durham, N.C.: Duke University Press, 2001.

Chae Chan Ping v. U.S. 130 U.S. 581 (1889).

Chan, Sucheng. "A People of Exceptional Character: Ethnic Diversity, Nativism, and Racism in the California Gold Rush." In *Rooted in Barbarous Soil: People, Culture, and Community in Gold Rush California*," ed. Kevin Starr and Richard J. Orsi, 44–85. Berkeley: University of California Press, 2000.

Chang, Gordon. "China and the Pursuit of America's Destiny: Nineteenth-Century Imagining and Why Immigration Restriction Took So Long." *Journal of Asian American Studies* 15, no. 2 (June 2012): 145–169.

Chapman, Mary. "Cross-Cultural Affinities between Native American and White Women in 'The Alaska Widow' by Edith Eaton (Sui Sin Far)." *Melus* 38, no. 1 (Spring 2013): 155–163.

"The Chinese: Many-Handed But Soulless." *Wasp*, vol. 15 (July–December 1885).

Chinese Consolidated Benevolent Association. *Memorial of the Six Chinese Companies. An Address to the Senate and House of Representatives of the United States. Testimony of California's Leading Citizens*. San Francisco: Alta Print, 1877.

Chinese Immigration: The Social, Moral, and Political Effect of Chinese Immigration: Testimony Taken Before a Committee of the Senate of the State of California Sacramento, Calif.: State Printing Office, 1876.

"chinese oaths." *Country Gentleman* 3, no. 1 (January 4, 1853): 66.

Chinn, Sarah E. *Technology and the Logic of American Racism: A Cultural History of the Body as Evidence*. Critical Research in Material Culture. New York: Continuum, 2000.
Clemmer, Mary. "Ah Sin," *San Francisco Daily Evening Bulletin* (21 May 1877).
Cole, Simon A. *Suspect Identities: A History of Fingerprinting and Criminal Identification*. Cambridge, Mass.: Harvard University Press, 2002.
———. "Twins, Twain, Galton, and Gilman: Fingerprinting, Individualization, Brotherhood, and Race in *Pudd'nhead Wilson*." *Configurations* 15, no. 3 (Fall 2007): 227–265.
"The Coming Man: Allee Sammee 'Melican Man Monopoleeee." *Wasp*, vol. 6 (January–June 1881).
Constitution of the State of California. San Francisco: Bancroft-Whitney Co., 1902.
Cosco, Joseph. *Imagining Italians: The Clash of Romance and Race in American Perceptions, 1880–1910*. Albany, N.Y.: SUNY Press, 2003.
Coulombe, Joseph. *Mark Twain and the American West*. Columbia: University of Missouri Press, 2003.
Courtney, Steve. *Joseph Hopkins Twichell: The Life and Times of Mark Twain's Closest Friend*. Athens: University of Georgia Press, 2008.
Crawford, Richard. "Introduction." In *The Civil War Songbook: Complete Original Sheet Music for 37 Songs*, ed. Richard Crawford, v–x. New York: Dover, 1977.
Cresswell, Tim. *The Tramp in America*. London: Reaktion, 2001.
The Critic; an Illustrated Monthly Review of Literature, Art, and Life. Unsigned review. 26 (May 11, 1895): 338–339. In Mark Twain, *Pudd'nhead Wilson and Those Extraordinary Twins*, ed. Sidney E. Berger, 243–244. New York: Norton, 2005.
"Cues Must Come Off." *The Washington* (December 20, 1897), 4–5.
Daniels, Roger. "The Immigrant Experience in the Gilded Age." In *The Gilded Age: Perspectives on the Origins of Modern America*, ed. Charles William Calhoun, 63–89. Lanham, Md.: Rowman & Littlefield, 2007.
Dayan, Joan [Colin]. "Legal Slaves and Civil Bodies." *Nepantla: Views from South* 2, no. 1 (2001): 3–39.
De Graaf, Lawrence, and Quintard Taylor. "Introduction: African Americans in California History, California in African American History." In *Seeking El Dorado: African Americans in California*, ed. Lawrence De Graaf, Kevin Mulroy, and Quintard Taylor, 3–69. Los Angeles: Autry Museum of Western Heritage, 2001.
Dekker, George. *The American Historical Romance*. Cambridge: Cambridge University Press, 1990.
De Leeuw, Karl, and Jan Bergstra. *The History of Information Security: A Comprehensive Handbook*. Amsterdam: Elsevier, 2007.
Denning, Michael. *Mechanic Accents: Dime Novels and Working-Class Culture in America*. London: Verso, 1987.
DePastino, Todd. *Citizen Hobo: How a Century of Homelessness Shaped America*. Chicago: University of Chicago Press, 2003.
Dillon, Elizabeth Maddock. "Fear of Formalism: Kant, Twain, and Cultural Studies in American Literature." *Diacritics* 27, no. 4 (1998): 46–69.

Dimock, Wai Chee. "Deep Time: American Literature and World History." *American Literary History* 13, no. 4 (Winter 2001): 755–775.

Donnelly, Ignatius. *Caesar's Column: A Story of the Twentieth Century.* Chicago: Schulte & Co., 1890.

Douglass, Frederick. "Our Composite Nationality: An Address Delivered in Boston, Massachusetts, on 7 December 1869." In *The Frederick Douglass Papers*, ser. 1: *Speeches, Debates, and Interviews*, vol. 4: *1864–1880*, ed. John Blassingame and John McKivigan, 240–259. New Haven, Conn.: Yale University Press, 1991.

Dreger, Alice Domurat. *One of Us: Conjoined Twins and the Future of the Normal.* Cambridge, Mass.: Harvard University Press, 2004.

Driscoll, Kerry. "'Man Factories' and the 'White Indians' of Camelot: Re-reading the Native Subtext of *A Connecticut Yankee in King Arthur's Court*." *Mark Twain Annual* 2, no. 1 (September 2004): 7–23.

Du Bois, W. E. B. *The Souls of Black Folk: Essays and Sketches.* Cambridge, Mass.: A. C. McClurg, 1903.

———. "Reconstruction and Its Benefits." In *W. E. B. Du Bois: A Reader*, 174–192, ed. David Levering Lewis. New York: Henry Holt & Co., 1995.

Duckett, Margaret. *Mark Twain and Bret Harte.* Norman: University of Oklahoma Press, 1964.

Eliot, T.S. "Introduction to Adventures of Huckleberry Finn." In *Mark Twain, Adventures of Huckleberry Finn*, ed. Thomas Cooley, 348–354. New York: Norton, 1999.

Epstein, Dena. *Music Publishing in Chicago before 1871: The Firm of Root & Cady, 1858–1871.* Detroit: Information Coordinators, Inc., 1969.

Eyler, John. *Victorian Social Medicine: The Ideas and Methods of William Farr.* Baltimore: Johns Hopkins University Press, 1979.

Fabian, Johannes. *Time and the Other: How Anthropology Makes Its Object.* New York: Columbia University Press, 2002.

Farrell, Molly. "'Beyond My Skil': Mary Rowlandson's Counting." *Early American Literature* 47, no. 1 (2012): 59–87.

Faust, Drew Gilpin. "'Numbers on Top of Numbers': Counting the Civil War Dead." *Journal of Military History* 70, no. 4 (October 2006): 995–1009.

A Few Particulars Concerning Chang-Eng, the United Siamese Brothers. New York: John M. Elliott, 1838.

Fiedler, Leslie. "Come Back to the Raft Ag'in, Huck Honey!" In *Leslie Fiedler and American Culture*, ed. Steven G. Kellman and Irving Malin, 26–36. Newark: University of Delaware Press, 1999.

———. "'As Free as Any Cretur . . .'" In *The Devil Gets His Due: The Uncollected Essays of Leslie Fiedler*, ed. Samuele Pardini, 77–85. Berkeley, Calif.: Counterpoint Press, 2008.

Fishkin, Shelley Fisher. *Was Huck Black? Mark Twain and African-American Voices.* New York: Oxford University Press, 1994.

———. "Mark Twain and Race." In *A Historical Guide to Mark Twain*, ed. Shelley Fisher Fishkin, 127–162. New York: Oxford University Press, 2002.

———. "Race and the Politics of Memory: Mark Twain and Paul Laurence Dunbar." *Journal of American Studies* 40 (2006): 283–309.

———, ed. *The Mark Twain Anthology: Great Writers on His Life and Work*. New York: Library of America, 2010.

Foucault, Michel. *"Society Must Be Defended": Lectures at the Collège de France, 1975–1976*, trans. David Macey. New York: Picador, 2003.

Fredricks, Nancy. "Twain's Indelible Twins." *Nineteenth-Century Literature* 43, no. 4 (March 1989): 484–499.

Freeman, Elizabeth. "The Political Sensuality of the Archive: A Roundtable." Conference presentation. "C19: The Society of Nineteenth-Century Americanists." Berkeley, Calif.: April 12, 2012.

"A Fresh Eruption of the Pacific Coast Vesuvius." *Wasp*, vol. 8 (January–June 1882).

Galton, Sir Francis. *Finger Prints*. New York: Macmillan & Co., 1892.

Gates, Henry Louis, Jr. "Frederick Douglass and the Language of the Self." In *Figures in Black: Words, Signs, and the "Racial" Self*. New York: Oxford University Press, 1987.

Gerber, John C. "Sources for Characters." In *The Adventures of Tom Sawyer: 135th Anniversary Edition* by Mark Twain, ed. Paul Baender, 270–271. Berkeley: University of California Press, 2010.

Gillman, Susan. *Blood Talk: American Race Melodrama and the Culture of the Occult*. Chicago: University of Chicago Press, 2003.

Gillman, Susan, and Forrest Glen Robinson, eds. *Mark Twain's Pudd'nhead Wilson: Race, Conflict, and Culture*. Durham, N.C.: Duke University Press, 1990.

Gilmore, Ruth Wilson. *Golden Gulag: Prisons, Surplus, Crisis, and Opposition in Globalizing California*. Berkeley: University of California Press, 2007.

Glass, Loren. *Authors Inc.: Literary Celebrity in the Modern United States, 1880–1980*. New York: NYU Press, 2004.

Grady, Henry Woodfin. *The New South*. New York: Robert Bonner's Sons, 1890.

———. "The South and Her Problems." In *The Complete Orations and Speeches of Henry W. Grady*, ed. Edwin Shurter, 23–64. New York: Hinds, Noble, & Eldredge, 1910.

Haggard, H. Rider. *King Solomon's Mines*. New York: Oxford University Press, 2006. Originally published 1886.

Hall, Stuart. "Race, Articulation, and Societies Structured in Dominance." In *Sociological Theories: Race and Colonialism*, 305–345. Paris: UNESCO, 1980.

Hamilton, Anne. "From China to Hartford, a Historic Connection." *Hartford Courant* (June 14, 2009). http://articles.courant.com/2009-06-14/news/exlife0614.art_1_first-chinese-graduate-chinese-government-chinese-families.

Harris, Helen. "Mark Twain's Response to the Native American." *American Literature* 46, no. 4 (January 1975): 495–505.

Harris, Susan. *God's Arbiters: Americans and the Philippines, 1898–1902*. New York: Oxford University Press, 2011.

Harris, William. *Deep Souths: Delta, Piedmont, and Sea Island Society in the Age of Segregation*. Baltimore: Johns Hopkins University Press, 2001.

Harte, Bret. "Indiscriminate Massacre of Indians, Women and Children Butchered." *Northern Californian* 2, no. 9 (February 29, 1860).
———. Harte, Bret. "The Iliad of Sandy Bar." In *The Luck of Roaring Camp and Other Writings*, ed. Gary Scharnhorst, 87–97. New York: Penguin Books, 2001.
———. "Plain Language from Truthful James." In *The Luck of Roaring Camp and Other Writings*, ed. Gary Scharnhorst, 215–216. New York: Penguin Books, 2001.
———. "Three Vagabonds of Trinidad." In *The Luck of Roaring Camp and Other Writings*, ed. Gary Scharnhorst, 155–167. New York: Penguin, 2001.
———. "Wan Lee, the Pagan." In *The Luck of Roaring Camp and Other Writings*, ed. Gary Scharnhorst, 123–137. New York: Penguin Books, 2001.
Hartman, Saidiya V. *Scenes of Subjection: Terror, Slavery, and Self-Making in Nineteenth-Century America*. New York: Oxford University Press, 1997.
———. "The Time of Slavery." *South Atlantic Quarterly* 101, no. 4 (Fall 2002): 757–777.
Hayot, Eric. *The Hypothetical Mandarin: Sympathy, Modernity, and Chinese Pain*. New York: Oxford University Press, 2009.
"A Heathen Missionary." *Shaker Manifesto* 9, no. 11 (November 1879): 259–260.
Hebard, Andrew. "Romantic Sovereignty: Popular Romances and the American Imperial State." *American Quarterly* 57, no. 3 (September 2005): 805–830.
———. *The Poetics of Sovereignty in American Literature, 1885–1910*. Cambridge: Cambridge University Press, 2012.
Heym, Stefan. "Introduction." In *King Leopold's Soliloquy* by Mark Twain, 11–26. New York: International Publishers, 1970.
Higgens-Evenson, Ronald Rudy. *The Price of Progress: Public Services, Taxation, and the American Corporate State, 1877 to 1929*. Baltimore: Johns Hopkins University Press, 2003.
Hodes, Martha. "Fractions and Fictions in the United States Census of 1890." In *Haunted by Empire: Geographies of Intimacy in North American History*, ed. Ann Laura Stoler, 240–270. Durham, N.C.: Duke University Press, 2006.
Holland, Sharon. *Raising the Dead: Readings of Death and (Black) Subjectivity*. Durham, N.C.: Duke University Press, 2000.
Hollander, Gail M. "'Subject to Control': Shifting Geographies of Race and Labour in US Sugar Agroindustry, 1930–1950." *Cultural Geographies* 13, no. 2 (April 2006): 266–292.
Hong, Grace Kyungwon, and Roderick A. Ferguson, eds. *Strange Affinities: The Gender and Sexual Politics of Comparative Racialization*. Durham, N.C.: Duke University Press, 2011.
Horwitz, Morton J. *The Transformation of American Law, 1870–1960: The Crisis of Legal Orthodoxy*. New York: Oxford University Press, 1992.
Howells, William Dean. "The New Historical Romance." *North American Review* 171 (1900): 935–948.
Hsu, Hsuan L. "Wong Chin Foo's Periodical Writing and Chinese Exclusion." *Genre: Forms of Discourse and Culture* 39, nos. 3–4 (Fall/Winter 2006): 83–105.

———. "A Connecticut Yankee in Wu Chih Tien's Court." *Common-Place: The Interactive Journal of Early American Life*, vol. 11, no. 1 (October 2010). www.common-place.org/vol-11/no-01/hsu/.

"The Hydra-Headed Vampire-Contending Contentments." *Wasp*, vol. 4 (August 1879–July1880).

"Immigration East and West." *Wasp* 7 (July–December 1881): cover.

Inge, M. Thomas. "About the Illustrations." In *A Connecticut Yankee in King Arthur's Court*, ed. M. Thomas Inge, xx–xxi. New York: Oxford, 1997.

Jackson, John L., Jr. "Censoring Twain." *Chronicle of Higher Education* (January 5, 2011). http://chronicle.com/blogs/brainstorm/censoring-mark-twains-ghost/30789.

Jorland, Gérard, et al., eds. *Body Counts: Medical Quantification in Historical and Sociological Perspectives*. Montreal: McGill-Queens University Press, 2005.

Jun, Helen Heran. *Race for Citizenship: Black Orientalism and Asian Uplift from Pre-Emancipation to Neoliberal America*. New York: NYU Press, 2011.

Jung, Moon-Ho. *Coolies and Cane: Race, Labor, and Sugar in the Age of Emancipation*. Baltimore: Johns Hopkins University Press, 2006.

———. "Coolie." In *Keywords for American Cultural Studies*, ed. Bruce Burgett and Glenn Hendler, 64–66. New York: NYU Press, 2007.

Kaplan, Amy. *The Anarchy of Empire in the Making of U.S. Culture*. Cambridge, Mass.: Harvard University Press, 2002.

———. "Romancing the Empire." In *The Anarchy of Empire in the Making of U. S. Culture*, 92–120. Cambridge, Mass.: Harvard University Press, 2002.

———. "Imperial Melancholy in America." *Raritan* 28, no. 3 (Winter 2009): 13–31.

Keenan, Danny. *Wars without End: The Land Wars in Nineteenth Century New Zealand*. New York: Penguin, 2009.

Keller, G. Frederick. "The Curse of California." *Wasp* 9, no. 316 (August 19, 1882): 520–521.

———. "The Ogre of Mussel Slough." *Wasp* 8 (March 12, 1882).

———. "What Shall We Do With Our Boys?" *Wasp* 8 (March 3, 1882): 136–137.

Knoper, Randall. *Acting Naturally: Mark Twain in the Culture of Performance*. Berkeley: University of California Press, 1995.

Krauth, Leland. *Mark Twain & Company: Six Literary Relations*. Athens: University of Georgia Press, 2003.

Kremer, Gary. "Politics, Punishment, and Profit: Convict Labor in the Missouri State Penitentiary, 1875–1900." *Gateway Heritage* 13 (Summer 1992): 28–41.

Kusmer, Kenneth. *Down and Out, on the Road: The Homeless in American History*. New York: Oxford University Press, 2002.

LaFargue, Thomas. *China's First Hundred: Educational Mission Students in the United States, 1872–1881*. Pullman: Washington State University Press, 1987.

Lai, Chun-chuen. *Remarks of the Chinese Merchants of San Francisco, upon Governor John Bigler's Message and some Common Objections*, trans. William Speer. San Francisco: Whitton, Towne, & Co., 1855.

Lao, She. "Mark Twain: Exposer of the 'Dollar Empire.'" In *The Mark Twain Anthology: Great Writers on His Life and Work*, ed. Shelley Fisher Fishkin, 283–288. New York: Library of America, 2010.

Laufer, William S. *Corporate Bodies and Guilty Minds: The Failure of Corporate Criminal Liability*. Chicago: University of Chicago Press, 2008.

Lears, T. J. Jackson. *No Place of Grace: Antimodernism and the Transformation of American Culture, 1880–1920*. Chicago: University of Chicago Press, 1994.

Lee, James Kyung-Jin. *Urban Triage: Race and the Fictions of Multiculturalism*. Minneapolis: University of Minnesota Press, 2004.

Lee, Julia H. *Interracial Encounters: Reciprocal Representations in African and Asian American Literatures, 1896–1937*. New York: NYU Press, 2011.

Lee, Robert. *Orientals: Asian Americans in Popular Culture*. Philadelphia: Temple University Press, 1999.

Lee, Yan Phou. "The Chinese Must Stay." *North American Review* 148 (1889): 476–483.

LeMenager, Stephanie. *Manifest and Other Destinies: Territorial Fictions of the Nineteenth-Century United States*. Lincoln: University of Nebraska Press, 2004.

Lichtenstein, Alex. *Twice the Work of Free Labor: The Political Economy of Convict Labor in the New South*. London: Verso, 1995.

Lindsay, Nicholas Vachel. "The Golden-Faced People: A Story of the Chinese Conquest of America." *Crisis* 9, no. 1 (November 1914): 36–42.

"Literary Chat." *Munsey's Magazine* 13, no. 3 (June 1895): 310–315.

"Literary Intelligence." *Trübner's American, European and Oriental Literary Record* 4 (1883): 2–6.

Liu, Haiming. "Mark Twain in China," trans. Stephen Fleming. *Chinese Literature: Fiction Poetry Art*, ed. Wang Meng (Autumn 1987): 179–192. Beijing: Foreign Language Press.

Loewen, James W. *Lies across America: What Our Historic Sites Get Wrong*. New York: New Press, 1999.

London, Jack. "The Yellow Peril." In *Jack London Reports: War Correspondence, Sports Articles, and Miscellaneous Writings*, ed. King Hendricks and Irving Shepard, 340–350. New York: Doubleday, 1970.

Lott, Eric. *Love and Theft: Blackface Minstrelsy and the American Working Class*. New York: Oxford University Press, 1995.

Lowe, Lisa. "The Intimacies of Four Continents." In *Haunted by Empire: Geographies of Intimacy in North American History*, ed. Ann Laura Stoler, 191–212. Durham, N.C.: Duke University Press, 2006.

Lwin, Sanda Mayzaw. "'A Race So Different from Our Own': Segregation, Exclusion, and the Myth of Mobility." In *AfroAsian Encounters: Culture, History, Politics*, ed. Heike Raphael-Hernandez and Shannon Steen, 17–33. New York: NYU Press, 2006.

Lye, Colleen. *America's Asia: Racial Form and American Literature, 1893–1945*. Princeton, N.J.: Princeton University Press, 2004.

———. "The Afro-Asian Analogy." *PMLA* 123, no. 5 (Oct 2008): 1732–1736.

MacLeod, Christine. "Telling the Truth in a Tight Place: Huckleberry Finn and the Reconstruction Era." *Southern Quarterly* 34 (Fall 1995): 5–16.

Mancini, Matthew. *One Dies, Get Another: Convict Leasing in the American South, 1866–1928*. Columbia: University of South Carolina Press, 1996.
"Mark Twain and Twin Cheer New Year's Party." *New York Times* (January 1, 1907).
"Mark Twain's New Book." *Cincinnati Commercial Gazette* (February 3, 1895): 23.
Marx, Karl. *Grundrisse: Foundations of the Critique of Political Economy*, trans. Martin Nicolaus. New York: Penguin, 1993.
Mbembe, Achille. "Necropolitics." Trans. Libby Meintjes. *Public Culture* 15, no. 1 (Winter 2003): 11–40.
McClain, Charles J. *In Search of Equality: The Chinese Struggle against Discrimination in Nineteenth-Century America*. Berkeley: University of California Press, 1994.
McClintock, Anne. *Imperial Leather: Race, Gender, and Sexuality in the Colonial Contest*. New York: Routledge, 1995.
McCoy, Alfred W. *Policing America's Empire: The United States, the Philippines, and the Rise of the Surveillance State*. Madison: University of Wisconsin Press, 2009.
McIntyre, Michael, and Heidi J. Nast, eds. "Bio(necro)polis: Marx, Surplus Populations, and the Spatial Dialectics of Reproduction and 'Race.'" Special issue of *Antipode: A Radical Journal of Geography*, vol. 43, no. 5 (November 2011).
McKelvey, Blake. "Penal Slavery and Southern Reconstruction." *Journal of Negro History* 20 (1935): 153–179.
McNutt, James. "Mark Twain and the American Indian: Earthly Realism and Heavenly Idealism." *American Indian Quarterly* 4, no. 3 (August 1978): 223–242.
Metzger, Sean. "Charles Parsloe's Chinese Fetish: An Example of Yellowface Performance in Nineteenth-Century American Melodrama." *Theatre Journal* 56, no. 4 (December 2004): 627–651.
Michelson, Bruce. "Realism, Romance, and Dynamite: The Quarrel of *A Connecticut Yankee in King Arthur's Court*." *New England Quarterly* 64, no. 4 (December 1991): 609–632.
The Monument to Robert Gould Shaw: Its Inception, Completion and Unveiling, 1865–1897. Boston: Houghton, Mifflin, & Co., 1897.
Moreheid, J. N. *Lives, Adventures, Anecdotes, Amusements, and Domestic Habits of the Siamese Twins*. Raleigh, N.C.: E. E. Barclay, 1850.
Morris, Roy, Jr. *Lighting Out for the Territory: How Samuel Clemens Headed West and Became Mark Twain*. New York: Simon & Schuster, 2010.
Morrison, Toni. *Playing in the Dark: Whiteness and the Literary Imagination*. Cambridge, Mass.: Harvard University Press, 1992.
Moy, James. *Marginal Sights: Staging the Chinese in America*. Iowa City: University of Iowa Press, 1993.
Mullen, Bill, and Cathryn Watson, eds. *W. E. B. Du Bois on Asia: Crossing the World Color Line*. Jackson: University Press of Mississippi, 2005.
Murphy, Brenda. *American Realism and American Drama, 1880–1940*. Cambridge: Cambridge University Press, 1987.
Murphy, Gretchen. *Shadowing the White Man's Burden: U.S. Imperialism and the Problem of the Color Line*. New York: NYU Press, 2010.

Nace, Ted. *Gangs of America: The Rise of Corporate Power and the Disabling of Democracy*. San Francisco: Berrett-Koehler Publishers, 2005.
"New Books." *Hartford Times* (February 18, 1895), 8.
"Ng Poon Chew: Chinese Statesman and Journalist." Pamphlet. Boston: Redpath Lyceum Bureau, [1910s]. 4 pages.
Ng Poon Chew Papers. Asian American Studies Archive, University of California, Berkeley.
"Ng Poon Chew Speaks for China." *National Civic Federation Review* 1–2 (January–February 1906): 16.
Ngai, Mae. *The Lucky Ones: One Family and the Extraordinary Invention of Chinese America*. New York: Houghton Mifflin Harcourt, 2010.
Nissen, Axel. *Bret Harte: Prince and Pauper*. Jackson: University Press of Mississippi, 2000.
———. "A Tramp at Home: Huckleberry Finn, Romantic Friendship, and the Homeless Man." *Nineteenth-Century Literature* 60 (June 2005): 57–86.
Nixon, Rob. *Slow Violence and the Environmentalism of the Poor*. Cambridge, Mass.: Harvard University Press, 2011.
Norris, Frank. *The Octopus*. New York: Penguin, 1986.
Okihiro, Gary Y. *The Columbia Guide to Asian American History*. New York: Columbia University Press, 2001.
Ou, Hsin-yun. "Mark Twain, Anson Burlingame, Joseph Hopkins Twichell, and the Chinese." *Ariel: A Review of International English Literature* 42, no. 2 (2012): 43–74.
Paddison, Joshua. *American Heathens: Religion, Race, and Reconstruction in California*. Berkeley: University of California Press, 2012.
Paine, Albert Bigelow. *Mark Twain, a Biography: The Personal and Literary Life of Samuel Langhorne Clemens*. New York: Harper, 1912.
Parenti, Christian. *The Soft Cage: Surveillance in America from Slavery to the War on Terror*. New York: Basic Books, 2003.
Park, John S. W. *Illegal Migrations and the Huckleberry Finn Problem*. Philadelphia: Temple University Press, 2013.
Parker, Hershel. *Flawed Texts and Verbal Icons: Literary Authority in American Fiction*. Evanston, Ill.: Northwestern University Press, 1984.
Payson, L. E. "Texas and Pacific Railroad Company." *Executive Documents of the Senate of the United States for the First Session of the Forty-Eighth Congress*, vol. 1, no. 27. Washington, D.C.: U.S. Government Printing Office, 1884.
Penner, Louise. *Victorian Medicine and Social Reform: Florence Nightingale among the Novelists*. New York: Palgrave, 2010.
Penry, Tara. "The Chinese in Bret Harte's Overland: A Context for Truthful James." *American Literary Realism* 43, no. 1 (Fall 2010): 74–82.
People v. Elyea. 14 Cal. 144 (1859).
People v. Hall. 4 Cal. 399 (1854).
People of the State of California v. Brady. 40 Cal. 198 (1870).
Peters, John Durham. *Courting the Abyss: Free Speech and the Liberal Tradition*. Chicago: University of Chicago Press, 2005.

Peyser, Thomas. "Mark Twain, Immigration, and the American Narrative." *ELH* 79, no. 4 (December 2012): 1013–1037.

Pfaelzer, Jean. *Driven Out: The Forgotten War against Chinese Americans*. Berkeley: University of California Press, 2007.

Plessy v. Ferguson, 163 U.S. 537 (1896).

"Pudd'nhead Wilson." *Public Opinion* 18, no. 7 (February 14, 1895): 161.

Pun, Chi. "A Remonstrance from the Chinese in California to the Congress of the United States," trans. William Speer. In *The Oldest and the Newest Empire: China and the United States* by William Speer, 588–603. Cincinnati: National Publishing Co., 1870.

Qien, Kung, and J. Hu. *Chinese Educational Commission Studies*. Hong Kong: Chinese Books, 2003.

Rabinow, Paul. "Galton's Regret: Of Types and Individuals." In *DNA on Trial: Genetic Identification and Criminal Justice*, ed. Paul R. Billings, 5–18. Plainview, N.Y.: Cold Spring Harbor Laboratory Press, 1992.

Rafael, Vicente. *White Love and Other Events in Filipino History*. Durham, N.C.: Duke University Press, 2000.

Railton, Stephen. "Twain and Twins." *Mark Twain in His Times*. http://etext.virginia.edu/railton/wilson/mttwins.html.

Raphael-Hernandez, Heike, and Shannon Steen, eds. *AfroAsian Encounters: Culture, History, Politics*. New York: NYU Press, 2006.

Reesman, Jeanne Campbell. *Jack London's Racial Lives: A Critical Biography*. Athens: University of Georgia Press, 2009.

Rhoads, Edward. *Stepping Forth into the World: The Chinese Educational Mission to the United States, 1872–81*. Hong Kong: Hong Kong University Press, 2011.

Rizal, José. "My Last Thought." In *An Eagle Flight*, xii–xiii. New York, McClure, Phillips, & Co., 1901.

Robbins, William G. *Colony and Empire: The Capitalist Transformation of the American West*. Lawrence: University Press of Kansas, 1994.

Robinson, Forrest. "Mark Twain, 1835–1910: A Brief Biography." In *A Historical Guide to Mark Twain*, ed. Shelley Fisher Fishkin, 13–54. New York: Oxford University Press, 2002.

Rohe, Randall E. "After the Gold Rush: Chinese Mining in the Far West, 1850–1890." In *Chinese on the American Frontier*, ed. Arif Dirlik, 3–26. Lanham: Rowman & Littlefield, 2001.

Root, George. "Tramp, Tramp, Tramp." In *The Civil War Songbook: Complete Original Sheet Music for 37 Songs*, ed. Richard Crawford, 45–48. New York: Dover, 1977.

Rowe, John Carlos. "Fatal Speculations: Murder, Money, and Manners in *Pudd'nhead Wilson*." In *Mark Twain's Pudd'nhead Wilson: Race, Conflict, and Culture*, ed. Susan Gillman and Forrest Glen Robinson, 137–154. Durham, N. C.: Duke University Press, 1990.

———. Rowe, John Carlos. *At Emerson's Tomb: The Politics of Classic American Literature*. New York: Columbia University Press, 1997.

———. "Highway Robbery: 'Indian Removal,' the Mexican-American War, and American Identity in *The Life and Adventures of Joaquin Murieta*." *NOVEL* 31 (Spring 1998): 149–173.

———. *Literary Culture and U.S. Imperialism: From the Revolution to World War II*. New York: Oxford University Press, 2000.

Ruffin v. Commonwealth, 62 Va. 790 (1871).

Russell, Emily. *Reading Embodied Citizenship: Disability, Narrative, and the Body Politic*. New Brunswick, N.J.: Rutgers University Press, 2011.

Salvant, Shawn. "Mark Twain and the Nature of Twins." *Nineteenth Century Literature* 67, no. 3 (December 2012): 366–396.

Santa Clara County v. Southern Pacific R. Co. 118 U.S. 394 (1886).

Saxton, Alexander. *The Indispensable Enemy: Labor and the Anti-Chinese Movement in California*. Berkeley: University of California Press, 1971.

———. *Rise and Fall of the White Republic: Politics and Mass Culture in Nineteenth-Century America*. New York: Verso, 2003.

Scarpaci, Vincenza. "Walking the Color Line: Italian Immigrants in Rural Louisiana, 1880–1910." In *Are Italians White? How Race Is Made in America*, 60–76. New York: Routledge, 2003.

Scharnhorst, Gary. *Bret Harte: Opening the American Literary West*. Norman: University of Oklahoma Press, 2000.

Schmidt, Barbara. "*San Francisco Daily Morning Call*, 1863–1864." *Mark Twain Quotations, Newspaper Collections, and Related Resources*. www.twainquotes.com/callindex.html.

Schmitz, Neil. "Twain, Huckleberry Finn, and the Reconstruction." *American Studies* 12–13 (1971–1972): 59–67.

Scott-Childress, Reynolds J. "Race, Nation, and the Rhetoric of Color: Locating Japan and China, 1870–1907." In *Race and the Production of Modern American Nationalism*, ed. Reynolds J. Scott-Childress, 3–20. New York: Taylor & Francis, 1999.

Scott v. Sandford, 60 U.S. 407 (1856).

Seligman, Scott D. *The First Chinese American: The Remarkable Life of Wong Chin Foo*. Hong Kong: Hong Kong University Press, 2013.

Shah, Nayan. *Contagious Divides: Epidemics and Race in San Francisco's Chinatown*. Berkeley: University of California Press, 2001.

———. *Stranger Intimacy: Contesting Race, Sexuality and the Law in the North American West*. Berkeley: University of California Press, 2012.

Shih, Shu-Mei, ed. "Comparative Racialization." Special issue of *PMLA* 123, no. 5 (October 2008).

Sklar, Martin J. *The Corporate Reconstruction of American Capitalism, 1890–1916: The Market, the Law, and Politics*. Cambridge: Cambridge University Press, 1988.

Smith, Harriet Elinor, et al., eds. *Autobiography of Mark Twain*, vol. 1. Berkeley, Calif.: University of California Press, 2010.

Speer, William. *An Humble Plea, Addressed to the Legislature of California, in Behalf of the Immigrants from the Empire of China to this State*. San Francisco: Office of the Oriental, 1856.

———. *An Answer to the Common Objections to Chinese Testimony; and an Earnest Appeal to the Legislature of California, for Their Protection by our Law*. San Francisco: Chinese Mission House, 1857.

———. *The Oldest and the Newest Empire*. Hartford, Conn.: S. S. Scranton & Co., 1870.

The Statutes of California Passed at the First Session of the Legislature. San José: J. Winchester, State Printer, 1850.

Steinroetter, Vanessa. "'Reading the List': Casualty Lists and Civil War Poetry." *ESQ: A Journal of the American Renaissance* 59, no. 1 (2013): 48–78.

Storey, Moorfield, and Julian Codman. *Secretary Root's Record: "Marked Severities" in Philippine Warfare*. Boston: Geo. H. Ellis Co., 1902.

Sumida, Stephen H. "Reevaluating Mark Twain's Novel of Hawaii." *American Literature* 61, no. 4 (December 1989): 586–609.

Sundquist, Eric J. *To Wake the Nations: Race in the Making of American Literature*. Cambridge, Mass.: Harvard University Press, 1992.

Takaki, Ronald. *A Different Mirror: A History of Multicultural America*. Boston: Back Bay Books, 2008.

Taylor, Henry Osborn. *A Treatise on the Law of Private Corporations Having Capital Stock*. Philadelphia: Kay & Bro., 1898. Originally published 1884.

"Theres Millions In It." *Wasp*, vol. 21 (July–December 1888).

Thomas, Brook. *American Literary Realism and the Failed Promise of Contract*. Berkeley: University of California Press, 1997.

———. *Civic Myths: A Law-and-Literature Approach to Citizenship*. Chapel Hill: University of North Carolina Press, 2007.

Thomas, Ronald. *Detective Fiction and the Rise of Forensic Science*. Cambridge: Cambridge University Press, 1999.

Thomason, Jerry. "Ah Sin: The Heathen Chinee." In *The Mark Twain Encyclopedia*, ed. J. R. LeMaster and James D. Wilson, 17. New York: Routledge, 2011.

Thompson, E. P. "Time, Work-Discipline, and Industrial Capitalism." *Past and Present* 38, no. 1 (1967): 56–97.

"Thumbs Down! The Latest Plan for Outwitting the Chinese." *San Francisco Daily Report* 34, no. 67 (September 19, 1885): 8.

"The Tocci Twins." *Scientific American* 65, no. 24 (December 12, 1891): 374.

Trachtenberg, Alan. *The Incorporation of America: Culture and Society in the Gilded Age*. New York: Hill & Wang, 1982.

Trinculo. "Causerie." Review of *Ah Sin. New York Spirit of the Times* (August 4, 1877).

Twain, Mark. "The China Trial." *Territorial Enterprise* (February 19, 1863). In *Early Tales and Sketches*, vol. 1: *1851–1864*, ed. Edgar Branch and Robert Hirst, 402–403. Berkeley: University of California Press, 1979.

———. "Horrible Affair." *Virginia City Territorial Enterprise*, April 16–18, 1863. In *Early Tales and Sketches*, vol. 1: *1851–1864*, ed. Edgar Branch and Robert Hirst, 246–247. Berkeley: University of California Press, 1979.

———[attributed]. "Astonishing Freak of Nature." *San Francisco Daily Morning Call* (July 22, 1864): 3.

———— [attributed]. "Discharged." *San Francisco Daily Morning Call* (September 10, 1864): 3.

———— [attributed]. "In Bad Company." *San Francisco Daily Morning Call* (September 7, 1864): 3.

———— [attributed]. "The Battered Chinaman Case." *San Francisco Daily Morning Call* (September 11, 1864): 3.

———— [attributed]. "Police Court." *San Francisco Daily Morning Call* (September 18, 1864): 3.

————. "What Have the Police Been Doing?" *San Francisco Golden Era*, vol. 14 (January 21, 1866).

————. "Curtain Speech. Opening of *Ah Sin*, Fifth Avenue Theatre, New York, July 31, 1877." In *Mark Twain Speaking*, ed. Paul Fatout, 103–105. Iowa City: University of Iowa Press, 1976.

————. *A Tramp Abroad*. 2 vols. London: Chatto & Windus, 1880.

————. "A Connecticut Yankee in King Arthur's Court." MS. 1885–1889. Henry W. and Albert A. Berg Collection, Berg Coll. MSS Clemens, New York Public Library, New York. Copy in the Mark Twain Papers, box 41, Bancroft Library, University of California, Berkeley.

————. "Pudd'nhead Wilson." MS. 1892. Mark Twain Papers, box 40, MS1, Bancroft Library, University of California, Berkeley. Supplemental title page from the Shaun Speer Collection, available through the Mark Twain Project, Bancroft Library, University of California, Berkeley.

————. "Pudd'nhead Wilson." MS. 1893. Literary and Historical Manuscripts MA 881-2, Morgan Library. Copy in the Mark Twain Papers, Bancroft Library, University of California, Berkeley, box 40, 1892.00.00-1893.00-00.

————. "Notebook #38." Supplemental pages from the Henry W. and Albert A. Berg Collection, Berg Coll. MSS Clemens, New York Public Library, New York. Typescript, May 4, 1896, in the Mark Twain Papers, Bancroft Library, University of California, Berkeley.

————. *Following the Equator*. Hartford, Conn.: American Publishing Co., 1898.

————. "Introduction Speech." Quoted in Major J. B. Pond, *Eccentricities of Genius: Memories of Famous Men and Women of the Platform*. New York: G. W. Dillingham Co., 1900.

————. "How to Tell a Story." In *How to Tell a Story and Other Essays*, 7–15. Hartford, Conn.: American Publishing Co., 1901.

————. "The Fable of the Yellow Terror." MS. 1904–1905. Mark Twain Papers, MS171, DV359a, typescript, 8 pp., Bancroft Library, University of California, Berkeley.

————. "King Leopold's Soliloquy" MS. 1905. Mark Twain Papers, 32v. Bancroft Library, University of California, Berkeley, CU-MarkWritingsFile 1905.09.00.

————. "Autobiographical Dictation." Transcript. September 12, 1908. Mark Twain Papers, Bancroft Library, University of California, Berkeley.

————. *Extract from Captain Stormfield's Visit to Heaven*. New York: Harper & Bros., 1909.

———. "Public Education Association. Address at a Meeting of the Berkeley Lyceum, New York, Nov. 23, 1900." In *Mark Twain's Speeches*, ed. William Dean Howells, 144–146. New York: Harper & Bros., 1910.

———. "Letter to Fred J. Hall." In *Mark Twain's Letters*, ed. Alfred Bigelow Paine, 2:590–592. New York: Harper & Bros., 1917.

———. "Letter to William Dean Howells." In *Mark Twain's Letters*, ed. Alfred Bigelow Paine, 1:410–412. New York: Harper & Bros., 1917.

———. *Tom Sawyer Abroad, Tom Sawyer Detective, and Other Stories, Etc., Etc.* New York: Harper & Bros., 1923.

——— [attributed]. "California's Dull." In *On the Poetry of Mark Twain: With Selections from His Verse*, ed. Arthur Lincoln Scott, 69. Urbana: University of Illinois Press, 1966.

———. "My Last Thought." In *On the Poetry of Mark Twain with Selections from His Verse*, ed. Arthur Lincoln Scott, 129–131. Urbana: University of Illinois Press, 1966.

———. "Three Thousand Years among the Microbes." In *Mark Twain's "Which Was the Dream?" and Other Symbolic Writings of the Later Years*, ed. John S. Tuckey, 433–473. Berkeley and Los Angeles: University of California Press, 1968.

———. *No.44: The Mysterious Stranger*. Berkeley: University of California Press, 1969.

———. *King Leopold's Soliloquy*. New York: International Publishers, 1970.

———. *Mark Twain's Letters from Hawaii*, ed. A. Grove Day. Honolulu: University of Hawaii Press, 1975.

———. "Sandwich Islands Lecture." In *Mark Twain Speaking*, ed. Paul Fatout, 4–14. Iowa City: University of Iowa Press, 1976.

———. "Woman—the Pride of Any Profession, and the Jewel of Ours." In *Mark Twain Speaking*, ed. Paul Fatout, 20–22. Iowa City: University of Iowa Press, 1976.

———. *Notebooks and Journals*, vol. 3, *1883–1891*, ed. Frederick Anderson et al. Berkeley: University of California Press, 1979.

———. *The Prince and the Pauper*. Berkeley: University of California Press, 1979.

———. "The Fable of the Yellow Terror." In *The Devil's Race-Track: Mark Twain's Great Dark Writings*, ed. John S. Tuckey, 369–372. Berkeley: University of California Press, 1980.

———. *The Works of Mark Twain: Early Tales and Sketches*, vol. 2: *1864–1865*, ed. Edgar Marquess Branch, Robert H. Hirst, and Harriet Elinor Smith. Berkeley: University of California Press, 1981.

———. *A Connecticut Yankee in King Arthur's Court*, ed. Allison Ensor. New York: Norton, 1982.

———. *Autobiography of Mark Twain*, ed. Charles Neider. New York: Harper, 1990.

———. "Concerning the Jews." In *The Complete Essays of Mark Twain*, ed. Charles Neider, 235–250. Cambridge, Mass.: Da Capo Press, 1991.

———. "Disgraceful Persecution of a Boy." In *The Complete Essays of Mark Twain*, ed. Charles Neider, 7–9. Cambridge, Mass.: Da Capo Press, 1991.

———. "To My Missionary Critics." In *The Complete Essays of Mark Twain*, ed. Charles Neider, 296–311. Cambridge, Mass.: Da Capo Press, 1991.

———. "The United States of Lyncherdom." In *The Complete Essays of Mark Twain*, ed. Charles Neider, 673–679. Cambridge, Mass.: Da Capo Press, 1991.

———. "Aguinaldo." In *Mark Twain's Weapons of Satire: Anti-imperialist Writings on the Philippine-American War*, ed. Jim Zwick, 88–108. Syracuse, N.Y.: Syracuse University Press, 1992.

———. "Comments on the Moro Massacre." In *Mark Twain's Weapons of Satire: Anti-imperialist Writings on the Philippine-American War*, ed. Jim Zwick, 170–178. Syracuse, N.Y.: Syracuse University Press, 1992.

———. "A Defence of General Funston." In Mark Twain's *Weapons of Satire: Anti-imperialist Writings on the Philippine-American War*, ed. Jim Zwick, 120–132. Syracuse, N.Y.: Syracuse University Press, 1992.

———. "The Fall of the Great Republic." Excerpted in *Mark Twain's Weapons of Satire: Anti-imperialist Writings on the Philippine-American War*, ed. Jim Zwick, 74–80. Syracuse, N.Y.: Syracuse University Press, 1992.

———. "Goldsmith's Friend Abroad Again." In *Collected Tales, Sketches, Speeches, and Essays: 1852–1890*, ed. Louis Budd, 455–70. New York: Library of America, 1992.

———. "History 1,000 Years from Now: A Translation." In *Mark Twain's Weapons of Satire: Anti-imperialist Writings on the Philippine-American War*, ed. Jim Zwick, 70–73. Syracuse, N.Y.: Syracuse University Press, 1992.

———. "Letter to Daniel Beard." In *Mark Twain's Weapons of Satire: Anti-imperialist Writings on the Philippine-American War*, ed. Jim Zwick, 111. Syracuse, N.Y.: Syracuse University Press, 1992.

———. "Letter to Olivia L. Langdon, Appendix B." In *Mark Twain's Letters*, ed. Victor Fischer and Michael Frank, 3:469. Berkeley: University of California Press, 1992.

———. "Notes on Patriotism." In *Mark Twain's Weapons of Satire: Anti-imperialist Writings on the Philippine-American War*, ed. Jim Zwick, 113–115. Syracuse, N.Y.: Syracuse University Press, 1992.

———. "Personal Habits of the Siamese Twins." In *Collected Tales, Sketches, Speeches, and Essays, 1852–1890*, ed. Louis Budd, 296–299. New York: Library of America, 1992.

———. "Salutation Speech from the Nineteenth Century to the Twentieth." In Mark Twain's *Weapons of Satire: Anti-imperialist Writings on the Philippine-American War*, ed. Jim Zwick, 12–13. Syracuse, N.Y.: Syracuse University Press, 1992.

———. "The Secret History of Eddypus, the World Empire." Excerpted in *Mark Twain's Weapons of Satire: Anti-imperialist Writings on the Philippine-American War*, ed. Jim Zwick, 81–85. Syracuse, N.Y.: Syracuse University Press, 1992.

———. "The Stupendous Procession." In *Mark Twain's Weapons of Satire: Anti-imperialist Writings on the Philippine-American War*, ed. Jim Zwick, 43–56. Syracuse, N.Y.: Syracuse University Press, 1992.

———. "To the Person Sitting in Darkness." In *Mark Twain's Weapons of Satire: Anti-imperialist Writings on the Philippine-American War*, ed. Jim Zwick, 24–39. Syracuse, N.Y.: Syracuse University Press, 1992.

———. *Roughing It*, ed. Harriet Elinor Smith and Edgar Marquess Branch. Berkeley: University of California Press, 1993.

———. *The Adventures of Huckleberry Finn*, ed. Justin Kaplan. New York: Ballantine, 1996.

———. *The Adventures of Tom Sawyer*, ed. Shelley Fisher Fishkin. New York: Oxford University Press, 1996.

———. "John Chinaman in New York." In *The Complete Humorous Sketches and Tales of Mark Twain*, ed. Charles Neider, 134–135. Cambridge, Mass.: Da Capo Press, 1996.

———. *The Adventures of Huckleberry Finn*, ed. Thomas Cooley. New York: Norton, 1999.

———. "A Tribute to Anson Burlingame." In *Mark Twain at the Buffalo Express: Articles and Sketches by America's Favorite Humorist*, ed. Joseph B. McCullough and Janice McIntire Strasburg, 153–157. DeKalb: Northern Illinois University Press, 1999.

———. "To William Dean Howells, 20 November 1874." In *Mark Twain's Letters*, vol. 6: *1874–1875*, ed. Michael Frank and Harriet Elinor Smith, 289–292. Berkeley: University of California Press, 2002.

———. "The Chronicle of Young Satan." In *The Mysterious Stranger Manuscripts*, ed. William Gibson, 35–174. Berkeley: University of California Press, 2005.

———. "*Pudd'nhead Wilson*" and "*Those Extraordinary Twins*," ed. Sidney Berger. New York: Norton, 2005.

———. *Those Extraordinary Twins*. In *Pudd'nhead Wilson and Those Extraordinary Twins*, ed. Sidney E. Berger, 125–185. New York: Norton, 2005.

———. "The Treaty with China: Its Provisions Explained." *Journal of Transnational American Studies*, 2, no.1 (2010): 1–12. http://escholarship.org/uc/item/2r87m203.

———. *Mark Twain's Adventures of Tom Sawyer and Huckleberry Finn*, ed. Alan Gribben. Montgomery, Ala.: NewSouth, 2011.

Twain, Mark, and Bret Harte. *Ah Sin*. In *The Chinese Other, 1850–1925: An Anthology of Plays*, ed. Dave Williams, 40–95. Lanham, Md.: University Press of America, 1997.

Twichell, Joseph H. "An Address by the Rev. Joseph H. Twichell." April 10, 1878. In Yung Wing, *My Life in China and America*, 247–273. New York: Henry Holt & Co., 1909.

"Uncle Sam's Farm in Danger." *Wasp*, vol. 2 (August 1877–July 1878).

Wacquant, Loïc. "From Slavery to Mass Incarceration: Rethinking the 'Race Question' in the US." *New Left Review* 13 (January 2002): 41–60.

Wagner, Bryan. "Helen Hunt Jackson's Errant Local Color." *Arizona Quarterly* 58, no. 4 (Winter 2002): 1–23.

———. *Disturbing the Peace: Black Culture and the Police Power after Slavery*. Cambridge, Mass.: Harvard University Press, 2009.

Walker, Richard A. "California's Golden Road to Riches: Natural Resources and Regional Capitalism, 1848–1940." *Annals of the Association of American Geographers* 91, no. 1 (March 2001): 167–199.

Wallace, Amy, and Irving Wallace. *The Two*. New York: Simon & Schuster, 1978.

Washington, Booker T. *Up From Slavery*, ed. W. Fitzhugh Brundage. Boston: Bedford/St. Martin's, 2003.

Washington, Harriet. *Medical Apartheid: The Dark History of Medical Experimentation on Black Americans from Colonial Times to the Present*. New York: Doubleday, 2006.

Wigger, Anne P. "The Composition of Mark Twain's 'Pudd'nhead Wilson and Those Extraordinary Twins': Chronology and Development." *Modern Philology* 55, no. 2 (November 1957): 93–102.

———. "The Source of Fingerprint Material in Mark Twain's *Pudd'nhead Wilson and Those Extraordinary Twins*." *American Literature* 28, no. 4 (January 1957): 517–520.

Wildman, Rounsevelle. *China's Open Door: A Sketch of Chinese Life and History*. Boston: Lothrop Publishing Co., 1900.

Williams, Dave. *Misreading the Chinese Character: Images of the Chinese in Euroamerican Drama to 1925*. Asian Thought and Culture no. 40. New York: Peter Lang, 2000.

Williams, Harry R. "'Ah Sin.' Chinese Song." Detroit: Roe Stephens, 1877. https://jscholarship.library.jhu.edu/handle/1774.2/9681?show=full.

Williams, Nathaniel. "Frank Reade, Jr. in Cuba: Dime-Novel Technology, U.S. Imperialism, and the 'American Jules Verne.'" *American Literature* 83, no. 2 (June 2011): 279–303.

Wilson, Theodore. *The Black Codes of the South*. University: University of Alabama Press, 1965.

Wilson Moore, Shirley Ann. "'We Feel the Want of Protection': The Politics of Law and Race in California, 1848–1878." In *Taming the Elephant: Politics, Government, and Law in Pioneer California*, ed. John F. Burns and Richard J. Orsi, 96–125. Berkeley: University of California Press, 2003.

"Wong Chin Foo." *New York Times* (October 4, 1873): 4.

Wong, Chin Foo. "Political Honors in China." *Harper's New Monthly Magazine* (July 1883): 298–303.

———. "Why Am I a Heathen?" *North American Review* 145, no. 369 (August 1887): 169–179.

———. *Wu Chih Tien, The Celestial Empress: A Chinese Historical Novel*. Published in installments in *Cosmopolitan*: 6, no. 4 (February 1889): 327–334; 6, no. 5 (March 1889): 477–485; 6, no. 6 (April 1889): 564–572; 7, no. 1 (May 1889): 65–72; 7, no. 2 (June 1889): 128–132; 7, no. 3 (July 1889): 289–299; 7, no. 4 (August 1889): 361–368; and 7, no. 5 (September 1889): 449–459.

Wong, Edlie. "In a Future Tense: Immigration Law, Counterfactual Histories, and Chinese Invasion Fiction." *American Literary History* (in press).

Wong, Sau-Ling Cynthia. *Reading Asian American Literature: From Necessity to Extravagance*. Princeton, N.J.: Princeton University Press, 1993.

Wonham, Henry B. *Playing the Races: Ethnic Caricature and American Literary Realism*. New York: Oxford University Press, 2004.

Wu, Cynthia. "The Siamese Twins in Late-Nineteenth-Century Narratives of Conflict and Reconciliation." *American Literature* 80, no. 1 (2008): 29–55.

Wunder, John R. "Chinese in Trouble: Criminal Law and Race on the Trans-Mississippi West Frontier." *Western Historical Quarterly* 17, no. 1 (January 1986): 25–41.

Yung Wing. *My Life in China and America*. New York: Henry Holt & Co., 1909.

The Yurok Tribe. "The Yurok Tribe: Background Information." www.yuroktribe.org/culture/history/history.htm. Accessed March 1, 2008.

Zehr, Martin. "Mark Twain, 'The Treaty with China,' and the Chinese Connection." *Journal of Transnational American Studies*, vol. 2, no. 1 (2010). http://escholarship.org/uc/item/5t02n321.

Zwick, Jim. Introduction to *Mark Twain's Weapons of Satire: Anti-imperialist Writings on the Philippine-American War*, ed. Jim Zwick. Syracuse, N.Y.: Syracuse University Press, 1992.

———, ed. Mark Twain's Weapons of Satire: Anti-imperialist Writings on the Philippine-American War. Syracuse, N.Y.: Syracuse University Press, 1992.

———. "Mark Twain and Imperialism." In *A Historical Guide to Mark Twain*, ed. Shelley Fisher Fishkin, 227–255. New York: Oxford University Press, 2002.

———, ed. *Confronting Imperialism: Essays on Mark Twain and the Anti-Imperialist League*. West Conshohocken, Pa.: Infinity Publishing, 2007.

———. "'Prodigally Endowed with Sympathy for the Cause': Mark Twain's Involvement with the Anti-Imperialist League." In *Confronting Imperialism: Essays on Mark Twain and the Anti-Imperialist League*, ed. Jim Zwick, 109–140. West Conshohocken, PA: Infinity Publishing, 2007.

Index

Aarim Heriot, Najia, 77
aborigines, 150
Act for the Government and Protection of Indians (1850), 69
Acting Naturally (Knoper), 43, 180n62
"An Act to Amend the Vagrant Laws of the State" (1865), 70
The Adventures of Huckleberry Finn. See Huckleberry Finn
The Adventures of Tom Sawyer, 55, 57–58
African American(s): in antebellum era, 5, 71–72, 77, 114, 139, 168; and black codes, 14, 65–66, 68–71, 76, 81, 186n36; and Chinese immigrants, 29, 37, 81, 85, 90, 107–108, 195n96; as counted individuals, 149; immobilization of, 54–55, 68–71, 186n40; and Italian immigrants, 90, 191n29; land ownership, 69, 186n36; legal status in California, 3; male suffrage, 76; and Shaw monument, 156; and "southern enclosure," 69–70, 186n44; and Twain's cross-racial critiques, 5–9, 13–14. *See also* labor; vagrancy
"AfroAsia Encounters" (Raphael-Hernandez and Steen, eds), 8, 173n30
"The Afro-Asian analogy" (Lye), 6
"After the Explosion" (Beard), 127, 129 *fig. 4.4*
Aguinaldo (Wildman), 139, 152
Aguinaldo, Emilio (President), 119, 139, 207n69
Ah Sin (Harte and Twain), 39–49; collaboration on, 27, 39–40, 73–74, 188n60, 200n57; friendship in, 47–48, 181n69, 181n74; poker scene in, 48, 181n71; and *Pudd'nhead Wilson* trials compared, 28, 50; representation against stereotype in, 21; as response to *People v Hall*, 24, 27–28, 43, 48–49, 50; reviewers on, 40–41, 42, 43, 180n62–64; synopsis of, 41–42
"Ah Sin" (Williams), 45, 46 *fig 1.1*
Ah Song Hi (fictional character), 56–57, 80–81
"The Alaska Widow" (Sui Sin Far), 169, 208n3
Alexander, Michelle, 69–70, 71
Ament, William Scott (Reverend), 22, 159–160
American Board of Foreign Missions, 159
American exceptionalism, 113, 196n13, 203n7
Anderson, Benedict, 155–156
Angell Treaty (1880), 122
"Another Miracle" (Beard), 127, 128 *fig 4.3*
"An Answer to the Common Objections" (Speer), 30–32, 178n15
antebellum era, 5, 71–72, 77, 114, 139, 168
anthropometry, 51–52
anti-Chinese movement, 29–39; and anti-Italian intersections, 97; and CEM students recall, 122; and Governor's speech, 32; and immigration law, 77, 135, 193n71; *Memorial of the Six Chinese Companies* on, 49; violence reports, 35–36. *See also* California; Chinese Exclusion Act; Geary Act; *People v. Hall*
anti-corporate movement, 84, 87–88, 91, 97–100, 189n2. *See also* industrial capitalism; labor
Anti-Imperialist League, 22, 139, 151, 203n1, 203n6
anti-modernists, 112–119
Arlington National Cemetery, 155
Armstrong, Nancy, 132, 142

Article 8, Burlingame Treaty, 120, 199n37-38
Art of War (Sun Tzu), 127
"Atlanta Compromise" (Washington speech), 107, 195n96
Australians (indigenous), 150
Autobiography (Twain), 1, 16–17, 39, 60, 109–110, 152

Barbary narratives, 142
Barnum, P. T., 89
baseball club, of CEM, 120, 121 *fig 4.1*
"Battle Hymn of the Republic," 160
"The Battle of the Sand Belt" (Twain), 118–119
Beard, Daniel Carter, 125–128, 126 *fig. 4.2*, 128 *fig. 4.3*, 129 *fig. 4.4*, 200n64
Bees and Butterflies (unpublished fable), 21, 136–138
Bellew, Frank, 66–67 *fig. 2.2*, 68, 185n30
Ben-Hur (Wallace), 113–114
Bertillon, Alphonse, and Bertillonage, 52, 105, 182n86, 194n86
Beveridge, Albert (Senator), 140
Bible, swearing on, 33–34
Bigler, John, (Governor), 32
"biopower," and biopolitics, 103, 105–106, 141–143, 147
"black" (term), 6, 27–28, 29
blackbirding, 143–144, 150
black codes, 14, 65–66, 69–70, 76, 186n39
blackface, 40, 184n20
"black Orientalism," 8
blacks. *See* African Americans
"Blessings-of-Civilization Trust," 92
Blyn, Robin, 84, 189n2
Bob Skinner (fictional character), 75–76, 79
body counts. *See* statistics
Boxer Relief Expedition, 140
Boxer uprising, 22–23, 139, 142, 159–160, 207n66
Braun, Bruce, 80
Brechin, Gray, 12
British colonial conditions, 143–146, 204n19

Broderick (fictional character), 42–48, 50, 181n71, 181n74
Brooks, Van Wyck, 87
Browne, J. Ross, 111
Buffalo Daily Courier (newspaper), 133
Burlingame, Anson, 17, 111, 183n9, 196n4, 204n19
Burlingame Treaty: and academy study, 122; Article 8 of, 120, 199n37–38; Chang on, 196n5; provisions of, 17; renegotiation of, 49; Twain on, 17, 22, 111, 120, 196n5, 199n37–38
Bush, Harold, 41
Butler, Judith, 147–148, 153, 206n48
Butterflies and Bees (unpublished fable), 21, 136–138

Cable, George Washington, 168, 208n3
Caesar's Column (Donnelly), 102, 118, 198n30
California: Act for the Government and Protection of Indians (1850), 58; Chinese testimony in, 27–37; Constitution, 70, 77, 98; Criminal Procedures ban, 29; financial and imperial status, 14; Governor's anti-Chinese speech, 32; Humboldt purges, 78; Miners' tax, 30–31, 48, 177n13, 178n16, 181n72; penal and civil codes (1872), 49; racialized labor and economy in, 8, 10–12; Senate Committee report, 49; Supreme Court, 27, 34–35. *See also* Chinese Exclusion Act; *People v. Hall*
Campomanes, Oscar, 156–157, 205n40
capitalism. *See* corporation(s); U.S. (imperial and colonial policy)
Captain Jinks, Hero (Crosby), 200n64
caricatures (Chinese), 19, 21, 40–41, 100, 175n62–64. *See also* Chinese immigrant(s); corporation(s)
Castronovo, Russ, 183n7
CEM. *See* Chinese Educational Mission
census, in U.S. and Philippines, 142, 203n13. *See also* population(s); statistics
Census of the Philippine Islands (1905), 203n13

Central Pacific Railroad, 97, 102
chain gangs, 54
"Chains Repaired," 139
Chan, Sucheng, 30
Chang, Gordon, 196n5
Chang and Eng Bunker, 16, 88, 89–90, 96
Charles L. Webster & Co., 97
Chartered Company, Rhodes, 144
Chesnutt, Charles, 168, 208n3
China: Boxer uprising, 22–23, 139, 142, 159–160, 207n66; CEM (*see* Chinese Educational Mission); Cixi *versus* Gong, 133; disparate views of, 110; European incursions into and migration results, 204n19; "Ever Victorious Army," 116; against foreign invasion (embodied by Yung and Wong), 21; military defeats of, 120; missionaries (*see* missionaries); and modernization (*see* Chinese modernization); Office of Foreign Affairs (Zongli Yamen), 120; Opium Wars, 120, 204n19; railroads in, 120, 157, 199n37–38; reformists in, 120, 133, 201n80; Self-Strengthening movement, 110–112, 116, 120–121, 133–134, 135; and Taiping Rebellion, 116, 120, 204n19; technology access, 112; western representations of, 135; Wong on, 110, 112, 134–135, 201n81. *See also* Burlingame Treaty; Twain, Mark (on China and Chinese)
"Chinaman" (term), 102
Chinatowns, 54
Chinese-American (newspaper), 131
"Chinese-American" (term), 125, 200n59
Chinese and Indian migrants, 144–145 *fig* 5.1, 146
Chinese Educational Mission (CEM), 119–124; baseball club, 121 *fig 4.1*; connection with Twain's work, 25, 112, 200n57; returned students in China, 200n55; Twichell's involvement with, Twain on, 199n44
Chinese Exclusion Act (1882): and anti-corporatism, 13, 97–100; and Bertillonage, 194n86; Congress on, 32–33, 98; and Geary Act, 49, 78–79, 84, 105, 188n70, 195n87; and immigration, 13, 96–97, 104; and Jim Crow, 1–2, 87; before passage of, 49, 81, 120, 196n5; Yan on, 120–121
Chinese immigrant(s): and African Americans, 29, 37, 81, 85, 90, 107–108, 195n96; and anti-corporation movement, 84, 87–88, 91, 97–100, 189n2; caricatures, 19, 40–41, 100, 175n62–64; "coolie" (*see* "coolie(s)"); crime victims described, 35–36; and domestic labor, 15, 77; Douglass on, 34; and dynamite, 116–118, 158–159, 198n27–28; and Geary Act, 49, 78–79, 84, 105, 188n70, 195n87; Grady on exclusion of, 107; health norms imposed on, 142; Henry George on, 97, 192n60; Humboldt purges of, 78; Irish animosity towards, 19; Jack London on, 137, 138, 202n92; labor and U.S. West development, 13; miner Ling murder, 29; miners, 30–31, 48, 177n13, 178n16, 181n72; and Native Americans, 80; portrayal in *Roughing It*, 132; registration of, 84, 103–104, 194n81; settlements attack, 31–32; status *versus* slave status, 36–37; stereotypes and testimony ban, 28, 30, 49; stoning of, 16–17, 36–37, 39, 48, 149; and U.S. West development, 13; western descriptions of, 30, 49, 97–102, 104, 194n81–83; women prohibited from entering, 77; Wong on, 130–136, 200n59. *See also* labor; *People v. Hall*; Twain, Mark (on China and Chinese)
Chinese Immigrants, African Americans, and Racial Anxiety in the United States (Aarim Heriot), 77
Chinese Immigration (1876 report), 49
Chinese invasion narratives: and miners' tax, 30, 177n12; proliferation of, 102, 193n71; Twain on, 109, 136–139
"the Chinese Mark Twain" (Ng), 135–136, 202n86

Chinese modernization, 109–138; CEM students and, 119–124, 200n55; influence on *Connecticut Yankee*, 110, 112, 114–119, 124; reformists and defense technology, 120–122; "Self-Strengthening" movement, 110–112, 116, 120–121, 133–134, 135; Twain on, in Howells letter, 109–110; white anxieties on (*see also* Chinese invasion narratives), 118; and Wong's *Wu Chih Tien*, 124, 125–128, 126 *fig 4.2*, 131–135; Yung and Wong as embodiment of, 21, 25

"The Chinese Must Stay" (Yan), 120

"chinese oaths," 27, 176n2

Chinn, Sarah, 51, 103, 106

chivalric ideals, 115, 119

Christianity, 113–114, 153–154, 196n13. *See also* missionaries; U.S. (imperial and colonial policy)

"The Chronicle of the Young Satan" (Twain), 23

Citizen of the World, A (Goldsmith), 56, 183n9

city, as social and economic force, 93, 191n38

civil death, 71–72

civil disobedience, 78–79, 188n70

Civil Rights Act (1870), 48–49

Civil War, 62, 63 *fig 2.1*, 147, 155, 185n21

Cixi (Empress), 133

Cole, Simon, 104–105, 194n86–88, 195n88

"Come Back to the Raft Ag'in, Huck Honey!" (Fiedler), 47

The Comedy of Those Extraordinary Twins. See *Those Extraordinary Twins*

comparative racialization (overview), 1–10, 13–14, 26, 168–169

"Concerning the Jews" (Twain), 21, 91–92

Congo deaths, 160–164, 207n71

A Connecticut Yankee in King Arthur's Court (Twain): alternative monument in, 157–158; CEM influence on, 124; chivalric ideals in, 115; corporate form in, 94; on "dream of a republic," 110; dungeon conditions in, 73; dynamite use in, 159; excised passage from, 117; as imperial romance critique, 112–119, 197n19; innovations in, 201n81; massacre in, 116–117, 149; *Wu Chih Tien* compared with, 25, 124, 127, 135, 136

convict-lease system, 55, 69–71, 182n5, 184n16, 186n44, 187n46. *See also* vagrancy

"coolie(s)": contested status of, 14; and corporate association, 102, 193n70; figure and term, as indentured *versus* slave, 1, 7–8, 173n21; legal fiction of, 84; *versus* "loafer," 57; as mechanical labor, 21, 175n68; myth of, 57, 183n10; stereotype and CEM students, 120; as threat to anti-modernists, 85, 110–111; Twain on, 10–11, 21, 175n68, 193n70. *See also* caricatures; corporation(s); labor

"Coolies for California" (Twain), 10–11, 193n70

corporation(s): anti-corporate movement on, 84, 87–88, 91, 97–100, 189n2; and Chinese labor, 11–12, 21; civil rights of, 95, 192n47; *versus* individualism, 21, 88–91, 97, 102, 111, 149; personhood (legal attribute), 84–85, 94–95, 102–103, 189n2; public to private incorporation, 93–94; as temporary Chinese allies, 97; and twin representation, 21, 83–85, 95–96, 102–103. *See also* anti-Chinese movement

Cosco, Joseph, 97

Cosmopolitan (periodical), 125, 127

Country Gentleman (magazine), 176n2

counts (body). *See* statistics

Courtney, Steve, 123

Crisis (periodical), 118

Crosby, Ernest Howard, 200n64

Cubic Air Ordinance (1870), 78

"The Curse of California" (Keller), 100

Daily Alta California (newspaper), 15

Daniels, Roger, 96

Danites, The (Miller), 40

Dawes Act (1887), 79

Dawson Landing, 92–93, 106
Dayan, Joan, 55, 71, 183n6, 184n16, 187n49
"dead in law," 60, 71–72, 149, 184n16
"dead people," theme, 57–59, 184n12
death-worlds of Mbembe, 143
Defense of General Funston, A (Twain), 119, 207n69
Democratic Vistas (Whitman), 18
Democrats (southern), 3, 14, 29, 76, 79
Denning, Michael, 66
DePastino, Todd, 69, 186n34
Dillon, Elizabeth Maddock, 87, 97
"Disgraceful Persecution of a Boy" (Twain), 6, 18, 36–37, 149
dispossession, and mass migration, 143–146, 150, 204n19–20
"Dog Tag Law," 78–79, 188n70
Donnelly, Ignatius, 102, 118, 193n72, 198n30
Douglass, Frederick, 33–34, 187n53
Dred Scott v. Sandford (1856), 37
Dreger, Alice Domurat, 88–89, 190n22
Driven Out (Pfaelzer), 78
Du Bois, W. E. B., 70, 118, 168, 187n52, 208n3
Duckett, Margaret, 5, 39
dynamite, 116–118, 158–159, 198n27–28

Eagle Flight, An (Rizal), 165
Eaton, Winifred, 169, 208n3
Eliot, T. S., 53, 54, 65, 66
epidemiologists, 146, 204n22
eugenics, 103, 146, 149–150, 204n22
evidence, 28, 43–45, 50–52. See also *People v. Hall*; testimony ban
Exclusion Act. See Chinese Exclusion Act
"The Explosion" (Beard), 126–127 *fig 4.2*
Extract from Captain Stormfield's Visit to Heaven (Twain), 154–155, 206n50
"Extract from Cross-Examination of the Future," 104, 194n83

"Fable of the Yellow Terror" (Twain), 21–22, 136–138
Farr, William, 146, 149–150
Farrell, Molly, 146

Faust, Drew Gilpin, 146–147
Fiedler, Leslie, 47, 85, 87
Filipino(s): casualties, 148, 151–154, 157, 205n39–40, 206n44; file cards on, 52; health norms imposed on, 142. See also Philippines; U.S.-Philippine War
fingerprinting: evidence, Pudd'nhead Wilson on, 50–52, 103; for identifying race, 103, 193n75, 194n86, 195n89, 195n91; and policing methods, 51–52, 103–106, 194n81
Finger Prints (Galton), 103
Fishkin, Shelley Fisher, 4, 6, 17
Following the Equator (Twain), 21, 108, 141, 143–146, 149–150, 158
Foreign Miners' Tax (1852), 6–7, 30–32, 48, 177n13, 178n16, 181n72
Foucault, Michel, 141–143, 147–148
14th Amendment cases, 95, 192n47–48
Frames of War (Butler), 147
Frank Reade (fictional character), 114, 197n16
Fredricks, Nancy, 87
Freeman, Elizabeth, 115
Funston, Frederick, 119

Galaxy Magazine, 18, 36–37, 179n36
Galton, Francis, 103, 104, 146, 193n75, 195n91, 204n22
Gates, Henry Louis, 187n53
Geary Act (1892), 49, 78–79, 84, 105, 188n70, 195n87
George, Henry, 97, 192n60
Gerber, John, 60, 184n17
German Catholic reparations, 159, 160
Gilded Age, 2, 84, 93, 103
The Gilded Age (Twain and Warner), 91
Gillis, Steve, 14, 16
Gillman, Susan, 143
Gilmore, Ruth Wilson, 143, 204n16
"The Golden-Faced People" (Lindsay), 118, 198n31
Golden Gulag (Gilmore), 204n16
Goldsmith, Oliver, 56, 183n9

"Goldsmith's Friend Abroad Again" (Twain): Ah Song Hi's vision in, 80–81; and Burlingame obituary, 183n9; described, 55–57; first person narration of, 18, 25, 56, 183n8; as *Huckleberry Finn* antecedent, 37–38, 179n36; vagrancy in, 55–57, 61, 80–81
Gong (Prince), 120, 133
Gordon, Charles George, 116
Grady, Henry, 107
Grant, Ulysses S. (President), 123
grave robbing, 184n12
'Greasers', 69, 73
Gribben, Alan, 167
"grievable" lives, 147–148
gunpowder, 127

Haggard, H. Rider, 114, 197n17
Hall, George W., 29
Hamilton, Anne, 122
Hamlet soliloquy, 71–72, 187n52
Han *versus* Manchu, 122
Harlan, John Marshall (Justice), 107–108, 195n96
Harris, Susan, 115–116, 165, 166
Harte, Bret: *Ah Sin* collaboration, 27, 39–41, 73–74, 180n63, 188n60, 200n57; on effects of *People v. Hall*, 39; on mobility access, 24–25, 54, 73–81, 168, 208n3; "Plain Language from Truthful James," 39, 179n41, 181n71; popularity of, 5, 39; threatened with lynching, 79; and "Three Vagabonds of Trinidad," 25, 55, 73–80, 188n60
Hartman, Saidiya, 68–69
Hawai'ian dispatches (Twain), 5, 10–13, 21, 173n33, 174n34. *See also Mark Twain's Letters from Hawaii*
Hawai'i annexation, 74, 142
Hawai'ian novel (Twain, unpublished), 115–116, 197n22
Hayot, Eric, 193n71
health and hygiene: and eugenicists, 146, 149–150; extralegal policing of, 54, 76, 78; norms, state imposed, 142; tracking birth and death statistics for, 146–150, 204n22; Twain on blackbirding and, 143–144, 150. *See also* "biopower," and biopolitics; vagrancy
heaven, white populations in, 154–155
"Hiker" monuments, 156–157
historical romances, 112, 113–115, 131, 196n13, 197n16–17
history, as non progressive, 127, 200n65
History of England in the Eighteenth Century (Lecky), 115
History of European Morals from Augustus to Charlemagne (Lecky), 115
"Horrible Affair" (Twain), 60–61
Horwitz, Morton, 95
Howells, William Dean, 109–110, 196n13, 197n22, 199n44
Huckleberry Finn (fictional character): on black as "negative" person, 71; river experience *versus* Jim's, 65–66, 68, 185n26
Huckleberry Finn (Twain), 53–82; and *Ah Sin* similarities, 40, 42–43; convict-lease context in, 182n5; and "dead in law" blacks, 71–73, 149, 184n16; death references in, 65–73; Eliot on, 53, 54, 65, 66; "Goldsmith's Friend" as antecedent, 37–38, 179n36; *Hamlet* soliloquy in, 71–72, 187n52; Injun Joe haunting plot of, 59; mobility in, 54, 65–66; and "negative personhood," 71–72, 187n49; precursor texts to, 36–37, 55, 179n36; and "Three Vagabonds," 74, 188n60; and "tramping," 61–68; walking dead in, 56, 183n7; white vagabonds in, 55
"human shields," 153, 206n48
Humboldt County purges, 78
"hygiene." *See* health and hygiene
The Hypothetical Mandarin (Hayot), 193n71

"The Iliad of Sandy Bar" (Harte), 39
Illegal Migrations and the Huckleberry Finn Problem (Park), 168
immigrants. *See specific groups*
imperialism / imperialists: on colonies as backward, 135; in *Connecticut Yankee*,

115–116, 118–119, 197n19; counteractions against, 110–112; in popular stories, 113–116, 197n16–17; in "To the Person Sitting in Darkness," 139–140, 203n1. *See also* romance novels; U.S. (imperial and colonial policy)
imperial romance, 112–119; overview, 25
"In a Future Tense" (Wong), 193n71, 198n31
"Indian" (term use), 29
"Indians and Chinamen" (illustration), 145 *fig 5.1*
"Indiscriminate Massacre of Indians, Women and Children Butchered" (Harte), 79
individualism: and classification systems, 149, 195n88; in *Connecticut Yankee*, 117, 149; *versus* corporation(s), 21, 88–91, 97, 102, 111, 149; *versus* interdependence, 88–89, 190n22; and racialization, 21, 80, 97, 105–106, 111; twin analogy and, 83–84, 88, 89, 102–103, 107. *See also* romance novels; statistics
industrial capitalism: and individualism, 88; populist rhetoric on, 90; in postbellum period, 25, 70, 84; and racial tensions, 96
"information revolution," 51–52
Injin Jim (fictional character), 71, 75–77, 79–80
Injun Joe (fictional character), 44, 57–61, 116, 157, 184n12, 184n15
The Innocents Abroad (Twain), 157
In re Tiburcio Parrott (1880 legal ruling), 98
Iraq Body Count project, 148, 205n29
Irish immigrants, 19
Isaiah's prophecy, 165
Israeli assault on Palestinians, 147, 206n48
Italian immigrants, 90, 96–97, 191n29

Jackson, Helen Hunt, 168, 208n3
Jackson, John L., 167
Jackson's Island retreat, 74, 75–76
A Japanese Blossom (Eaton), 169, 208n3
Jim (fictional character): captivity of, 2, 42–43, 59, 71–73, 187n52; and grave robbing, 184n12; mobility of, 55, 71, 167–168; on Pap's death, 42–43; rescued from sphinx, 197n16; river experience, 25, 65–66
Jim Crow: and biopolitics, 142; and Chinese Exclusion, 1–2, 87; compared with colonialism, 22; critiqued in Lindsay story, 118; and policing methods, 51, 191n36; and "southern enclosure," 69–70, 186n44; vigilantism, and "law's delay," 72, 187n51; in western states, 13, 55, 90. *See also* African American(s); mobility; vagrancy
"Jim Smiley and His Jumping Frog" (Twain), 10
"John Chinaman in New York" (Twain), 18–19, 20 *fig I.1*, 166, 175n62–64, 184n11
Jun, Helen, 8–9
Jung, Moon-Ho, 7–8, 14

Kanaka, 10, 144
Kaplan, Amy: on *Connecticut Yankee*, 115; on "romance[s] of empire," 113, 196n13; on Twain's American exceptionalism, 203n7; on Twain's western and Hawai'ian writings, 10, 173n33; on *Wu Chih Tien*, 132
Keller, G. Frederick, 100
King Leopold's Soliloquy (Twain), 151, 160–164, 207n69–71
Knoper, Randall, 43–44, 180n62, 180n64

labor: Chinese as emergent form of, 7; Chinese domestic, 15, 77; convict lease system (captive), 55, 69–71, 182n5, 186n44, 187n46; "coolie" (*see* "coolie(s)"); and Exclusion Act, 13; indentured and involuntary, 7–8, 70–72, 143–146, 186n44; Irish *versus* Chinese, 19; "new economic servitude," 93; in postbellum era, 43, 53–55, 68–71; postbellum responses to immigrants', 25, 84; sources, after Emancipation, 10–11; wage slavery, 183n10; white *versus* Chinese, 13, 14, 57, 78, 118, 193n70, 198n28

Lai Chun-chuen, 32
Lao She, v, 5, 172n14
"the law's delay," 72, 187n52
Lears, T. J. Jackson, 112–113
Lecky, William, 115
Lee, Julia, 8–9, 174n43
"Legal Slaves and Civil Bodies (Dayan), 183n6, 184n16
LeMenager, Stephanie, 155
Leopold II, 163–164
Letters from Hawai'i (Twain), 73, 141, 174n34
Li Hongzhang, 120, 122, 123
Lindsay, Vachel, 118
Li Tan (fictional character), 131–132, 134
Li Tee (fictional character), 75, 77–78
"loafer," 56–57
Loewen, James, 156, 207n60
London, Jack, 137, 138, 169, 202n92, 208n3
Lott, Eric, 40, 184n20
Lowe, Lisa, 7
Lowell, James Russell, 156
Luigi and Angelo Cappello (fictional characters), 83–97, 106–107, 149, 189n2
Lye, Colleen, 6, 8, 21, 101–102
lynchings, 72, 84, 150–151, 187n51

Malory, Thomas, 114, 115
Manchu leaders, 120, 122, 133, 201n80
manhood/masculinity, 29, 59, 113, 115, 127, 132, 196n13
Maoris, 158–159
"Mark Twain, 'The Treaty with China,' and the Chinese Connection" (Zehr), 5–6
"Mark Twain: Exposer of the 'Dollar Empire'" (Lao She speech), 5
Mark Twain's Letters from Hawaii, 73, 141, 174n34
Mark Twain's Weapons of Satire (Zwick), 22
mass surveillance, 51–52, 105–106, 195n88. See also "biopower," and biopolitics; fingerprinting; policing methods; statistics

Mauritius, 21, 145–146
Mbembe, Achille, 143
McClain, Charles, 28–29
McClintock, Anne, 135
McCoy, Alfred, 51–52
media: "assault on the senses," 147–148, 153, 206n48; disinformation, in U.S. wars, 154, 205n29
medieval romance novels, 112, 113–115, 196n13, 197n17
"Memoranda" in *Galaxy* (Twain), 18
"A Memorial for the Perpetuation of My Name" (Twain), 161 *fig 5.2*
Memorial of the Six Chinese Companies (address to senate), 49
memorials. See monument(s)
Metzger, Sean, 40–41
Mexican Americans, 8, 13, 24, 30, 52, 69, 73
microorganisms, in "Three Thousand Years," 73, 188n58
migrations, involuntary, 143–146, 150, 204n19–20
"The Mill Among the Mill-Hands" (Twain), 98–100, 99 *fig. 3.1*
Miller, Joaquin, 40
miners' tax (California), 6–7, 30–32, 48, 177n13, 178n16, 181n72
minstrelsy, 40, 184n20 See also missionaries: and Boxer uprising, 139, 142, 159–160, 207n66; on Chinese women, 132; as colonizing reformists, 22, 115–116, 119, 124, 160; and "Lyncherdom" proposal, 22, 150–151; and Reverend Ament, 22, 159–160; and "trader-bugs," 22, 136–138; Twain's satires on, 22–23; "usual cargo" (Howells letter), 109–110, 197n22; Wong on, 130. See also *A Connecticut Yankee in King Arthur's Court*; "To the Person Sitting in Darkness"; U.S. (imperial and colonial policy)
Mississippi Black Codes, 70, 186n39. See also black codes
"Mi Ultimo Adiós" (Rizal), 165–166

mobility: access to, 24, 54, 66, 68–71, 77, 80–81; Hartman on, 68–69; in postbellum U.S., 43, 53–55, 68–71; to seek work, 57; in "Three Vagabonds of Trinidad," 74, 80. *See also* African American(s); vagrancy; *specific immigrant groups*
mob violence, 72, 187n51
modernization. *See* Chinese modernization
Monopoly (board game), 192n60
monument(s), 155–166; to Ament, Twain's proposal, 159–160; Leopold's, 160–165, 161 *fig 5.2*, 164 *fig 5.3*, 207n69; and mortality statistics, 140, 151; public interest in war dead, 151, 155, 205n39–40; War of 1898, 156–157, 207n60. *See also* statistics; U.S. (imperial and colonial policy); U.S.-Philippine War
Moore, Shirley Ann Wilson, 58
Moreheid, J. N., 96
Morgan Library's manuscript, 85, 103, 107
Moro Massacre (Philippines), 118, 152–154
Morrison, Toni, 1, 7
Morse, Harry, 51
Moy, James, 41
Mr. Skinner (fictional character), 75, 76
multicultural fictions, 77, 188n64
Murphy, Brenda, 41
Murray, Hugh (Justice), 27, 29–30
Mussel Slough incident, 91
"*Mutilated Figure in Chains*" (Twain), 139
"My Last Thought" (Twain), 165–166
My Life in China and America (Yung), 119
"The Mysterious Chinaman" (Twain), 14–15, 166

nationalism. *See* monument(s)
Native Americans: and dislocated Chinese, 80; displacement of, 8, 53–55, 58, 79; Lai on, 32; and monuments, 157; testimony ban, 24, 30, 32; Twain on, 168, 174n42; vagrancy laws, 24, 52, 76
Necro Citizenship (Castronovo), 183n7
necropolitics, 143, 204n16

"negative personhood," 71–72, 184n16, 187n49
"Negro Problem" and the "Yellow Peril," 13–14, 174n43
The New Jim Crow (Alexander), 69
NewSouth edition, 1, 167–168
New Zealand Land Wars, 158
Ng Poon Chew, 135–136, 202n86
Nightingale, Florence, 146, 204n22
Nissen, Axel, 39, 66
No. 44, The Mysterious Stranger (Twain), 88, 149, 190n20
Noli Me Tangere (Rizal), 165
No Place of Grace (Lears), 112–113
Norris, Frank, 91

oaths (Chinese), 33–34, 176n2, 178n15
The Octopus (Norris), 91, 191n31
Office of Foreign Affairs (Zongli Yamen), 120
"The Ogre of Mussel Slough" (Keller), 100
One of Us (Dreger), 88, 190n22
Opium Wars, 120, 204n19
The Ordeal of Mark Twain (Brooks), 87
Ou, Hsin-Yun, 17, 41, 175n57
"Our Composite Nationality" (Douglass), 33
"Our Fellow Savages of The Sandwich Islands" (Twain), 10

Pacific Islands, 143–144, 150
Pacific Railroad Company, 11
Packard's Monthly (periodical), 88
Paddison, Joshua, 3–4
palmistry in *Pudd'nhead*, 51, 106, 195n91. *See also* fingerprinting
Panics (financial crises), 93
Pap (fictional character), 61–62, 64, 65
Park, John, 168
Parslow, Charles, 40–41, 45, 46 *fig 1.1*, 179n46
patriotism. *See* monument(s)
People of the State of California v. Brady (1870), 34

People v. Hall (1854), 27–49; *Ah Sin* as response to, 24, 27–28, 43, 48–49, 50; critique of effects, 34–35; examples of policing after, 35; extension of "not white," 3, 6, 27, 77, 181n75; and Harte's stories, 39; Lai on, 32–33; McClain on, 28–29; and miners' tax collusion, 30–31; Murray on, 27, 29–30; reversal of, 48–49, 181n75; *Roughing It* chapter on, 38; Speer on, 27–28, 30–31, 32, 38–39, 181n73
"Personal Habits of the Siamese Twins" (Twain), 16, 88–89, 175n54
Peters, John Durham, 29
Peyser, Thomas, 149
Pfaelzer, Jean, 76
Philippines: Beveridge's speech on, 140; Filipino losses, 148, 151–154, 157, 205n29, 205n39–40; flag proposed for (Twain's), 160; José Rizal, 165–166; Moro Massacre, 118, 152–154; national resistance of, 156–157; "philopena" reference, 106; and President Aguinaldo, 119, 139, 207n69; U.S. police surveillance in, 52, 106; U.S. state control in, 116, 118, 142, 203n13; U.S. war effect on Twain, 10, 22, 118–119, 139, 202n90. *See also* Twain, Mark (on U.S.-Philippine War); U.S.-Philippine War
"Plain Language from Truthful James" (Harte), 39, 179n41, 181n71
Plessy, Homer, 192n48
Plessy v. Ferguson, 107–108, 195n96
Plunkett (fictional character), 42–50, 169, 181n71, 181n74
Poe, Edgar Allan, 14
Policing America's Empire (McCoy), 51–52
policing methods, 34–38, 51–52, 54, 103–106, 175n59, 194n81. *See also* fingerprinting; surveillance technology
"Political Honors in China" (Wong), 134, 201n81
Pond, James B., 129
population(s): biometric identification of, 103–106, 141–143, 147; *versus* character, in Twain's later works, 154; colonized, 52, 143, 203n13; eugenicists and health statistics, 149–150; framed as war target, 147–148; in heaven, 154–155; management of, 52, 142–150, 182n86; mobility/immobility of (social and physical), 69, 143; racialized counting of, 103, 146; state control of, 142–150. *See also* statistics
"post-racial" racism, 167–169
The Prince and the Pauper (Twain), 73, 89
Prince Gong, 120
prison inmates. *See* convict lease system
Pudd'nhead Wilson (Twain): and *Ah Sin* trials compared, 28, 50; and anti-Italian sentiment, 191n29; biometric identification in, 106, 141; counting bodies in, 149; courtroom farce in, 24, 28, 50–51; "evidence" in, 28, 50–52; financial speculations in, 93; fingerprints in, 103–104, 105–106, 193n75; legal and race fictions in, 23, 25, 84; link to Twain's Asian commentaries, 5, 23, 25, 106; Morgan Library version, 85, 103, 107; reviewers and critics on, 86–89, 93, 97; revision of, with *Twins*, 106–107, 189n7; separated from *Twins*, 9, 85, 97, 106, 108; title page fingerprints, 193n75; Twain on origin of, 86–87, 189n7; and white tramp mobility, 73. See also *Those Extraordinary Twins*
(David) Pudd'nhead Wilson (fictional character): calendar entries of, 108, 114; and fingerprints, 50–51, 103, 104, 105, 194n81; and Italian twins, 92–93, 95; legal defenses of, 86
Pun Chi, and "catalogue of crimes," 32–33
"punishment for crime" (13th Amendment), 70, 77
purges, in Humboldt County, 78

Qing dynasty, 122, 130, 133, 201n80
Queensland, 143, 150

race: establishment and identification of, 68, 103–104, 194n86, 195n88–89; Galton on, 103–104, 193n75, 195n91;

London on, 137, 138, 202n92; registration of, 84, 103–104, 194n81; and the "ungrievable," 147–148
racialization (overview), 1–10, 13–14, 26, 168–169
Raphael-Hernandez, Heike, 173n30
Redpath, James C., 129, 135
Revolution of 1911, 133, 135, 201n80
Rhoads, Edward, 122
Rhodes, Cecil, 144
Ridge, John Rollin, 168, 208n3
Rizal, José, 165–166
Robbins, William, 12
Robinson, Forrest, 4
Rohe, Randall E, 181n72
romance novels, 112, 113–115, 131, 196n13, 197n16–17
"Romancing the Empire" (Kaplan), 113, 196n13
Roosevelt, Theodore, 153
Root, George, 62, 63 fig 2.1, 185n22
Roughing It (Twain): Chinese descriptions in, 19–21, 38–39, 132, 175n68; as early formative piece, 10; tax abuses enumerated in, 178n16; "vagrant Mexicans" in, 73
Rowe, John Carlos, 93, 114, 115, 116
Ruffin v. Commonwealth case, 70
Russell, Emily, 50, 87, 190n16

Sacramento Daily Union (newspaper), 10, 15, 173n33
Saint-Gaudens, Augustus, 156
"Salutation Speech from the Nineteenth Century to the Twentieth" (Twain), 139
Sandwich Islands, 10–11, 174n34
San Francisco Alta California (newspaper), 111
San Francisco Daily Morning Call (newspaper), 15, 16–17, 28, 35–36, 78
San Francisco Daily Report (newspaper), 104, 106, 194n81–83, 195n89
Santa Clara County v Southern Pacific Railroad, 95, 98, 192n47
Saxton, Alexander, 13, 97, 118
Scott, Walter, 114

"Self-Strengthening" movement, 110–112, 116, 120–121, 133–134, 135
Shah, Nayan, 181n69
Shaker Manifesto (journal), 130
Shaw monument, 156
sheet-music industry, 62, 185n21
"Siamese twins" (Moreheid), 96
Siamese Twins metaphors, 16, 88–91, 102–103, 175n54
Six Chinese Companies (address), 49
skeletons, 160–166
slavery: after Emancipation and Reconstruction, 7, 93; and India castes, 22; "slaves of the state," 70–71, 139, 187n48; status, *versus* Chinese immigrant, 36–37. *See also* labor
"Society Must Be Defended" (Foucault), 141
"The South and Her Problems" (Grady), 107
Southern black codes, 14, 65–66, 69–70, 76, 186n39
Southern Democrats, 3, 14, 29, 76, 79
"southern enclosure," 69–70, 186n44
Southern Pacific Railroad, 91, 102
Speer, William: on Foreign Miners' Tax, 30–32, 178n15–16; on *People v. Hall* effects, 27–28, 30–32, 38–39, 178n15, 181n73; on Tuolomne County evidence, 27–28
statistics: casualty, 151–154, 205n39–40, 206n44; of Filipino casualties (unrecorded), 151, 205n40, 206n44; for health tracking, 146–150, 204n22; for imperial and domestic racialization, 140, 141–143, 146–155, 149, 203n13; public fascination with war dead, 151, 155, 205n39–40; war body counts withheld, 148
Steen, Shannon, 173n30
stoning, of Chinese, 16–17, 36–37, 39, 48, 149
Stowe, Harriet Beecher, 113, 143
Stranger Intimacy (Shah), 48, 181n69
"stranger intimacy," in *Ah Sin*, 48, 181n69, 181n74

structural inequality and violence: California Supreme Court support of, 34–35; Gilmore on U.S. racism and, 143; legalization of, 34–35, 61; Twain critiques of, 1–2, 23–26, 167–169

"The Stupendous Procession" (Twain), 139, 160

"sublimity of *incongruity*," in "Disgraceful Persecution," 37, 179n35

Sucheng Chan, 30

Sui Sin Far, 168–169, 208n3

Sumida, Stephen, 10, 115–116

Sun Tzu, 127

Sun Yat-Sen, 201n80

Supreme Court (U.S.), on harm and intent, 184n16

surveillance technology, 51–52, 105–106, 195n88. *See also* "biopower," and biopolitics; fingerprinting

Taber, Isaiah West, 103–104, 194n81

Taiping Rebellion, 116, 120, 204n19

Tammany Hall, 139

Taney, Roger (Justice), 37

Taylorism, 92, 191n37

Technology and the Logic of American Racism (Chinn), 103

Tennenhouse, Leonard, 142

Tennyson, Alfred, 114

Territorial Enterprise (newspaper), 103, 194n78

testimony ban: after reversal of *People v. Hall*, 49, 181n75; alternatives to (evidence), 50–51; "black" term extended, 6, 27–28, 29; Chan on, 30; Chinese stereotypes and, 30, 49; Douglass on, 33; *Memorial of the Six Chinese Companies* on, 49; merchants Lai and Pun on, 32–33; and miners' tax, 6–7; and Native Americans, 24, 30, 32; political effects of, 28; Southern Democrats and, 3; Speer on, 27–28, 30–32, 38–39, 178n15, 181n73; "testify" provenance, 29; in *Tom Sawyer*, 44, 60; Twain's news reports on, 35–39. See also *Ah Sin*; Foreign Miners' Tax; *People v. Hall*

"Testimony of California's Leading Citizens" (1877), 49

13th Amendment exception, 77

Thomas, Brook, 84, 88, 189n2

Thomason, Jerry, 41

Those Extraordinary Twins (Twain), 83–108; and anti-corporate movement, 84, 87–88, 91, 97–100, 189n2; and Chinese immigrant labor, 96–97, 102; corporate body of, 90–91, 92–94, 95, 101–103; deleted section, 106–107; Judge's speech in, 83; legal logic in, 95–96, 107, 149; Morgan Library manuscript of, 85, 103, 107; physical ease of, 92, 191n36; reviewers and critics on, 86–87; separated from *Pudd'nhead Wilson*, 9, 85, 97, 106, 108; synopsis of, 86. See also *Pudd'nhead Wilson*

"Three Thousand Years among the Microbes" (Twain), 73, 188n58

"Three Vagabonds of Trinidad" (Harte), 25, 55, 73–81, 188n60

thumbprints, 51, 103–104, 194n81–83. *See also* fingerprinting; policing methods

"Thumbs Down!" *San Francisco Daily Report*, 104, 106, 194n81–83, 195n89

time, deprivation of, 72, 187n53

"time-discipline," 92, 191n37

Tocci brothers, 90, 191n27

Tom Driscoll (fictional character), 50–51, 73, 85, 107

"Tom Driscoll's demonstrative body" (Russell), 50

Tom Sawyer (fictional character), 44, 59, 184n15

"To My Missionary Critics" (Twain), 22

"To the Person Sitting in Darkness" (Twain): Harris on, 166; imperialist and domestic connections in, 22, 73, 92, 139–140, 203n1, 203n7; and *King Leopold's Soliloquy*, 151; monument to Ament imagined in, 159–160; title provenance, 165; "two Americas," v, 113

Trachtenberg, Alan, 84, 90, 91–92, 94, 96–97, 191n38

The Tramp (Bellew), 66–68, 67 *fig* 2.2, 185n30
A Tramp Abroad (Twain), 73
tramp(s): divergent attitudes towards, 66, 68, 186n34; in Pap's dream, 61–64; portrayals of, 64, 66, 67 *fig* 2.2, 68; racialized forms of, 61–62, 65–66, 72; as romanticized figure, 53–54, 66, 68, 185n30; and vagrancy codes, 66, 69, 185n27. *See also* vagrancy
"Tramp-tramp-tramp" (song), 61–64, 63 *fig* 2.1, 185n22
The Transformation of American Law (Horwitz), 94–95
Treaty of Guadalupe Hidalgo, 3, 8
"The Treaty with China" (Twain), 17–18, 157, 172n14
Twain, Mark: on "blackbirding," 143–144, 150; Burlingame's obituary, 183n9; on corporate form and stockholders, 94; on editors, 36; exposure to racialized laws, 13; fingerprinting depictions, 105–106; flag proposal for Philippines, 160; on Funston and Aguinaldo, 119; Hawai'ian dispatches, 5, 10–13, 21, 173n33, 174n34; investment failures of, 93; on Kanaka, 144; links to larger contexts, 22–23; on migrants adaptation, 145–145, 204n19; name incorporation, 92; on Native Americans, 168, 174n42; as policing/trial witness, 35–36, 38; shifts in perspective, 21, 24–26; story settings, 5; structural inequalities examined by, 1–2, 23–26, 167–169; on transpacific commerce, 11–12; western move during Civil War, 54
Twain, Mark (in California): on coolie labor, 10–11, 21, 175n68, 193n70; friends' influence on, 17, 175n57; newspaper writings on "Chinese Question," 14–21, 174n52; patronizing writing during, 14–16, 174n52; on police practices, 35–38; social dynamics exposure during, 14
Twain, Mark (literary forms): allegorizing U.S.-Asia relationship, 15, 16, 136–138, 202n90; break with journalism, 16–17; comparison method of critique, 139; courtroom farces, 24, 28; fascination with duplicity, 88; in "Goldsmith's Friend," 18, 25, 56, 183n8; Hawai'ian novel (unfinished), 115–116, 197n22; in Howells correspondence, 109–110, 197n22, 199n44; international interest in, 1, 172n2; irony and first-person narrative, 18; lecture tour in 1895, 108; letter to Beard, 200n64; *versus* Melville, Stowe, Tyler, 143; "Memoranda" to *Galaxy Magazine*, 18; multiple racial contexts of, 9–10; narrative interruptions in, 169; newspaper reports, 10–13, 35–36, 38; on origins of *Pudd'nhead* and *Twins*, 85–86, 189n7; on politics of counting lives, 148–149; population *versus* character studies, 141; as precursor of comparative racialization, 169; revision of *Pudd'nhead* and *Twins*, 106–108; satires and fables listed, 21–23; shift to fiction, 4, 6; speculative fiction, 109–110, 202n90; on storytelling and 'linking absurdities,' 37, 179n35; styles listed, 26; on vagrancy, incarceration, race, 73; western and transpacific influence on, 10
Twain, Mark (on China and Chinese): Boxers and missionaries, 159–160; Burlingame Treaty, 17, 22, 111, 120, 196n5, 199n37–38; CEM, 122–124, 200n57; civilization of, 109–110, 137, 202n90; crimes against, in *Roughing It*, 38–39, 132; descriptions in legal cases, 35–36; early news reporting on, 4–5; *Galaxy* installments, 18–19; Hawai'ian contract laborers, 10–13; immigrants' conditions, 141; as indisdinguishable, 103, 194n78; informing *Connecticut Yankee*, 112, 114–119; interest in, throughout career, 4–6, 112; and Jewish diaspora relationship, 21; and *People v Hall*, 38–39; and police criminality, 17–18, 175n59; as policing/trial witness, 35–36, 38; responses to testimony of, 28;

Twain, Mark (*continued*)
versus slave, 37; on tax collectors' abuses, 178n16; transpacific commerce, 11–12, 193n70; on U.S. missionaries to U.S. south, 22; Virginia City's population, 19–21; and vulnerability linked with other groups, 23–26; and Wong's *Wu Chih Tien*, 25, 125–128, 131–132

Twain, Mark (on U.S. imperial policy): American exceptionalism views, 139, 168, 203n7; in Anti-Imperialist League, 22, 139, 151, 203n1, 203n6; critique in comparative contexts, 22–23, 139; death rates in colonies, 150; heroics and chivalry invalidated, 119; and Leopold analogy, 160–166, 207n71; migrants description, 144, 145 *fig 5.1*, 204n19; opening markets with missionaries, 21–22; Philippine slaughter and Christianity, 153–154; transpacific commerce, 11–12, 193n70; and two Americas, v, 113

Twain, Mark (on U.S.-Philippine War): counting dead, 151–154; effect of, 10, 22, 118–119, 139, 202n90; and Funston and Aguinaldo, 119; Moro Massacre, 118, 152–154; response to in "My Last Thought," 165–166; and U.S. in China, 139–140

Twain, Mark (travelogues): on British colonial conditions, 143–146, 204n19; chapter epigraphs in, 108, 114; on indigenous Australians, 150

Twichell, Joseph Hopkins, 17, 119–120, 122–123, 199n44, 204n19

"Twins, Twain, Galton, and Gilman" (Cole), 194n86–88

twins metaphor: as corporation representation, 21, 83–85, 95–96, 102–103; and individuality, 83–84, 88, 89, 102–103, 107, 190n18; as U.S. body politic, 16, 175n54

Two Men of Sandy Bar (Harte), 40

Tyler, Royall, 142

Uncle Tom's Cabin (Stowe), 113
"The United States of Lyncherdom" (Twain), 22, 150–151

unknown soldiers' tombs, 155–156

U.S. (imperial and colonial policy): annexation of Guam and Philippines, 22; atrocities in Philippines and China, 119; on both domestic and colonized populations, 143; capitalists' funding of Leopold II, 163–164; colonial administration, 52; exceptionalism, in romance novels, 113, 196n13; Ng on, 135

U.S.-Philippine war: body counts withheld, 148, 151–154, 205n29, 205n39–40, 206n44; as media disinformation inception, 148, 205n29; for transpacific access, 142; and War monument, 156–157, 207n60

vagabonds: antitramp anxiety, 66; generousity to, 69, 186n34; romance of, 53–54, 64, 66, 76; whiteness of, 54–55, 76, 80. *See also* tramp(s)

vagrancy, 53–81; and captive labor, 55, 69–71, 182n5, 186n44, 187n46; in *Goldsmith's Friend*, 55–57, 61, 80–81; and Humboldt purges, 78; laws, 54, 55, 70, 74, 78, 186n40; Native Americans and, 24, 53–55, 58, 61, 76, 79; in *Roughing It*, 73; white *versus* the racialized, 54, 60, 64, 69, 80, 184n16. *See also* health and hygiene; labor; mobility; tramp(s)

Vagrancy Act (1547), 187n49
Vagrancy Act (1855), 69
vigilantism, 72, 187n51
Virginia City Territorial Enterprise (newspaper), 15, 103, 194n78

Wagner, Bryan, 70
Wallace, Lew, 113
"Wan Lee, the Pagan" (Harte), 39
Warner, Charles Dudley, 91
War of 1898, 22, 142, 156
War of Philippine Independence. *See* U.S.-Philippine War
Washington, Booker T., 107, 195n95
Wasp (periodical), 98–100, 99 *fig 3.1*
"What Have the Police Been Doing?" (Twain), 6, 18, 175n59

"What Shall We Do With Our Boys?" (Keller), 100, 101 *fig 3.2*
When I was a Boy in China (Yan), 120
"white Indians," 116, 155, 159
white(s): labor, 25, 57, 183n10, 184n11; laborers on Chinese, 13, 14, 57, 78, 118, 198n28; masculinity, 113, 127, 196n13; miners and dynamite, 118, 198n28; and mobility, 54, 64, 69, 80; population, in heaven, 154–155; testimony ban effects on (Speer), 27–28, 30–32, 38–39, 178n15, 181n73. *See also* vagrancy
Whitman, Walt, 18
"Why Am I a Heathen?" (Wong), 134
Wildman, Edwin, 139, 152
Wildman, Rounsevelle, 134
Williams, Dave, 41
Williams, Harry, 45, 46 fig 1.1
Williams, True, 19, 20 *fig I.1*
Wilson Moore, Shirley Ann, 58
witnesses. *See* testimony ban
Wiyot Indians, 79
Wong, Edlie, 193n71, 198n31
Wong, Sau-Ling Cynthia, 54
Wong Chin Foo, 125–136; on China and Chinese, 110, 112, 134–135, 201n81; misogyny of, 132; on missionaries, 130; political engagement of, 124–125, 128, 130–131, 133–134, 201n80; public persona, 129–130, 200n67, 201n69; writings, 25, 124, 128, 131, 201n72
"Wong Chin Foo's Periodical Writing and Chinese Exclusion" (Hsu), 130
Wu, Cynthia, 89–90, 175n54
Wu Chih Tien (Wong), 125–136; on China without colonialists, 124, 134, 135; and *Connecticut Yankee*, 25, 124, 127, 135, 136; portrayal of Chinese men, 25, 132, 134; sources for, 131, 201n72; summary, 131; and Twain motifs, 131–132
Wu Zideng, 122

Xinhai Revolution (1911), 133, 135, 201n80

Yan Phou Lee, 120–121
"Yellow Peril" (London), 137
"Yellow Peril" and "Negro Problem," 13–14, 174n43
Yung Wing, 21, 25, 110, 112, 119, 122–124, 200n57
Yurok Indians, 79

Zehr, Martin, 4, 5–6
Zongli Yamen, 120
Zwick, Jim, 22

About the Author

Hsuan L. Hsu is Associate Professor of English at the University of California, Davis, and author of *Geography and the Production of Space in Nineteenth-Century American Literature.*

www.ingramcontent.com/pod-product-compliance
Lightning Source LLC
Chambersburg PA
CBHW020403080526
44584CB00014B/1148